BILINGUAL FIRST LANGUAGE ACQUISITION

LANGUAGE ACQUISITION & LANGUAGE DISORDERS

EDITORS

Harald Clahsen
University of Essex

William Rutherford
University of Southern California

Volume 7

Jürgen M. Meisel

Bilingual First Language Acquisition

BILINGUAL FIRST LANGUAGE ACQUISITION

FRENCH AND GERMAN GRAMMATICAL DEVELOPMENT

JÜRGEN M. MEISEL
University of Hamburg

JOHN BENJAMINS PUBLISHING COMPANY
AMSTERDAM/PHILADELPHIA

TM The paper used in this publication meets the minimum requirements of American National Standard for Information Sciences — Permanence of Paper for Printed Library Materials, ANSI Z39.48-1984.

Library of Congress Cataloging-in-Publication Data

Bilingual first language acquisition : French and German grammatical development / edited by Jürgen Meisel.
    p.   cm. -- (Language acquisition & language disorders : ISSN 0925-0123; v. 7)
    Includes bibliographical references and index.
    Contents: Acquiring German and French in a bilingual setting / Peter Jordens -- The DUFDE project / Regina Köppe -- The acquisition of gender and number morphology within NP / Caroline Koehn -- Gender and number agreement within DP / Natascha Müller -- Getting FAT : fitness, agreement, and tense in early grammars / Jürgen M. Meisel -- More about INFL-ection and agreement : the acquisition of clitic pronouns in French / Georg Kaiser -- Case assignment and functional categories in bilingual children / Achim Stenzel -- NP-movement and subject raising / Regina Köppe -- Parameters cannot be reset : evidence from the development of COMP / Natascha Müller.
    1. Language acquisition. 2. Bilingualism in children. 3. French language--Acquisition. 4. German language--Acquisition. 5. Grammar, Comparative and general. I. Meisel, Jürgen M. II. DUFDE (Research Group) III. Series.
P118.B53   1994
401'.93--dc20   94-23215
ISBN 90 272 2470 6 (Eur.) / 1-55619-242-8 (US) (Hb; alk. paper)   CIP
ISBN 90 272 2471 4 (Eur.) / 1-55619-243-6 (Eur.) (Pb; alk. paper)

John Benjamins Publishing Co. • P.O.Box 75577 • 1070 AN Amsterdam • The Netherlands
John Benjamins North America • P.O.Box 27519 • Philadelphia, PA 19118 • USA

Contents

Preface
On the Initial States of Language Acquisition

Jürgen M. Meisel

University of Hamburg

The contributions to this volume represent the major part of the results obtained over the last three years in a research project studying the grammatical development of bilingual children who are acquiring two first languages simultaneously, French and German. It is the second volume published by the members of the research team DUFDE; the first appeared as J. M. Meisel (ed.) (1990). *Two First Languages – Early Grammatical Development in Bilingual Children (= Studies on Language Acquisition,* 10). Dordrecht: Foris.

The DUFDE research group (Deutsch und Französisch – Doppelter Erstspracherwerb/German and French – Simultaneous First Language Acquisition) has been operating at the University of Hamburg since 1980. From 1986 until 1992, it was generously supported by a research grant from the DFG (Deutsche Forschungsgemeinschaft) to the author of these lines. We have also benefitted from material assistance from the University of Hamburg. This support, both from the DFG and from the University, is hereby gratefully acknowledged.

A number of individuals have also been most helpful. In fact, without them the authors of the following chapters would not have been able to do their work, and we therefore want to thank them sincerely. This is addressed, first of all, to the children whose language development we have been studying and to their parents. I gladly repeat what I have said before, namely that knowing them has been a most rewarding experience for us. Nobody who has not lived through this experience can imagine the kind of inconvenience it represents in the daily life of a family to have two people with video equipment invading their homes every second week for four, five, and more years. We can only hope that our work will turn out to be useful for other bilingual families — and perhaps even for those who we studied. Merci infiniment.

Berthold Crysmann, Axel Mahlau, Gesche Seemann, and Martina Wulf have contributed to the studies published in this volume by helping in analyzing the data and by discussing the results with us. Without the help of Thomas Westphal, computers would not only be those mysterious beings which they are, they would even be frightening. Thanks to all of them. We are especially grateful to Susanne E. Carroll, Peter Jordens, Tom Roeper, and the anonymous readers recruited by the series editors for reading and commenting on earlier versions of the chapters in this volume.

Let me finally mention that all authors are or have been affiliated with the University of Hamburg and the research group DUFDE, except Peter Jordens (Free University, Amsterdam) who accepted our invitation to introduce us to the reader. I want to thank him and all other contributors for their cooperation.

Jürgen M. Meisel
Universität Hamburg
Romanisches Seminar

Acquiring German and French in a Bilingual Setting

Peter Jordens

Free University Amsterdam

The DUFDE-project on the simultaneous acquisition of German and French as first languages was carried out between 1986 and 1992 under the supervision of Dr. Jürgen M. Meisel. The acronym DUFDE stands for Deutsch und Französisch Doppelter Erstspracherwerb (German and French — Simultaneous Acquisition of Two First Languages). In the present volume, acquisition data from five children were analyzed: Caroline (1;06,26 – 4;01,06), Pierre (2;03,16 – 4;07,11), Ivar (1;10,12 – 3;04,23), Annika (1;10,18 – 4;05,09) and Pascal (1;08,22 – 3;04,14). These children grew up in families in which French was the native language of the mother, and accordingly prominent for those largely in the care of their mothers during the day, and German the native language of the father. In the course of the children's development the linguistic situation changes somewhat. As social relations beyond the family come into play, the role of German becomes more important. The details on data collection, transcription, computation of MLU, and coding conventions are given in the introduction by Regina Köppe. In the following, I would like to point out some of the highlights of this study which touches upon many of the main issues in first language acquisition research today.

The structure of the mental lexicon is relevant to the acquisition of plural morphology and gender attribution. In *The acquisition of gender and number morphology within NP*, Caroline Koehn provides evidence for a representation in terms of schema theory. Within this model, both simple and complex forms are represented independently in the lexicon. Classes of words are established through lexical connections based on shared semantic and phonological properties. The identification of specific phonological features for particular morphological classes, such as singular or plural, provides evidence that schemas play a major role in the organization of the mental lexicon. The internal structure of the lexicon is accounted for through the relations between the schemas that particular items belong to.

In her analysis of plural formation and gender attribution in Ivar (1;5 – 5;0), Koehn provides evidence for the adequacy of schema theory. In the acquisition of plural formation in German and French, there is first a stage (from 2;2 to 2;6) in which Ivar uses *deux* and *zwei* without number marking on the noun, as in *zwei kind*, to refer to two or more objects and *ein* and *un* with nouns to refer to single objects.

Evidence for the functioning of schemas in the acquisition of the grammatical notions of number and gender can be found in Ivar from 2;7 to 5;0. In French, Ivar learns the plural and singular forms of the article system before number distinctions on nouns. In German, on the other hand, number marking is learned first with nouns. With respect to number marking on nouns, there are two stages to be discriminated. First, there is a stage in which the plural and singular forms themselves are produced correctly but often used incorrectly: plural forms are used with singular reference while singular forms are used with plural reference. At this stage, the child appears to use particular schemas. Depending on the cue strengths for plural which are based on saliency, frequency, and reliability, the child discriminates between allomorphs that are more or less typical of plural morphology. See Table 1.

Table 1. Plural nouns – errors in reference

prototypical plural forms		errors in reference: plural nouns with single reference and single nouns with plural reference
polysyllabic -*s*	Autos	0
polysyllabic -*en*	Katzen	15,4
polysyllabic -*e*	Füße/Schuhe	18,2
polysyllabic -*er*	Kinder/Räder	33,3
umlaut	Mütter	50%

Then, from 3;5, allomorphs that were determined as plural forms are overextended. In nouns such as *tischen, keksen, tigern, büchern, froschen, schuhen, händen* -*en* is overgeneralized. Overgeneralization of -*s* only occurs with nouns ending in *-er*. Ivar has a schema in which *-er* is a cue for a singular form and, furthermore, for him plural forms apparently have to be different in shape.

In her analysis of gender attribution in definite articles, Koehn shows that in child French nouns ending in a nasal or *-o* are treated as masculine: *le train*, **le main*; *le garçon*, **le maison*; *le manteau*, **le photo*. In child German, nouns ending in *-er* and *-en* are masculine: *der tiger*, *der räuber*, **der ufer*, **den zimmer*; *der wagen*, *der besen*, **der mädchen*, **der essen*; and nouns ending in *-e* are feminine: *die sonne*, **die hase*. Application of these schemas even leads to the creation of target deviant forms such as **der aff*, **die plakate*.

In her study *Gender and number agreement within DP*, Natascha Müller observed Caroline and Ivar. In the early grammars of Caroline (1;5 – 1;9/2;0) and Ivar (1;6 – 2;4), number and gender are semantic concepts. As far as the concept of singular vs. plural is concerned, numerals are used referentially correctly. Hence, *deux schuhe* 'two shoes' and *deux paket* 'two parcel' refer to two objects and *anot schuhe* 'another shoes', *un autre zu* 'another shoe', *un autre zamono* (animaux) 'another animals' to one object. However, as Müller points out, these number distinctions are used "irrespective of the gender and number specification of the co-occurring nouns." The same holds for gender. Caroline uses *das* 'this' to refer to non-animates, and Ivar uses *aman* 'ein Mann' for animates such as 'a man', 'a woman', 'Ivar's mother', 'a cowboy' and 'a snake'. Summarizing, initially the grammatical features of number and gender are absent. Furthermore, Müller notes that as far as NP syntax is concerned there are two positions available. Consequently, prenominal elements such as numerals, adjectives, and the presyntactic elements [ë], [dë], [a] are used in a mutually exclusive way.

With Caroline at 1;10/2;0 – 2;11 and Ivar at 2;4 – 2;8, indefinite and definite articles are introduced into the children's grammars. Syntactically, however, these articles are part of different systems. Indefinite articles behave like numerals. They have a referential meaning and do not enter into an agreement relation with nouns. Therefore, *ein schwein* 'a pig' or *ein schweine* 'a pigs', *ein kuh* 'a cow' or *ein kühe* 'a cows', and *un autre zenfant* 'another children' are used with singular reference, *zwei kind* 'two child' or *zwei kinder* 'two children' and *zwei aff* 'two monkey' or *zwei affe* 'two monkeys' are used with plural reference. Definite articles, on the other hand, are analyzed as functional elements. They agree with nouns. In German *der* and *die* – in NPs such as *die puppe* 'the doll', *die tasche* 'the bag' – and in French *le/la* are always used with singular nouns. Hence, noun phrases such as **der schweine* 'the=sg pigs', *le/la zamono* 'the=sg animals', *le/la chevaux* 'the=sg horses' or *ce zamono* 'this animals' do not occur. This means that singular nouns are systematically used for singular reference. Plural articles *die* and *les* also agree, as in *die tiere* 'the=pl animals', *les poupées* 'the=pl dolls', *ces zamono* 'these animals' and *diese deckel* 'these covers'. However, they may be used with plural and singular reference. Interestingly, the same holds for bare plurals such as *kinder* 'children', *schuhe* 'shoes' and *zoreilles* 'ears', which can be used with both singular and plural reference, whereas *schuh* 'shoe' and *kind* 'child' are only used with singular reference. Given the fact that plural NPs can be used with either singular or plural reference and that the finite verb form is the unmarked option, children produce utterances such as *où l'est les poussettes* (sing.ref.) 'where they is the baby carriages', *und eh schiffe* (sing.ref.) *paßt* 'and eh boat fits', *les poupées* (plur.ref.) *va pas manzer* 'the dolls will=sg not eat', and *oui les poupées* (plur.ref.) *elles arrivent* 'yes the dolls they arrive'.

As far as gender is concerned, again the definite article has the wrong form only with a few nouns. In French *le* is used with nouns that have a nasal vowel, such as *main* 'hand', *dent* 'tooth', *maison* 'house', *maman* 'mother'; in German *der* and *dieser* are used with monosyllabic words, such as *zahl* 'number', *tür* 'door'; *dach* 'roof', *bett* 'bed', *loch* 'hole', *schiff* 'ship', *boot* 'boat', *bein* 'leg', and *die* is used with words ending in *-a* or *-e*, such as *die opa* 'the grand-pa', *die papa* 'the daddy', *die sofa* 'the sofa'; *die hase* 'the bunny'. The indefinite article, however, is frequently used with the wrong gender. Both indefinite articles can often be used with the same noun.

In his study *Finiteness, agreement and tense in early grammars*, Jürgen Meisel claims that there is no reason to believe that children have access to hierarchical X-bar structure before the age of 2;0. With Bickerton (1990), Meisel believes that around this particular age UG, and with it the properties of X-bar structure, become available through neurological maturation. This means that before children have access to UG principles, early multi-word utterances are organized according to pragmatic principles. As soon as X-bar structure has become available with UG, however, certain options are given with respect to the architectural development of functional categories. What is of crucial importance for the acquisition of the hierarchical structure of a particular language is the discovery of syntactic categories. A major role is given to the acquisition of finite verb forms. According to Meisel, they "enable the learner to identify verbal elements and distinguish them from other predicates." This certainly holds for French. As soon as children are able to identify verbal elements, their grammars have VPs structured as in Figure (1).

(1)   Early VP in French

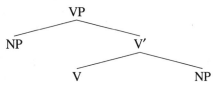

(2)   Early VP in German

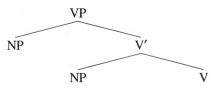

For German, however, it is not immediately obvious how the acquisition of *finite* verb forms leads to VPs structured as in Figure (2). The majority of utterances have a *non-finite* verb in final position. Meisel suggests that initially German children might use both (1) and (2) simultaneously. This is probably true given the fact that initially there are distributional differences between verb forms with finite and non-finite morphology. Stative verbs with a present tense form occur in non-final position, while action verbs and change of state verbs with non-finite verb forms occur in final position. For a similar situation in Dutch child language, see also Jordens (1990).

Given the structural conditions of VP structure, it is Meisel's main objective to discover how children acquire functional categories, mainly IP. The availability of IP in the child's grammar means that there must be a position to which finite verbs are moved. It is Meisel's aim to investigate what exactly the properties of finiteness are which are correlated with evidence of movement. Both agreement and tense have to be considered properties of finiteness. Evidence for the presence of IP in the child's grammar is found (a) if the verb can be preceded by either a subject or a topicalized constituent, (b) when finite verb forms occur before and non-finite verb forms after the negation *nicht* in German or *pas* in French, and (c) if modal verbs are used.

As far as the acquisition of German is concerned, Meisel's investigation shows that subject-verb agreement in German is acquired in two stages by all three subjects investigated: Caroline, Ivar and Pascal. First, the 3rd person singular is acquired as an agreement marker, and 2 to 5 months later the 1st and 2nd person singular forms are learned. The same is true in French for the acquisition of subject clitics, which are relevant for person and number marking. Here, the 3rd person singular clitics (*il* 'he', *elle* 'she', *on* 'one') are acquired two to three months before the 1st and 2nd person singular clitics (*je* 'I' and *tu* 'you'). Evidence for tense distinctions in German is the use of present tense forms alongside auxiliary and past-participle constructions, the use of the verb *war* 'was', and the use of predicates with a modal and a non-finite verb form. Meisel's analysis, first, shows that tense is acquired significantly later than agreement morphology. Furthermore, it turns out that the phenomena that are evidence of movement are acquired simultaneously with 1st and 2nd person singular morphology, but before tense distinctions. Hence, Meisel concludes that finiteness and, therefore, INFL as a position that the finite verb can be moved to, is acquired due to the acquisition of agreement. According to Meisel "agreement alone is sufficient as an instantiation of finiteness." Another interesting finding is that 3rd person singular morphology is used before the acquisition of INFL. Interestingly, a similar observation has been made by Clahsen (1986), who attributes it to the semantico-pragmatic function of low-transitivity. Meisel, however, claims that these early 3rd person singular markings within VP are evidence of an elementary version of agreement. It marks the syntactic specifier-head relation between two elements without the sharing of features. Hence, it is representative of the default agreement value which is used when other options are not yet available.

Having implemented IP, Meisel's subjects end up with structures without CP. At this point in the children's development, French and German child grammars differ only with respect to headedness within VP. Due to the lack of CP, German child grammar is not yet a true V2 language. One may ask if German/French bilingual children are any different from monolingual German children in this respect.

In *More about INFL-ection and Agreement: The acquisition of clitic pronouns in French*, Georg Kaiser investigates the acquisition of subject and object clitics in Pascal and Ivar learning French. For adult French it is assumed that both subject clitics, as in *Jean il mange* 'John he eats' and *il mange Jean* 'he eats John', and object clitics, as for example in *Marie le lui a donné le livre à Jean* 'Mary it to him has given the book to John', are to be seen as agreement markers. However, subject and object clitics have a different linguistic status. Subject clitics are generated in INFL and object clitics are base-generated in V. Given this analysis and assuming that functional categories are lacking initially, Kaiser expects subject clitics to become available as soon as children have access to functional categories.

From the analysis of Pascal's and Ivar's data it can be shown that within one or two months, the 3rd person singular clitics *il/elle* 'he/she' and somewhat later *on* 'one', *je* 'I' and *tu* 'you' are acquired. Interestingly, *on*, formally a 3rd person singular clitic which functions semantically as a 1st person clitic, as in *ici, on peut dormir* 'here we can sleep', is acquired simultaneously with *je* and *tu*. With respect to object clitics, Kaiser observes that these were not used productively during the time that subject clitics were acquired. Kaiser argues that subject clitics also function in acquisition as agreement markers. Evidence is, first, the productive use of subject clitics simultaneously with the acquisition of the morphological distinction between finite and non-finite verbs (Meisel, this volume). Secondly, Kaiser observes that Pascal never uses a subject clitic in combination with a non-finite verb form. Finally, both children use subject clitics together with subject NPs or subject pronouns, as for example in *la grand-mère elle est là* 'the grand-mother she is here' (Pa 2;3) and *Ivar i répare* 'Ivar he repairs' (Iv 2;5).

In particular cases clitics are absent. This can also be seen as evidence that clitics are used as agreement markers. Firstly, clitics are absent in sentences with *être* 'be', *avoir* 'have' and *aller* 'go'. Examples are *est pas là* 'is not here' (Pa 2;10); *ai mal oreille(s) avant* 'have [1st person sg] bad ear(s) before' (Pa 2;9); *ai bien ai bien souri* 'have well have well smiled' (Iv 2;10); *va va après manger* 'will will afterwards eat' (Iv 2;8). Kaiser argues that this is what should be expected. Verbs such as *être*, *avoir* and *aller* have complex inflectional morphology and, therefore, clitics are not needed as agreement markers. Furthermore, sentences with intransitive verbs such as *dormir* 'sleep' and *tomber* 'fall' and sentences with modals verbs such as *vouloir* 'want' and *pouvoir* 'can' are used without subject clitics too. Examples are *dort bébé* 'sleeps baby' (Iv 2;0); *tombé berg* 'fallen mountain-[Germ.]' (Iv 2;4); *veux roir[=voir] aussi* 'will see too' (Pa 2;9); *peut avec l'auto aussi* 'can with the car too' (Pa 2;11); *veux courir* 'will run' (Iv 2;6); *peut peut pas rouner [rouler]* 'can can not go' (Iv 2;7). Kaiser claims that this is because the intransitive verbs *dormir* and *tomber* are used like impersonal verbs such as *falloir* 'have to', *paraître* 'appear' and *y avoir* 'there be' in *faut mett(re) des petites* 'have to put some little ones' (Pa 2;6); *y a rien* 'there is nothing' (Iv 2;9). He argues that in sentences in which there is no thematic subject, agreement does not apply. Here, it should be pointed out that this holds for modal verbs too. In Hoekstra & Jordens (1993) it was shown that in Dutch child language modals such as *kunnen* 'can' and *mogen* 'may' are first used non-thematically the same way as in the adult language. Adult French should have this option too. I would argue, therefore, that for *peut avec l'auto aussi* 'can with the car too' (Pa 2;11) and *peut peut pas rouner [rouler]* 'can can not go' (Iv 2;7) a similar analysis is possible. Summarizing, Kaiser's study provides sound evidence that subject clitics in French are acquired as agreement markers and, hence, the acquisition of subject clitics is evidence that children have access to INFL.

Achim Stenzel analyses German and French data from Pascal (1;8 – 4;10) and Annika (2;0 – 3;10) in *Case assignment and functional categories in bilingual children: Routes of development and implications for linguistic theory.* This study investigates what determines the acquisition of case marking or, put differently, what triggers abstract case. Theoretically, case marking is related to the category INFL. As illustrated in Figure (3), INFL is a prerequisite for structural case because it licenses NPs at the level of S-structure.

(3)   IP in German and French

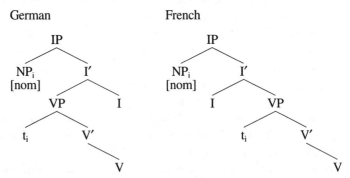

Furthermore, both INFL and DET are functional categories. That is, INFL functionally selects a VP and DET functionally selects an NP. In other words, VP is the complement of the functional head INFL, while NP is the complement of the functional head DET. As Stenzel argues, this structural equivalence corresponds to a semantic similarity as well: Determiners specify the reference of an NP, while tense, as a property of INFL, locates a particular event in time. The structural equivalence of DPs to IPs can be inferred from a comparison of an IP structure such as in (3) and a DP structure such as in Figure (4).

(4)   DP in German and French

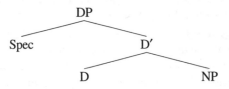

From the analysis of the data as produced by Pascal, it appears that evidence of INFL, such as finiteness, and V2 effects in German and clitics in French, is used before children are able to discriminate between nominative and accusative case. From this Stenzel concludes that "with the implementation of INFL [around 2;2 or 2;3] in the child's grammar, the structural necessity for case is introduced as the child is pressed to find an element [around 2;4] that discharges Nominative case included in INFL." The same holds for the implementation of DET with respect to nominative and accusative Case. Structural case can only be licensed after the child's grammar has the functional category DET.

The relevance of the DP analysis for the acquisition of Case is also demonstrated with respect to the acquisition of the Genitive.

(5)   DP with genitive Case

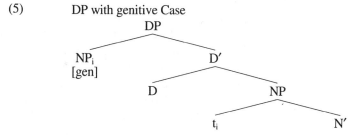

Figure (5) illustrates that structural case is licensed by DET, while semantic features are assigned within NP. This explains why in early child grammars without functional categories Genitives are used without the syntactic context of a possessor-possessed construction, as in *das meins* 'that one's mine' (Pa 2;1) and *mamas* [picking up the earrings]: 'mummy's' (An 2;0). For examples such as these, Tracy (1986) has claimed that the Genitive suffix only serves to indicate the semantic feature of possession. Hence, at the relevant stage she also found overgeneralizations of the Genitive suffix to Dative contexts involving possession, as in *das gehört Maltes* pointing to some object: 'that belongs to Malte's$_{GEN}$' (Ma 2;6).

Another observation discussed in Stenzel's study is the fact that in the domain of a preposition Pascal overgeneralizes the dative to accusative contexts, as in *und nur noch für dir* 'and still for you$_{DAT}$' (Pa 2;6). Furthermore, Stenzel argues that although she is able to encode syntactic features, Annika applies a morphological avoidance strategy until she has to use the dative and the genitive in order to be able to meet her communicative needs.

In her paper *NP-movement and subject raising*, Regina Köppe discusses the question of the availability of NP movement in child language. More particularly, the aim of her study is to investigate whether or not the acquisition of subject raising is linked to the emergence of IP. Since IP is a functional category that provides a landing site for NP movement "most authors assume that if verb raising to INFL is possible, subject raising to SpecIP follows automatically." In Pierce (1989) and Deprez & Pierce (1991), however, a different view is given. There, it is claimed that children acquiring French have verb raising to INFL without subject raising. This would explain Deprez & Pierce's finding that in the initial stages lexical subjects occur in postverbal position, as in *pas manger la poupée* 'not eat the doll'; *assis la poupée* 'seated the doll'; *est froid le camion* 'is cold the truck'; *travaille papa* 'works papa'; *bois peu moi* 'drink little me' (Pierce 1989:32,33).

Given the fact that subject raising requires INFL to provide SpecIP as a landing site and that initially child grammars do not have INFL, Köppe's investigation focuses on the developmental stage, at which there is evidence that INFL becomes part of child grammar. In the early stages of German, children have OV order, therefore, SVO order is evidence for both INFL and subject raising. In French, however, word order may not provide clear evidence. This is because IP and VP order is the same for transitive and intransitive verbs. Only with ergative verbs, as in *il arrive Pierre* 'he-comes Pierre', the subject does originate in postverbal position. Ergative verbs, however, are not reliable either, because it is possible that subjects are simply adjoined to the right of VP, as in *il mange une pomme Pierre* 'he-eats an apple Pierre'. Hence, for subject and verb raising another criterion has to be found. Köppe decides on the position of the subject and the verb with respect to sentence-internal negation. Both subjects and INFL are judged to be raised if they occur before sentence-internal negation. Furthermore, subject raising can also be identified independently. Subjects are raised to SpecIP if they precede a finite verb.

In Köppe's analysis of the data from Pascal and Ivar, two stages appear to be relevant. Initially, there is no evidence for the availability of IP. Regarding the acquisition of French this is illustrated with utterances such as *ouvrir chaussures* 'open$_{inf}$ shoes' (Pa 1;10) and *mouton sauter* 'sheep jump$_{inf}$' (Iv 2;2). From about 2;2 (Pascal) and 2;4 (Ivar) there is evidence for INFL and subject raising: *margarine tombe pas* 'margarine falls not' (Pa 2;0) and *teddy tombe pas* 'teddy bear falls not' (Iv 2;4). Re-analysis of Pierce's data reveals that the finding of a decreasing number of postverbal subjects is an artifact of the way in which the data were analyzed. In German, Pascal and Ivar have early cases of verb and subject raising: *papa mach diese* 'daddy make these' (Pa 2;0), *ich will nich* 'I want not' (Pa 2;0), *das nimm en deddi* 'this takes a teddy bear' (Iv 2;3) and *kommt das (nich)* 'comes this not' (Iv 2;3). However, systematic evidence of utterances in which both subject and verb precede sentence-internal negation occur from about 2;2 (Pascal) and 2;4 (Ivar).

Köppe observes that in the French data ergative verbs are the first that have verb and subject raising, whereas in the German data it is the transitive verbs that have verb and subject raising first. For Köppe this is reason to advance the interesting speculation that "the recognition of structural differences in the ordering of verbs and their complements at the level of VP might serve as a trigger for the development of the functional projection IP."

In *Parameters cannot be reset: Evidence from the development of COMP*, Natascha Müller clearly distinguishes two phases in the use of functional categories in German and French. First, there is a phase in which the category C is absent. In the early grammars of Ivar (at 2;4), Caroline (at 2;1) and Pascal (at 2;2), INFL, AGR and German V2 patterns are present. Evidence for the unavailability of the C-system is the fact that there are no complementizers of any kind and no subordination. Examples are *guck mal – ich hab, hab ich* 'look I have, have I' (Ca 2;6), *kannst du ihn k-trag k-hast du auch ... so ein haus ne?* 'can you him ask have you such a house?' (Iv 3;4), and *demander maman – là il est* 'ask Mommy there it is' (Iv 2;6). Furthermore, in French there is no inversion in root interrogatives. One example is *où il est (le) nounours?* 'where it is the teddy?' (Iv 2;6). As has been pointed out by Weissenborn (1990) for this type of inversion in French, the C-system is also required.

The absence of the functional category COMP implies that there are no embeddings with *wh*-elements either. At the relevant stage, however, main clauses can be introduced by *wh*-words, as in *wo is der auto?* 'where is the car?' (Iv 2;8). This can be explained by the syntactic difference between a lexically selected *wh*-specification in embedded clauses occurring in COMP and a non-selected *wh*-specification in main clauses occurring in INFL.

In the second phase, Ivar appears to acquire the C-system in German and French around 2;11, Caroline at 2;6 in French and 3;1 in German, Pascal at 2;5 in French and 2;9 in German. With respect to the integration of COMP in French, Müller observes that inversion in root sentences is acquired simultaneously with the use of complementizers in embedded sentences.

In German, Pascal and Caroline follow a route different from Ivar. As soon as Pascal and Caroline use complementizers, embedded clauses also have the verb-final pattern. The presence of a complementizer prevents the finite verb from moving to the V2 position. Hence, it can be concluded that both finite verbs and lexically selected *wh*-constituents are assigned to the same syntactic position. The data from Ivar show, however, that he does not analyze complementizers as functional categories, unlike Pascal and Caroline. Firstly, he uses only complementizers such as *weil* 'because', *als* 'when', *wenn* 'if' which cannot occur as moved *wh*-specifications, unlike *was* 'what', *wo* 'where', *wie* 'how'. Furthermore, he seems to develop COMP out of a lexical category. Evidence for this is the use of *für* in *f[o] de f[o] de reiten komm du* 'for it ride come you' (Iv 2;9), and *das ist für der rauch geht hoch, in das hau* 'this is for the smoke goes up, in the house' (Iv 3;4). The fact that lexically selected WH and F are distributed across different categories in Ivar's grammar explains V2 effects in subordinate clauses as in *erst wenn wir sind fertig mit das* 'just when we have finished with it' (Iv 3;4) about 3;2. At later stages of acquisition, Müller has found evidence that Ivar learns to use verb-final in embedded sentences for each lexical C-element separately. It demonstrates her hypothesis that as soon as a parameter has been set, resetting is impossible.

References

Bickerton, Derek. 1990. *Language and Species*. Chicago: The University of Chicago Press.

Clahsen, Harald. 1986. "Verb Inflections in German Child Language: Acquisition of agreement markings and the functions they encode." *Linguistics* 24.79–121.

Deprez, Viviane & Pierce, Amy. 1991. "Negation and Functional Categories in Early Grammar." Paper presented at the GLOW meeting, Leiden, March 1991.

Hoekstra, Teun & Peter Jordens. 1993. "From Adjunct to Head." Paper presented at the GLOW meeting, Leiden, March 1991.

Jordens, Peter. 1990. "The Acquisition of Verb Placement." *Linguistics* 28.1407–1448.

Pierce, Amy. 1989. *On the Emergence of Syntax: A crosslinguistic study*. Dissertation, Massachusetts Institute of Technology.

Tracy, Rosemarie. 1986. "The Acquisition of Case Morphology in German." *Linguistics* 24.47–78.

Weissenborn, Jürgen. 1990. "Functional Categories and Verb Movement in Early French and German." Paper presented at DFG-colloquium in Nijmegen, 1990.

The DUFDE Project

Regina Köppe
University of Hamburg

1. Introduction

The purpose of this chapter is to give a brief description of the DUFDE project[1] as well as of the methodology used for data collection, transcription and analysis.[2]

2. Design of the Study

In the DUFDE project, the simultaneous acquisition of German and French by children of preschool age was studied longitudinally. From the beginning of linguistic development (age 1;0–1;6)[3] up to the age of at least 5 years, the children's speech has been videotaped every second week. The bilingual children taking part in the study are growing up in middle-class families in Hamburg, Germany. In general, one, or even both parents, holds a university degree. French is the native language of the mothers, while the fathers' native language is German. Each parent uses his or her respective native tongue when communicating with the children. This principle of *une personne – une langue* (Ronjat 1913) has been judged as particularly successful in promoting the development of a balanced bilingualism (e.g. Grosjean 1982).

As of May 1992, a total of 13 children have been recorded. Recordings with those children listed in the upper half of Table 1 had to be discontinued because they did not seem to develop the kind of balanced bilingualism required for our analyses. The recordings of Lena were used for comparison purposes. Finally, all seven children listed in the lower half were recorded up to age 5 and over, and their linguistic development has been studied in the DUFDE project. The speech of Pierre, Caroline, Christophe, François, and Ivar has been analyzed in the contributions in Meisel (ed.) (1990). The present volume is concerned with various aspects of the grammatical development of Pierre, Caroline, Ivar, Annika, and Pascal.

Table 1. Recording periods

Child	Recording period
Aline	0;11,19–2;02,14
Gerlinde	1;03,11–1;06,04
Claire	1;05,21–1;08,04
Fabrice	1;06,13–2;06,22
Maxime	2;02,17–2;06,02
Lena	3;01,15–5;02,26
Pierre	1;00,21–9;00,28
Caroline	1;01,28–5;00,06
Christophe	1;10,02–5;00,01
François	1;10,13–6;06,01
Ivar	1;05,24–6;03,03
Annika	1;04,12–5;07,01
Pascal	1;05,21–5;05,16

3. Data Collection

3.1. Video Recordings

The video recordings consist mainly of free interaction in play situations in the children's homes, lasting about 60 minutes each, half in German and half in French. The recordings have been made by two research assistants, one a native speaker of French, the other a native speaker of German. While the French assistant played with the child, the German assistant operated the video equipment, and vice versa; one person was therefore not involved in the interaction. Furthermore, the interviewers were required to keep languages strictly separated, i.e. to stick consistently to their native language and not to follow switches to the other language. In the first recordings, however, the French-speaking mother was usually present even during the German part.

In our experience, in most of the cases, this recording situation did not influence the child's behavior and linguistic production, as the assistants were generally regarded by the child as being friends, and the video equipment was seen as an integral part of the play situation.

3.2. *Situation Protocols*

At each recording session, situation protocols were established where changes in the child's general and linguistic development as well as changes in his/her linguistic environment (e.g. holidays in a French-speaking country or the presence of French-speaking persons in the child's home) were noted. In this way, the influence of external factors on the development of one or the other language could be controlled.

Some parents also helped us in establishing lists of new words the child used or diaries of his/her development, etc. Twice a year, a report on the social, biological and linguistic development of the child was written on the basis of these two data sources.

3.3. *Tape Recordings*

Approximately every three months, we asked the parents to make a tape recording of the child's speech, if possible without the child being aware of it. This enabled us to evaluate whether the video recordings are representative of the child's speech and to ensure that the presence of the video equipment did not distort the child's linguistic and other behavior.

4.   Transcriptions

At least one recording per month has been transcribed; i.e. every second session taped. The transcriptions contain both linguistic and nonlinguistic interactions as well as the relevant contexts. In general, the person who interacted with the child was responsible for transcribing the recording, if possible immediately after the session, so that details of the situation which might have been important for its interpretation were more easily remembered. The remaining recordings of the period in question were transcribed and analyzed especially during crucial phases of development, or if a specific hypothesis needed to be tested on further material.

The transcriptions approximate standard orthography, without, however, adding morphemes which are not yet present in the child's speech, e.g. inflectional suffixes. In cases where the utterance of the child was unclear, ambiguous, or strongly deviant from adult pronunciation, a phonetic transcription offering possible interpretations has been given. All utterances of the child and of the adult have been transcribed, including those of other persons present, e.g. the children's parents or siblings. The situational setting and the nonverbal communication have also been rendered in the transcriptions whenever such contextual features might be relevant for the interpretation of the child's utterance.

The transcript is divided into four columns. The leftmost column contains the nonverbal behavior of the adult, the second column the adult's utterances, the third column the child's utterances, the fourth and rightmost column the child's nonverbal behavior. Simultaneous behavior or utterances are written on the same line, and consecutive utterances and/or behavior are written on consecutive lines, respectively.

Once a transcript has been completed, it is double-checked by a different person who also notes different interpretations of the child's utterances, etc.

Table 2. Transcription conventions

[...]	phonetic transcription
(...)	possible interpretation in terms of target language
(xx)	uninterpretable utterances or parts of utterances, each x representing one syllable
( )	words which cannot be interpreted unambiguously
.	longer pause
,	shorter pause or intonation break
–	aborted utterances

5. Mean Length of Utterance (MLU)

MLU values have been computed for at least every second transcription. Their calculation is based on the number of morphemes, not of words. This is to say that *dies-e Kind-er* 'these child-ren' is counted as four morphemes. Once a lexical item appears in different forms in a child's speech, corresponding to contrasting inflectional morphemes (e.g. *suche – suchst* 'search 1SG' – 'search 2SG'), these morphemes are considered to be used productively by the child and are counted when computing the MLU values. If, for example, the child uses the pronouns *ich* 'I' and *du* 'you', each pronoun is awarded two points. No form is given more than two points. Although this is an arbitrary restriction, it avoids extreme discrepancies between German and French MLU values, in view of the fact that German has a richer inflectional system and an abundance of poly-functional forms. Since overt markings are sometimes lacking in French, when compared to their German equivalents, it would be impossible in principle to reach the same values in French as in German. Simple answers like *ja/oui* 'yes' and *nein/non* 'no' are calculated only once per transcription; formulas and direct imitations as well are assigned only one point.

We are, of course, aware of the fact that MLU values are problematic as indicators for linguistic development, for increasing length of utterance need not necessarily correspond to increasing complexity. To mention only some of the problems, it may be difficult to establish utterance boundaries, different persons may calculate formulas or imitations differently, and the first appearance of two forms of a word need not mean that a morpheme is used productively. Most importantly, the difference between paratactic and hypotactic constructions is not captured at all. If used in combination with qualitative analyses, MLU values may, nevertheless, serve as a possible measure of the developmental level reached by the child, and it enables one to establish an approximate means to compare children's linguistic achievements at given points.

6. Computer Analysis

The transcriptions have been entered into a computer, using the database dBase III+. Each utterance represents a separate entry which receives specific codings. The coding system is based essentially on Clahsen's profile analysis (Clahsen 1986) and on the program developed by Clahsen to calculate the "Profile Chart", although the program has been adapted for our purposes.

The system allows one to code different kinds of morphosyntactic information, e.g. the number of constituents, MLU values, the type of sentence structure, inflection of nominal, adverbial, and verbal elements, as well as negation, question, case marking, gender, etc. Attention has been paid to separate codings of form and function, in order to gain insights into how the child maps one onto the other. The program used also permits us to relate different kinds of information to each other, e.g. word order and inflectional markings, thus enabling us to verify hypotheses concerning developmental relationships between the different devices studied.

The linguistic analyses presented in this volume are based on all the data available: video recordings, hand-written transcripts, and computer-analyzed data.

7. Children Studied in this Volume

Before turning to the individual characterization of the children studied in this volume, I would like to point out one general observation which holds for all of them. Concerning the linguistic development, French initially appears to be the dominant input language, and during this period it is also the language preferred by the children. As soon as social relations beyond the family become more important (e.g. German-speaking playmates, kindergarten, etc.), the role of German as well as a preference for it increases. Note however that such a slight imbalance — mainly in terms of vocabulary — is quite natural under the given conditions of acquisition.

7.1. *Caroline*

Caroline (= C) is an only child. At the age of 9 months she started going to a German daycare center. Consequently, she has been exposed to German more frequently than to French, the language used primarily with her mother and with some French friends. The family usually spends holidays in France where French is spoken exclusively. On the average, this happens three times a year. During a period of several months, beginning at the age of about 3 years, Caroline stopped speaking French. Even when communicating with her mother, she would respond in German. Later, she spoke French more willingly, but her language behavior varied throughout the period studied, with more French production directly after a trip to France; this is reflected in the changes of her MLU values.

Table 3. MLU Caroline[4]

Recording	Age	MLU German	(base)	MLU French	(base)
08	1;06,26	1.19	(both languages)		
12	1;09,16	1.35	(31)	1.85	
15	1;11,04	1.55	(54)	2.13	(46)
18	2;00,09	2.23	(50)	——	(86)
20	2;01,13	1.93	(55)	2.09	(20)
24	2;03,11	2.30		2.50	(76)
26	2;04,08	2.12	(25)	3.23	(52)
33	2;07,20	3.08	(73)	3.16	(24)
38	2;10,28	3.62	(83)	3.68	(19)
40	3;00,02	3.96	(50)	——	
42	3;02,10	3.65	(41)	4.08	(34)
44	3;03,10	4.30		3.78	(41)
48	3;06,11	4.86	(59)	——	
56	3;10,20	5.99	(85)	5.61	
61	4;01,06	6.07	(40)	4.3	(40)

7.2. Pierre

Pierre (= P) is a second child; he usually speaks French with his sister who is three years older. At the age of 2;8 he began to attend a French kindergarten. Since their mother works in a shop the family owns, a young woman frequently looks after the children in the afternoon. Pierre and his sister speak German with their babysitter, and they communicate in French with their mother. Every year, the family spends approximately six or seven weeks in France or in the French-speaking part of Switzerland. During this time, they speak German only with their father. Pierre's linguistic development is generally somewhat slower than that of the other children, by at least three months, when compared to Ivar, Pascal, Annika, and Caroline.

Table 4. MLU Pierre

Recording	Age	MLU German	(base)	MLU French	(base)
22	2;03,16	1.3	(20)	1.26	(65)
29	2;07,06	1.52	(84)	1.97	(67)
33	2;09,02	2.32	(59)	3.06	(98)
38	2;11,10	2.46	(88)	3.72	(79)
42	3;01,09	3.18	(90)	4.29	
45	3;02,23	2.76		3.48	(72)
49	3;05,03	4.34	(99)	5.08	(50)
52	3;06,14	4.26	(96)	5.28	(73)
56	3;09,05	5.22	(95)	5.44	(50)
60	3;11,02	5.51	(49)	6.3	(48)
66	4;02,03	5.27	(83)	6.38	(98)
72	4;04,25	6.28		6.57	
76	4;07,11	6.41	(87)	6.6	(99)

7.3. Ivar

Ivar (=Iv), a boy, is a first child. His younger brother was born when he was 4;2. Ivar's parents use French as the language of communication. Ivar's mother takes him to France to see his grandparents and other relatives about twice a year. She also makes considerable efforts to ensure that he has sufficient opportunities to speak French by maintaining contact with French-speaking friends in Hamburg. Up to the age of 4 years, Ivar was looked after by a German sitter three times a week. Beginning at the age of 3;0, he also participated in a German-speaking playgroup; from 4;0 up to 4;9 he attended a French kindergarten three to four times a week before he returned to a German kindergarten. Finally, Ivar began to attend a German preschool.

Ivar's two languages have always been well in balance, except for a short period at age 2;3, when, according to our analyses, his French was weaker. His linguistic development is average, when compared to other children studied by our research team.

Table 5. MLU Ivar

Recording	Age	MLU German	(base)	MLU French	(base)
07	1;10,12	1.12	(69)	1.13	
09	1;11,17	1.41	(99)	1.31	(68)
10	2;00,02	1.68		insufficient base	
12	2;00,29	1.63		1.31	
14	2;02,07	1.71		1.47	
16	2;03,05	1.80		1.35	
18	2;04,09	1.83		1.29	
20	2;05,07	2.76		2.93	
22	2;06,06	3.03		3.58	
24	2;07,17	3.35		3.51	
26	2;08,15	3.52		3.96	
28	2;09,18	3.82		4.55	
30	2;10,24	4.29		4.90	
32	2;11,21	4.77		4.90	
34	3;01,03	4.55		5.47	
36	3;02,14	3.90		6.01	
40	3;04,23	5.68		6.67	

7.4. *Annika*

Annika (=A), a girl, is a first child. Her younger brother was born when she was 2;9. Annika's mother, a French and Malagasy bilingual herself, stayed home to take care of the children until Annika was 4;0. Annika's parents speak German with each other, but her mother insists on being addressed in French by the children. In addition, Annika speaks French with French friends in Germany and during stays in France or Madagascar (approximately six weeks every year). From the age of 2;11 onwards, Annika spent weekday mornings in a German daycare center.

Concerning Annika's linguistic development, both languages initially seem to have been well developed. Already before age 2;0, she clearly followed the one-person-one-language principle. After age 2;6, German began to be the more dominant language, and her German vocabulary expanded quickly. From about 3;0 onwards, we observed that Annika began to develop different avoidance strategies helping her to cope with increasing problems of vocabulary in French during later phases of development.

Table 6. MLU Annika

Recording	Age	MLU German	(base)	MLU French	(base)
11	1;10,18	1.35	(93)	1.14	(48)
12	2;00,10	1.12	(48)	1.15	(50)
13	2;00,17	1.48	(93)	1.59	
15	2;01,10	1.31		1.33	
19	2;03,16	2.05		1.83	
22	2;05,18	2.33		2.39	
26	2;07,29	2.3	(94)	2.16	(92)
29	2;10,00	3.5		3.55	
31	2;10,27	4.2	(20)	——	
32	2;11,27	4.26		2.87	(92)
34	3;00,29	3.16		2.8	
36	3;01,26	3.83		3.52	
40	3;03,21	5.41		3.37	
44	3;05,30	6.84		4.08	
47	3;07,13	9.94		4.24	
49	3;08,24	4.8		3.03	
50	3;09,19	5.24		5.21	
54	4;00,29	5.71		4.71	
57	4;02,26	5.15		4.42	
60	4;05,09	6.14		4.00	

7.5. *Pascal*

Pascal (=Pa), a boy, is the younger of two children. His mother has remained in the home to care for her children. With his sister, who is two years older, Pascal speaks French as well as German. At the age of three, he started going to a bilingual French–German daycare center. The family goes to France twice every year.

Pascal always used both languages, although, initially, French has been somewhat dominant, whereas later on German apparently began to be the slightly preferred language.

Table 7. MLU Pascal

Recording	Age	MLU German	MLU French
04	1;08,22	1.07	1.06
06	1;10,00	1.70	1.57
08	1;10,28	1.63	1.85
10	1;11,28	1.58	1.63
12	2;01,00	1.97	2.14
14	2;01,28	2.15	2.49
16	2;02,26	2.04	2.42
18	2;04,07	2.81	3.45
20	2;05,05	3.17	3.63
22	2;06,02	2.74	3.93
24	2;07,00	3.09	4.53
25	2;08,17	4.35	4.87
29	2;10,13	4.30	5.00
31	2;11,11	4.05	4.47
33	3;00,14	4.15	4.82
35	3;01,20	4.10	3.98
36	3;02,23	5.14	5.60
38	3;04,14	5.79	5.44

Notes

1. DUFDE = Deutsch und Französisch — Doppelter Erstspracherwerb (German and French — Simultaneous Acquisition of Two First Languages), a research project made possible by several research grants (1986–1992) by the Deutsche Forschungs- gemeinschaft to Jürgen M. Meisel. During the period when the contributions to this volume were written, the researchers in this team were Caroline Koehn, Regina Köppe, Natascha Müller, and Achim Stenzel. Students collaborating as research assistants were Cornelia Huβmann and Christophe Bresoli.

2. I would like to thank Suzanne Schlyter for her permission to use parts of her presentation of the DUFDE project in Schlyter (1990) as the basis of this chapter. Special thanks also go to Susanne E. Carroll who has lent me her competence as a native speaker.

3. The age of the children is given in years;months,days. Note that, in this volume, sometimes only years and months are indicated, whereas in other cases, the precise age is given. This is done in order to identify specific recordings, e.g. when two recordings made in the same month are analyzed.

4. The base for calculations is indicated only if it is lower than 100.

Bibliography

This bibliography, in addition to listing the titles quoted in the foregoing text, contains a number of unpublished studies which have been carried out by the following students and researchers working in the DUFDE project: Berkele, Dieck, Jekat, Kaiser, Klinge, Koehn, Köppe, Meisel, Müller, Parodi, Schlyter, Veh, and Williams.

References

Clahsen, Harald. 1986. *Die Profilanalyse: Ein linguistisches Verfahren zur Sprachdiagnose im Vorschulalter*. Berlin: Marhold.

Grosjean, François. 1982. *Life With Two Languages: An introduction to bilingualism*. Cambridge, Mass.: Harvard University Press.

Meisel, Jürgen M. (ed.). 1990. *Two First Languages: Early grammatical development in bilingual children (=Studies on Language Acquisition, 10.)*. Dordrecht: Foris.

Ronjat, Jules. 1913. *Le développement du langage observé chez un enfant bilingue*. Paris: Champion.

Schlyter, Suzanne. 1990. "Introducing the DUFDE project." Meisel 1990, 73–84.

DUFDE studies

Berkele, Gisela. 1983. *Die Entwicklung des Ausdrucks von Objektreferenz am Beispiel der Determinanten: Eine empirische Untersuchung zum Spracherwerb bilingualer Kinder (Französisch/Deutsch)*. "Staatsexamen"-thesis, University of Hamburg.

Dieck, Marianne. 1989. *Der Erwerb der Negation bei bilingualen Kindern (Französisch – Deutsch): Eine Fallstudie*. Masters thesis, University of Hamburg.

Jekat, Susanne. 1985. *Die Entwicklung des Wortschatzes bei bilingualen Kindern (Französisch – Deutsch) in den ersten vier Lebensjahren*. Masters thesis, University of Hamburg.

Jekat-Rommel, Susanne. 1992. *Zeitkonzept und Zeitreferenz bei bilingualen Kindern (französisch/deutsch) in den ersten fünf Lebensjahren*. Dissertation, University of Hamburg.

Koehn, Caroline. 1989. *Der Erwerb der Pluralmorphologie durch bilinguale Kinder (Französisch/Deutsch): Eine empirische Untersuchung*. Masters thesis, University of Hamburg.

Köppe, Regina. 1990. *Code-switching: Strategien und Funktionen der Sprachwahl bei bilingualen Kindern (Französisch–Deutsch) im Vorschulalter*. Masters thesis, University of Hamburg.

Köppe, Regina & Jürgen M. Meisel. To appear. "Code-switching in Bilingual First Language Acquisition." *One Speaker, Two Languages: Cross-discplinary perspectives on code-switching* ed. by Lesley Milroy & Pieter Muysken. Cambridge: Cambridge University Press.

Meisel, Jürgen M. To appear. "Code-switching and Related Phenomena in Young Bilingual Children: The acquisition of grammatical constraints." *Studies in Second Language Acquisition.*

Müller, Natascha. 1987. *Der Genuserwerb im Französischen und Deutschen: Eine empirische Untersuchung eines bilingualen Kindes.* Masters thesis, University of Hamburg.

————. 1991. *Komplexe Sätze: Der Erwerb von COMP und von Wortstellungsmustern bei bilingualen Kindern (Französisch/Deutsch).* Dissertation, University of Hamburg.

Schlyter, Suzanne. 1987. "Language Mixing and Linguistic Level in Three Bilingual Children". *Scandinavian Working Papers on Bilingualism* 7.29–48.

Veh, Birgitta. 1990. *Syntaktische Aspekte des Code-Switching bei bilingualen Kindern (Französisch–Deutsch) im Vorschulalter.* "Staatsexamen"-thesis, University of Hamburg.

Williams, Sarah. 1991. *A Study of the Occurrence and Functions of "da" in a Very Young Bilingual Child.* Dissertation, University of Hamburg.

The Acquisition of Gender and Number Morphology within NP

Caroline Koehn
Therapiezentrum Burgau

1. Introduction

In the acquisition of gender and number at least four different tasks have to be faced. First, the child has to develop the underlying semantic concept for number, namely the distinction between *one* and *more than one*. Furthermore, the child has to recognize that gender and number are systematically encoded on specific syntactic categories, i.e. the corresponding grammatical features have to arise. In addition to this, the appropriate morphological realizations of these features have to be acquired as well as the related agreement phenomena. For the acquisition of agreement phenomena within NP as a syntactic phenomenon, I refer the reader to Müller (this volume, chap. 3). The main interest of my paper will be the acquisition and representation of morphologically complex forms, which I suppose to be a matter of the lexicon. For this purpose, only nouns and articles will be considered.

Concerning the acquisition of morphological markings, I will show that the schema model, initially put forward by Bybee and Slobin (1982),[1] can provide an explanation for the development of both number and gender.

2. The Theoretical Framework

2.1. Rules and Representations

In morphology, the term *rule* is used to refer to at least two different concepts: On the one hand, processes underlying morphological behavior are termed *rules*. On the other hand, the term is meant to cover the regularities that can be observed in the morphological system of a particular language. In the following, the distributional patterns of allomorphic variation will be referred to as *regularities*. The term *rule* will be reserved for the process adding inflectional morphemes to base forms of words. I will argue, however, that mechanisms different from RULES are involved as well in the processing of morphological information (cf. the section on schemas below).

Traditional models of plural formation and of morphology in general postulate separate components for rules and representations. The most popular among these has been the *Item and Process* (IP) model (cf. Hockett 1954). This approach assumes one underlying form for each morpheme to be stored in the mental lexicon. The difference between alternating allomorphs is described as a feature changing *Process* that derives the different surface forms from the underlying *Item*. The various inflected forms of a given base are explained by the *Process* of suffixation. Irregular plurals are supposed to be stored as such in lists of exceptions.[2]

A crucial characteristic of this model is that it assumes the morphological realization of grammatical categories to be either categorically regular or arbitrarily exceptional. In the description of the model I will use for my own analysis (see below), I will show that no such sharp distinction can be drawn between rules and representations, but that they rather constitute the extreme poles of a continuum.

According to the *Item and Process* approach, the acquisition of plural morphology is conceived of as learning of forms (plural allomorphs) and rules. Consequently, errors observed during the acquisition process are usually explained as omissions of particular allomorphs or as non-applications of determined rules respectively (cf. Berko 1958).

2.2. *Evidence against Item and Process*

The results of an elicitation task carried out by Bybee and Slobin (1982) indicate that the omission of a morphological ending depends on the base form of the item to which it should have been added rather than to concern determined allomorphs or rules. Bybee and Slobin asked preschool children to provide the past-tense forms of regular as well as of irregular verbs. One of their findings was that the children showed a significant tendency not to add the past-tense affix ({/ed/}, {/d/} or {/t/}) to verbs ending in /t/ or /d/ respectively. This means that the children tended to leave verbs like e.g. *want* unchanged, accepting them as being already marked for past-tense. A reinterpretation of the observations made by other researchers (cf. Berko 1958; Anisfeld & Tucker 1967; Bryant & Anisfeld 1969; Graves & Koziol 1971; Ivimey 1975; Derwing & Baker 1980) with respect to the acquisition of plural markings yielded similar results. This led to the conclusion that children initially do not predominantly operate with a suffixation rule adding a given morpheme to base forms of nouns or verbs but that they also take into consideration the desired shape of the target-form. I.e. they initially seem to formulate generalizations concerning the shape of product-forms (here: plural-forms). This may lead the child to accept a stem-form ending in the required sound as being sufficiently marked for past-tense or plural respectively.

2.3. *The Schema Model*

The basic assumption made by this approach is that relations do not only exist between base-forms and derived ones in terms of affixation-rules but that generalizations can be formulated with respect to the phonological properties of the *product-class*, i.e. of plural-forms, as well. Central notions of the model are *lexical strength* and *lexical connection*. *Lexical strength* is an index of word frequency. The lexical strength of a stored form is reinforced whenever it is phonologically and semantically matched by an input form, or produced successfully; i.e., repeated processing of a word strengthens its mental representation. In case of a partial match, a *lexical connection* is established for the corresponding parts. Lexical connections may concern semantic or phonological features. *Morphological relations* consist of parallel semantic and phonological connections. They may refer to stems as well as to affixes (cf. example).

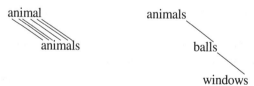

Figure 1. Morphological relations

These assumptions imply that affixes in general are not stored independently of the stems with which they occur and that the internal structure of morphologically complex forms is recognized by comparison with other forms containing the same elements. This is quite conceivable seen the fact that in language acquisition, rules have to be induced by comparison of related forms which are represented in the mental lexicon. This means that at least a certain amount of morphologically complex forms simply has to be learned in the sense that they have to be extracted from the input as a whole and, at least initially, have to be processed and stored as such.[3] It seems plausible to suggest that in languages where no regularities of a categorical type can be found (as it is the case for allomorphic variation in German noun plural formation) the number of forms that have to be learned in this way before the first rules can be induced is indeed very high.

On the basis of lexical connections, classes of words may be established that contain forms which share certain semantic and phonological features. At a higher level of abstraction, schemas may evolve which specify characteristic phonological features for a given morphological class (for example plural). For English plurals, such a schema may be stated for instance: "A noun form ending in /s/ or /z/, respectively, is likely to be a plural."

On the basis of a schema, the language-user may decide whether a given form is a plural or not. In addition to this, schemas may occasionally serve as a basis for new formations in so-called analogical formations. It has to be noted that there is no contradiction between the existence of affixation rules on the one hand and schemas on the other. Rather, they are to be understood as complementary to each other as far as the adult language is concerned. With respect to language acquisition, schemas may be hypothesized to be precursors to source-oriented rules. The perception of similarities between stored items and their organization is a prerequisite for the acquisition of combinatory rules anyway. In this sense, it is a further step to relate one class, described by a schema, to some other class by means of a rule that specifies how to proceed from the basic to the derived form.

Thus a picture emerges where we do not need separate components for rules and representations. Instead, we only have a lexicon. This lexicon necessarily contains representations of suppletive (plural-)forms but also a certain amount of "completely regular" forms. These stored forms are organized via a network of lexical connections which are more or less independent of their representations. One prediction made by the approach just described is that the child initially will only be able to associate given forms with their appropriate functions on the basis of phonological shape but s/he will not be able to create new forms on the basis of stored items. Furthermore, once the child has started to produce new formations, the occurrence of product-oriented errors is expected, i.e. singular forms matching a plural schema rather than other singular forms will be employed for reference to several objects and vice versa (for exemplification, see the application of the model to German plural formation below).

Köpcke (1988) has applied the model to the system of plural-inflection in German nouns. He organized form-classes of nouns on the basis of several criteria on a scale. A modified version of this scale is given in Figure 2.[4]

singular   plural

| monosyllabic | polysyllabic | polysyllabic | polysyllabic | polysyllabic |
| | final /ər/ | final /ə/ | final /s/ | final /ən/ |

Figure 2. Possible continuum of schemas for plural nouns, based on Köpcke (1988)

The endpoints of this scale are represented by prototypical singular- and plural-forms respectively. One of the ordering-criteria is the number of syllables: Monosyllabicity is a clear indicator of singularity. A further criterion is the *cue strength* of the ending which again is determined by three different criteria, namely *perceptual salience*, *type frequency* and *reliability*. *Salience* refers to the degree to which a marker is perceptually detectable by a listener. Thus, separable suffixing elements like the allomorphs {/(ə)n/} - {/s/} - {/ə/} - {/ər/} are supposed to be more salient than stem-changing processes like *Umlaut*.[5] *Type frequency* refers to the total number of lexical items that bear a particular allomorph. Here {/(ə)n/} is the most frequent, followed by {/ə/}. {/s/}, {/ər/} and *Umlaut* have low frequency. *Reliability* implies that high frequency of a given ending in the singular correlates with low reliability as a plural allomorph. For the different plural allomorphs of the nominal inflectional system of German the combination of these various factors results in the following rank order of plural allomorphs: {/(ə)n/} - {/s/} - {/ə/} - {/ər/} -{/0/} (cf. Figure 1). One prediction made by the approach presented so far for the acquisition of German is that errors in reference should concern plural forms ending in {/ər/} rather than plurals ending in {/(ə)n/} or {/s/}.

3.   The Gender and Number Systems in French and German

3.1 *Markings*

French has two genders, masculine and feminine. In French, gender is marked on articles, attributive and predicative adjectives, ordinal numbers and substantival and adjectival pronouns (cf. Table 1a). Number markings are provided for nouns and verbs as well. As only nouns and articles are considered in the present article, the description of the target systems will be limited to these categories. The declension of articles is to be found in Table 1a.

A peculiarity of the French gender system is that if a function word precedes a noun beginning with a vowel, the function word will be either elided (e.g. *l'image* 'the picture (f)' instead of **la image*) or a form ending in a consonant (predominantly the masculine form) will be chosen regardless of the gender of the noun (e.g. *mon image* 'my picture' instead of **ma image*).

As far as number is concerned, in these cases fusion of the final (plural-) {/s/} of the determiner with the following vowel is to be found, a phenomenon called *liaison*. The masculine definite article agglutinates with a preceding preposition, i.e. *de+le* ('of the') fuse as *du* and *à+le* ('to the') fuse as *au*. In the written language, number distinctions are generally marked by suffixation of {/s/} which, however, is pronounced in the cases of liaison only (see above). A variant of the plural morpheme occurs in forms ending in /al/ or /ail/, changing these final clusters into {/aux/}. Some of the nouns have separate plural forms.[6]

Thus, in French, for nouns no systematic overt number distinctions are provided. If we assume that a child acquiring a language needs a certain amount of positive evidence to perceive a given grammatical dimension, this implies that the acquisition of number in French is strongly dependent upon the acquisition of the target-like determiner system.

Table 1a. Declension of definite and indefinite articles in French

	definite/indefinite articles	
singular		plural
masculine	feminine	
D/I	D/I	D/I
le/un	*la/une*	*les/des*

German has three genders; masculine, feminine, and neuter. Gender is marked on singular forms only. The gender of the noun determines the form of articles, attributive adjectives, ordinal numbers, and substantival and adjectival pronouns. Morphological number marking occurs on nouns as well. An intricacy of the German system is that gender, number, and case markings are confounded: in most cases, they cannot be related to distinct forms, as it is the case, for example, in agglutinative languages. Another observation concerns the similarities of the paradigms: the feminine gender paradigm resembles the plural paradigm and, for some function words, such as the definite and indefinite article and the possessive pronoun in its adjectival use, the masculine gender paradigm is almost identical with the neuter gender paradigm. In rapid and colloquial speech the German articles are shortened, for example, *auf 'n/ein Baum klettern* corresponds to *auf einen Baum klettern* ('to climb a tree').

Table 1b. Declension of definite and indefinite articles in German

Case	definite/indefinite articles			
	singular			plural
	masculine	feminine	neuter	
	D/I	D/I	D/I	D/I
nominative	*der/ein*	*die/eine*	*das/ein*	*die*
accusative	*den/einen*	*die/eine*	*das/ein*	*die*
dative	*dem/einem*	*der/einer*	*dem/einem*	*den*
genitive	*des/eines*	*der/einer*	*des/eines*	*der*

With respect to number marking on nouns, the German target system provides four different suffixing allomorphs — ({/(ə)n/}, {/s/}, {/ə/}, {/ər/}) — in addition to {/0/}. Three of these allomorphs may be combined with *Umlaut*. For some examples see table 1c.

Table 1c. The allomorphs of the German plural morpheme

allomorph	example	
	singular	plural
1. {/s/}	*Auto*	*Autos*
2. {/(ə)n/}	*Katze*	*Katzen*
3. {/ə/}	*Tier*	*Tiere*
4. {/ə/ + Umlaut}	*Ton*	*Töne*
5. {/ər/}	*Kind*	*Kinder*
6. {/ər/ + Umlaut}	*Rad*	*Räder*
7. {/0/}	*Adler*	*Adler*
8. {/0/ + Umlaut}	*Mutter*	*Mütter*

3.2. Regularities

3.2.1. Regularities in gender assignment

Both French and German exhibit semantic, morphological, and phonological gender patterns. In this paper I will mainly consider generalizations which are based on the morphological or phonological shape of the noun.

For semantically based patterns I refer to Köpcke (1982) and Köpcke & Zubin (1984). Generalizations based on morphological cues predict the gender of nouns in accordance with derivational affixes and with respect to composition. For a detailed description of the generalizations based on affixation and compounding see Dubois (1965) for French and Hoeppner (1980), Ivanova (1985), Zubin & Köpcke (1984) for German.

The gender of morphologically simple nouns is partly predictable on the basis of their phonological characteristics. In German at least five different types of patterns can be formulated[7] whereas in French almost exclusively final sounds are considered. In what follows I will mainly refer to regularities concerning nominal endings. (Cf. examples in Tables 2a and 2b.)[8] It is clear that such regularities are not rules of a combinatory type but rather share the characteristics of schemas.

Table 2a. Phonological gender rules in French*

phonological form	associated gender†	number of nouns‡	exception§
1. [m]	M(1292) ca. 92%	1406	*la plume*(114) 'feather'
2. [n]	F(819) ca. 68%	1204	*le clown*(385) 'clown'
3. [ã]	M(1949) ca. 99%	1963	*la dent*(14) 'tooth'
4. [ɛ̃]	M(929) ca. 99%	938	*la faim*(9) 'hunger'
5. [o]	M(841) ca. 97%	865	*la photo*(24) 'photo'
6. [œ̃]	M(17) 100%	17	——
7. [õ]	F(1872) ca. 70%	2666	*le mouton*(794) 'sheep'

*   The basis referred to is the Petit Larousse (1959).

†   The number in parentheses refers to the absolute number of nouns for which the rule correctly predicts the gender.

‡   The number of nouns with this particular ending.

§   The number in parentheses refers to the absolute number of exceptions to the rule.

Table 2b. Phonological gender rules in German

phonological form	associated gender	number of nouns	exception
1. [ə]	ca. 90% F(1350)	15000	*der Hase** 'rabbit' *das Auge* 'eye'
2. [ən]	M†		*das Laufen* 'running'

* No exact numbers are available, cf. Mills (1986).

† No exact numbers are available, cf. Hoeppner (1980).

3.2.2. Regularities in allomorphic variation in German noun pluralization

The choice of the appropriate allomorph of the plural morpheme for German nouns is dependent on various phonological and morphological properties of the noun such as its final consonant/vowel, the derivational affix, gender assignment etc. Generalizations concerning the distribution of plural allomorphs in German nouns have been formulated by Mugdan (1977) and Köpcke (1987). Mugdan specifies 15 distinct patterns and 21 lists of exceptions. This clearly indicates that most of the generalizations are not of a categorical type but are rather stochastic. In what follows, only some examples for these patterns will be given.

(1) Nouns ending in /ə/ take {/(ə)n/} as a plural-allomorph
   (*Tanne-n (f), Löwe-n (m)*).
   Exceptions: Neuter nouns with the circumfix /gə-ə/ take {/0/}
   (*Gebirge-0 (n)*).

(2) Nouns ending in a full vowel take {/s/} (*Kino-s (n)*).
   Exceptions: Feminine nouns ending in /e/ or /i/ take {/(ə)n/}
   (*Fee-n (f)*).

(3) Nouns ending in /əC/[9] take
   a.   {/(ə)n/} if they are feminine (*Schüssel-n (f)*)
   b.   {/0/} if they are masculine or neuter (*Schlüssel-0 (m)*).
   Exceptions are given in lists.[10]

(4) Nouns ending in /C/ take
   a.   {/(ə)n/} if they are feminine (*Tür-en (f)*)
   b.   {/ə/} if they are masculine or neuter (*Ball-Bälle (m), Fell-e (n)*).
   Exceptions are given in lists.

(5)   A decision between M3 and M4 can be made on the basis of a
      general phonological rule for German that rules out the
      sequence /əCə/.

In addition to this, Köpcke formulates some categorical rules based on the
derivational suffix of the noun (cf. Table 3, for some examples).

4.   The Acquisition of Gender and Number in a Bilingual Child

This part is concerned with the analysis of Ivar's acquisition data. The
age-period studied covers the time-span of 1;5 to 5;0. In what follows, I will
refer to results of Müller's (1990) and my own research (cf. also Koehn 1989).

4.1. *The Developmental Phases*

As it is difficult to set up discrete developmental phases, I will state a
transitional stage between the two main phases, which in some sense belongs to
both — or, the other way around, to neither of them. It is for this reason, that
some of the tables go beyond the limits of a given stage (the age period referred
to is always indicated). For practical reasons, the order of presentation for the
acquisition data of German or French respectively will vary for the different
substages.

4.1.1. *Phase I (–2;4)*

During the first stage, no systematic grammatical markings of either number
or gender are employed in either language.

Gender. Ivar does not make productive use of determiners until the age of 2;5,
except for the numerals *un* and *ein*. In both languages, these forms are used with
nouns of all genders. No systematic contrastive use of *un/ein* vs. *0* can be
observed. Adjectives mostly appear without any inflectional markings during the
period discussed. Thus, up to this age, no gender distinctions are made.

Number. As for number, two different forms are used for a few of the German
nouns without, however, any systematic number distinction. This is evidenced
by the following observations:

I. Some of the forms are used independently of their number-specification, i.e. they are employed with reference to one as well as to several objects (cf. Figure 3).

Shape of the noun	Reference of the noun	Number of types
Npl ⟨	Rsg / Rpl	6
Npl ——	Rsg	5
Npl ——	Rpl	5
Npl ——	R?	3
Nsg ⟨	Rpl / Rsg	4
Nsg ——	Rpl	1

Figure 3. Reference of German nouns until 2;6,6.

II. Even in those cases where Ivar does know two different forms of a noun, he mainly makes use of one of them — independently of its number-specification, whereas the other one is used only once or twice.

III. There is no noun two different forms of which are employed contrastively to indicate a difference in number.

One possibility to explain the lack of systematic grammatical markings could be to say that the supposedly too complex underlying semantic concept is not mastered at this point of development. There exists evidence, however, that at age 2;2,21 at the latest the underlying semantic concept of *singularity vs. plurality* is recognized. From 2;2,21, in both languages, Ivar starts using the numerals *zwei* and *deux* respectively. This numeral, for the time being, is used as a sort of indeterminate plural marker, i.e. it is used with nouns referring to two or even more objects — irrespective of the number-specification of the noun. On the other hand, the forms of the indefinite article *ein* and *un* respectively, which are homophonous with the corresponding numerals, are used exclusively with nouns referring to single objects. Again, the number specification of the noun is not considered. This is to say that the numerals *un/deux* and *ein/zwei* respectively are used adequately with respect to the number of objects referred to. This clearly indicates that the relevant semantic concept is present at this point of development. We are thus faced with a situation where the child has mastered the underlying semantic concept, on the one hand, and where he does employ different forms for some of the nouns, on the other. The fact that these forms are nevertheless used unsystematically with respect to number, seems to indicate that the corresponding *grammatical feature* is not yet available.

With French nouns no number markings occur even with those nouns for which different forms for plural and singular are provided in the target-language.

In sum then, we may conclude, that by the age of 2;2,21, Ivar has recognized the semantic concept of singularity vs. plurality whereas the grammatical category number is not available until about 2;6.

4.1.2. *The transition from phase I to phase II (2;4,23–2;6,6)*

At this transitional stage, a great quantity of new forms is acquired. However, not all of them are used in a target-like fashion from the beginning.

Gender. Most of the forms of the definite and indefinite article are acquired within this period of a few weeks: In French, *le, la* and *une*, in German *der, die, das* and *eine*. Thus, from now on, Ivar is able to use contrasting gender forms for the definite and indefinite article in both languages. The attribution of the definite article is systematic[11] from the beginning (see Phase II).

Number. In French, the first number markings concern the definite article. The plural form of the definite article, *les*, shows up at age 2;5,21. There is only one occurrence of the form *les* during this recording and the utterance in which it appears refers to a single object. This means that at this point of development no distinction is made between the singular form *le* and the corresponding plural form *les*. In the next recording (2;6,6), the form appears more frequently and its use is target-like. From now on, nouns referring to several specific objects do not lack the appropriate article any more. This amounts to saying that the plural form of the French definite article is employed systematically from 2;6 onwards.

In German, first systematic number-distinctions are made with nouns. Whereas at the first stage Ivar used but one form of most nouns, at 2;6,6 a second form shows up for several nouns which, however, appear in free variation with those which he already used during phase I (cf. examples in (6)).

(6)
(Aa) C:*guck fü. ein fuß. ein fuß hat kindern* (Rsg)   (2;6,6)
      'look, a/one foot. a/one foot has children-PL/DAT'

(Ab)   A: *was ist das*   (2;6,6)
       'what's that?'
       C: *das? ein füßen* (Rsg)
       'that? a/one feet-PL/DAT'
       C: *füße(n)* (Rsg)
       'feet-PL/DAT'
(B)   A: *guck mal das buch mit den kindern*   (2;6,6)
       'look the book with the-PL/DAT children-PL/DAT'
       C: *zwei kindern* (Rpl)
       'two children-PL/DAT'
       A: *mhm*
       C: *zwei kindern* (Rpl)
       A: *mhm*
       C: *(xx) zwei kinder (de)* (Rpl)
       '... two children-PL/NOM'
       A: *mhm*
       C: *zwei kind* (Rpl)
       'two child-SG'
       Abbreviations: C=Child, A=Adult.

These observations indicate that at 2;6,6, the child realizes that nouns can vary in form but he is not yet able to associate these forms with different functions. Note that it is this recording during which the second highest rate of errors is displayed: 50% of all plural forms refer to single objects. I assume that the observed behavior reflects hesitations due to extensions of the mental lexicon. In the next recording then, at 2;6,27, Ivar for the first time uses two forms of a noun contrastively and both adequately with respect to their number-specification.

4.1.3. *Phase II (2;7–5;0)*

There is evidence that in both languages the grammatical notions of number and gender are available now. I will show that errors concerning the morphological realization can be explained by the — partly improper — application of schemas.

Number. In French, at this stage, Ivar acquires the plural form of the indefinite article des (2;8,15) which is used target-like from the beginning. In combination with what has been said in the preceding section on the use of the definite plural article, this amounts to saying that the French article system is mastered at this point of development as far as number is concerned. Number distinctions on French nouns do not occur until at least 3;5, i.e., only one form is used even for those nouns which have different forms for singular and plural.

As far as number marking on German nouns is concerned, phase II may be subdivided into two substages at about 3;6. The first of these substages (IIA) is characterized by the occurrence of product-oriented errors while overextension of determined allomorphs can be observed during the second period (IIB). I will describe both substages successively.

At 2;6,27, Ivar for the first time uses two forms of a noun contrastively and both adequately with respect to their number-specification. From now on until 3;5,7 all but four instances of deviations in reference occurring with plural nouns concern nouns of which Ivar never uses the corresponding singular-form. Target-deviant associations, either singular or plural, occur at the longest until a second form of the respective noun has been acquired. The few (systematic) exceptions will be discussed below. This indicates that the child, at least when he has acquired two different forms of a noun, is — from 2;6,27 onwards — able to associate them with their target-like number-reference. The observed behavior concerning the acquisition of the German system of plural marking can be accounted for within the schema-model: Once the child has acquired both the singular and the plural form of a noun, he is able to associate each — on the basis of schemas — with its target-like function. However, for the time being, the child is not able to productively create new (plural- or singular-) forms on the basis of stored items. This is evidenced by the fact that until about 3;5 no target-deviant *forms*[12] are used by Ivar, i.e. no overregularizations occur. If we consider the relative rates of error (cf. Table 3) we can observe the following rank order: {/0/}-{/ər/}-{/ə/}-{/(ə)n/}-{/s/} (for types). Except for {/(ə)n/} and {/s/}, this rank order meets the predictions made by the scale in Figure 1.

Table 3. Relative rates of errors, plural nouns, 2;6,7–3;5,7

allomorph	{/s/}	{/(ə)n/}	{/ə/}	{/ər/}	{Umlaut}
% types	0	15,4%	18,2%	33,3%	50%

There are only four nouns for which a plural form is used to refer to a single object, at a point of development where the corresponding singular form has already been acquired:

(7)	a.	*ich brauch die <u>vögel0</u>* (Rsg)	(2;8,15)
		'I need the birds'	
	b.	*oh. ich hab noch eine <u>klötzer</u>* (Rsg)	(2;11,17)
		'Oh. I have one more cubes'	
	c.	*das is <u>räder</u>* (Rsg)	(3;0,19)
		'that is the wheels'	
	d.	*ein <u>räder</u>* (Rsg)	(3;0,19)
	e.	*is das deine <u>kinder</u>. diesen?* (Rsg)	(3;2,24)
		'is this your children, this one?'	
	f.	*is das deine <u>kinder</u>?* (Rsg)	(3;2,24)

Here {/ər/} is affected three times (types), {/0/} once (cf. examples in (7)). Note that {/ər/} is an allomorph with low cue strength for plural. Thus, the target-deviant uses may be explained by the fact that the child associates these forms with a singular schema organizing forms ending in {/ər/} to a (form-) class and for this reason tends to use them with reference to one object.

For the second substage (IIB, 3;6–5;0) mainly two observations can be made. The first is that errors in reference constantly decrease, cf. Table 4.

Table 4. Errors in reference.* Phase 2;6,6–5;0

Use of plural nouns with reference to a single object†

Stage	IIA(–3;5)	IIB(–4;0)	IIB(4;1–)
Types	20,5%	8,5%	1,6%
Tokens	9,0%	5,9%	2,1%

Use of singular nouns for reference to several objects‡

Stage	IIA(–3;5)	IIB(–4;0)	IIB(4;1–)
Types	7,5%	6,9%	4,7%

* Percentages given in this table refer to the morphological markings of nouns only. Slightly different results are obtained if we consider full NPs, i.e. if we account for the specification of determining elements such as numerals and other quantifying elements as well. Cf. Koehn (1984:104) and Müller (this volume, chap. 3) for this matter.

† The basis referred to are all plural nouns used during the period indicated.

‡ The basis referred to are all obligatory contexts for a plural during the period indicated.

The second observation concerns the fact that at age 3;6 a new type of error occurs: The appearance of target-deviant forms indicates that Ivar begins to make productive use of the plural-allomorphs of the German target-language. We find double-marking as well as substitution of target-like allomorphs. The second substage may again be subdivided into two parts at about age 4;0, which are characterized by overgeneralization of {/(ə)n/}[13] and {/s/} respectively, cf. Table 5.

Table 5. Overextensions of plural allomorphs, 3;6–5;0

3;5,28	*tischen̲*	4;0,18	*räubers̲*	
3;7,9	*keksen̲*	4;2,4	*verkäufers̲*	
3;7,9	*tigern̲*	4;4,14	*ritters̲*	
3;8,1	*büchern̲*	4;4,14	*räubers̲*	
3;8,1	*froschen̲*	4;5,0	*lasters̲*	
3;8,29	*schuhen̲*	4;6,20	*kranken̲*	
4;0,4	*händen̲*	4;7,24	*gitters̲*	
		4;9,5	*flügeln̲*	
		4;8,17	*vaters̲*	(v ik)
		4;10,15	*räubers̲*	
		4;11,14	*käfers̲*	

Interestingly, the overgeneralizations of {/s/} exclusively concern nouns ending in /ər/ which in the target-language take {/0/} as a plural marker. This corroborates the findings obtained for stage IIA, that Ivar has established a schema according to which nouns ending in /ər/ are likely to be singular. It should be noted that the allomorphs used by Ivar are /en/ and /s/ which are prototypical plural allomorphs in German (see Figure 1).

The fact that all instances of {/s/} concern environments where {/0/} would be appropriate indicates that Ivar aims at providing a plural form different in shape from the corresponding singular noun. This suggests that iconicity as well plays a role in the acquisition of morphological markings. In Table 6 all instances of nouns ending in /ər/ and taking {/0/} as a plural allomorph are listed. The number of target-like uses (right column) is compared to the number of {/s/}-overextensions with these forms (left column).

From 2;8,15 onwards the definite article *die* shows up within NPs referring to several objects. Other forms of the definite article — including *den*, which would be the target-like dative plural form — are never used within plural NPs.[14] From now on the target-deviant use of *0*, i.e., the use within NPs referring either to several specific objects or to single objects in general, decreases drastically.

Table 6. Use of nouns ending in /ər/ with {/0/}-plural

N with additional {/s/} (target-deviant)		N ending in -ər without additional {/s/} (target-like)	
Types	Tokens	Types	Tokens
räubers̲	(13)	taler	(1)
verkäufer̲s̲	(1)	laster	(1)
ritters̲	(2)	fenster	(2)
lasters̲	(1)	räuber	(2)
gitters̲	(1)	verkäufer	(1)
vaters̲	(3)	teller	(1)
käfers̲	(1)	finger	(1)
tigers̲	(1)		
Total:	(23)		(9)

This means that the plural-indicating function of *die* as well as of *0* is recognized at this point of development.

In sum then, we find that the acquisition of the underlying semantic concept of *singularity vs. plurality* precedes the development of the grammatical notion *number*. The difference between *one* and *more than one* is first expressed by non-grammatical means of expression such as numerals and other quantifying elements. The fact that in French Ivar begins by marking number on articles while in German first systematic markings occur on nouns, suggests that unifunctionality plays a role in the acquisition process. Note that the plural article *die* is not reliable as a plural marker as it is homophonous with the feminine singular article. The observations that have been made concerning the use of German noun-forms indicate that Ivar takes into consideration the distribution of plural-allomorphs and singular-endings reflected by the target-system. Over-regularizations of {/s/} instead of {/0/} are evidence for a tendency to formally distinguish plurals from singulars by means of an iconic marker.

Gender. Further evidence in favor of the assumption that schemas indeed play a decisive role in the organization of the mental lexicon comes from the acquisition of gender attribution. There is clear evidence that the child from the beginning, i.e. from the moment the corresponding forms are available, makes use of formal as well as of semantic gender-patterns (cf. Müller 1990). I have already pointed out the fact that form-based gender-patterns are not rules of a combinatory type but rather have to be conceived of as schemas.

However, before we come to the presentation of evidence for the role of schemas in gender-attribution, it should be mentioned that in both languages a difference can be observed between the treatment of definite articles (and demonstratives) on the one hand and indefinite articles on the other. Whereas erroneous attributions of definite articles are relatively rare and can almost exclusively be explained by overextensive applications of gender-patterns exhibited by the respective target-language, the rate of target-deviant uses of indefinite articles is much higher and most of them are chaotic, i.e. do not conform to any patterns. Many of the target-deviant attributions of indefinite articles concern nouns which are used with the correct form of the definite article. Sometimes we even find free variation of different forms of the indefinite article with a given noun. For a further discussion of this problem I refer to Müller (this volume, chap. 3). In what follows, I will look at the attribution of definite articles only.[15]

Seen the fact that in the case of target-like gender attributions we cannot decide whether we are dealing with productive usage of the appropriate form of the function-word or with rote-learned combinations of article + noun, only target-deviant systematic associations can prove the existence of schemas. In French, we can observe target-deviant attribution of the definite article to nouns ending in a nasal or /o/ in addition to the target-like attributions with these endings (cf. examples in (8)).

(8) a. -nasal (M)

target-like	target-deviant
le train	*le main*
le capuchon	*le dent*
le garçon	*le maison*
le médecin	
le lapin	
——	

     b. -o (M)

target-like	target-deviant
le cacao	*le photo*
le manteau	*le moto*
le marteau	
——	

In German, Ivar first establishes a two-class system with a masculine and a feminine gender-class. Most of the neuter nouns are attributed masculine gender. Müller (1990) argues that the neuter — at least for this child — does not constitute a separate nominal class but rather has the status of a "subgender"[16] representing a subclass of the masculine. As an explanation she points out that in the target-language the neuter and the masculine gender paradigm are partially identical. Another factor could be the child's bilingualism i.e., the described behavior could reflect the tendency to transfer the French two-class-system to the German language. For the time being, no decision can be made about what the reasons are for the wrong classification of neuter nouns. However, there exist many patterns in the target-language which do not associate an ending with either masculine or neuter gender but which dissociate a given ending from feminine gender. Consequently, it seems plausible to suggest that attribution of masculine gender to neuter nouns within the child's two class system reflects rule-governed behavior.

In the target-language, /ən/ is associated with masculine gender and /ər/ exists as a masculine suffix. Examples for target-deviant use of the masculine definite article with nouns ending in these clusters are given in (9) (a) and (b).

(9) a.   -ər (M)
           target-like   *target-deviant*
           der busfahrer   *der wasser*   (N)
           der tiger   *der ufer*   (N)
           der anhänger   *den zimmer*   (N)
           der laster   *den fenster*   (N)
           der räuber   *den wohnzimmer*   (N)
           der verkäufer   *den feuer*   (N)
           ——   *den gitter*   (N)

     b.   -ən (M)
           target-like   *target-deviant*
           der wagen   *den häuschen*   (N)
           der boden   *der küken*   (N)
           der besen   *der mädchen*   (N)
           der rennwagen   *der essen*   (N)
           der faden   *der hühnchen*   (N)
                                             der männchen   (N)
                                             den märchen   (N)
                                             der pferdchen   (N)

In the case of /ə/ a schema — according to which nouns ending in this sound are likely to have feminine gender — apparently even leads to the creation of target-deviant *forms* (cf. (9c)).

(9)   c.   -ə (F)

	target-like	target-deviant	target-deviant *forms*
	die sonne	*die hase* (M)	*der aff*
	die hose		*die plakate* (*das plakat*)
	die puppe		
	die brücke		
	die küche		

This seems to indicate, that schemas are a useful device in (the acquisition of) gender-attribution, as well.

5.   Conclusion

In Ivar's acquisition data two main developmental phases can be observed. Within the first stage no grammatical markings of either number or gender are employed. However, at the same time, there is evidence from the use of numerals that the underlying semantic concept for number is already present.

Within a very short period of time, at the age of about 2;5/2;6 a multitude of new forms shows up which little later are employed in a systematic fashion. The fact that first number distinctions in French are made by use of the definite article, while in German the acquisition of nominal markings precedes target-like employment of articles suggests that unifunctional markings facilitate acquisition. Both the acquisition of nominal plural morphology in German and the gender classification of nouns (in both languages) indicate that schemas play a decisive role in organization and access of the mental lexicon. Initially, the child is capable of making phonologically based gender-attributions as well as of attributing stored forms to their target-like number-reference on the basis of phonological shape, but no creative construction is possible on the basis of stored items. Product-oriented errors occur. Only at a later point of development the child begins to produce newly created plural forms. Ivar then shows a tendency to use uniform, iconic markings even with nouns for which no distinct plural form is provided in the target-language.

Notes

1. Cf. also Bybee & Moder (1983), Bybee (1985) and Bybee (1988).

2. For a more detailed description of this model see Hockett (1954).

3. For further discussion of early processing of morphologically complex forms cf. MacWhinney (1978) and Peters (1983).

4. Köpcke (1988) used the form of the determiner as a further indicator of grammatical number: If a given form of a noun is used with either *der* or *das*, it has to be singular. To include the form of the article as a criterion implies that either noun forms have to be stored together with their corresponding article forms in the mental lexicon or that the model is one that is able to explain the perception but not the production. The first assumption is disproved by the fact that errors occur concerning the choice of the article (cf. Müller 1990). A closer look reveals that the test carried out by Köpcke is indeed designed as a decision task where subjects have to decide whether a given NP (definite article + noun) is marked for plural or not. For this reason, I have excluded the form of the article as a criterion in the scale and considered nominal endings only. In addition to this, I have integrated the {/s/}-allomorph, which has been omitted in Köpcke's scale.

5. *Umlaut* refers to the vowel changes [a, o, u] > [e, o, y], an originally (Old High German) phonologically conditioned assimilation process, which in Middle High German has become a morphological rule.

6. Cf. *oeil-yeux* ('eye/s').

7. We find generalizations referring to the structure of the whole word, patterns based on final, medial or initial sounds respectively and, finally, generalizations defining the gender of monosyllabic nouns on the basis of relations between final/medial/initial sounds.

8. For a more detailed description of phonologically based patterns see Tucker et al. (1977) for French and Köpcke (1982), Köpcke & Zubin (1983), Mills (1986) for German. The calculations for Tables 2c and 2d have been carried out by Müller (1990).

9. *C* is meant to indicate any type of consonants.

10. Cf. Mugdan (1977).

11. This does not necessarily imply that the attributions are target-like as well.

12. There are some instances of apparent overgeneralizations of {/(ə)n/} at 2;6 (e.g. *füßen*, *kindern*, *händen*). However, all the forms used have in common that they could be target-like dative plural-forms and thus do not necessarily have to be productively created by the child. The fact that these forms are used with reference to one as well as to several objects seems to indicate that this is indeed not the case.

13. Most of the resulting forms (except for *froschen*) correspond to target-like dative plural forms and thus do not necessarily have to be created productively (cf. note 12). However, the fact that these forms are not used for reference to single objects any more seems to indicate that {(ə)n} has been recognized as a plural allomorph by now.

14. Up to the age of 5;0 we find one occurrence of the form *den* in a plural NP (4;7,24). However, the form is employed in an accusative context, where *die* should be used.

15. There are only a few occurrences of demonstrative articles which however fit into the system evidenced by the attribution of definite articles.

16. Cf. Corbett (1989).

References

Anisfeld, Moshe & G. Richard Tucker. 1967. "English Pluralization Rules of Six-Year-Old Children." *Child Development* 38.1201–1217.

Berko Gleason, Jean. 1958. "The Child's Learning of English Morphology." *Word* 14.150–177.

Bryant, B. & Moshe Anisfeld. 1969. "Feedback versus No-Feedback in Testing Childrens Knowledge of English Pluralization Rules." *Journal of Experimental Child Psychology* 8.250–255.

Bybee, Joan. 1985. *Morphology: A study of the relation between meaning and form.* Amsterdam.

———. 1988. "Morphology as Lexical Organization." *Theoretical Morphology: Approaches in Modern Linguistics,* ed. by Michael Hammond & Maíre Noonan, 119–141. San Diego: Academic Press.

Bybee, Joan & Dan I. Slobin. 1982. "Rules and Schemas in the Development and Use of English Past." *Language* 58.265–289.

Bybee, Joan & C. L. Moder. 1983. "Morphological Classes as Natural Categories." *Language* 59.251–270.

Corbett, Greville G. 1989. "An Approach to the Description of Gender Systems." *Essays on Grammatical Theory and Universal Grammar,* ed. by Doug Arnold, Martin Atkinson, Jacques Durand, Claire Grover & Louisa Sadler, 53–89. Oxford: Clarendon Press.

Derwing, Bruce L. & William J. Baker. 1980. "Rule Learning and the English Inflections, With Special Emphasis on the Plural." *Experimental Linguistics: Interactions of theories and applications,* ed. by Gary D. Prideaux, Bruce L. Derwing & William J. Baker, 249–321. Ghent.

Dubois, Jean. 1965. *Grammaire structurale du français: Nom et pronom.* Paris: Larousse.

Graves, M. & S. Koziol. 1971. "Noun Plural Development in Primary Grade Children." *Child Development* 42.1165–1173.

Hockett, Charles F. 1954. "Two Models of Grammatical Description." *Word* 10.210–234.

Hoeppner, Wolfgang. 1980. *Derivative Wortbildung der deutschen Gegenwartssprache und ihre algorithmische Analyse.* Tübingen: Narr.

Ivanova, L. 1985. *Zum Genussystem des Deutschen und des Bulgarischen.* Diss., University of Jena.

Ivimey, G.P. 1975. "The Development of English Morphology: An acquisition model." *Language and Speech* 18.120–144.

Koehn, Caroline. 1989. *Der Erwerb der Pluralmarkierungen durch bilinguale Kinder (Französisch–Deutsch): Eine empirische Untersuchung.* Masters thesis, University of Hamburg.

Köpcke, Klaus-Michael. 1982. *Untersuchungen zum Genussystem der deutschen Gegenwartssprache.* Tübingen: Niemeyer.

————. 1987. "Die Beherrschung der deutschen Pluralmorphologie durch muttersprachliche Sprecher und L2-Lerner mit englischer Muttersprache: Ein Vergleich." *Linguistische Berichte* 107.23–41.

————. 1988. "Schemas in German Plural-Formation." *Lingua* 74.303–335.

Köpcke, Klaus-Michael & David A. Zubin. 1983. "Die kognitive Organisation der Genuszuweisung zu den einsilbigen Nomen der deutschen Gegenwartssprache." *Zeitschrift für germanistische Linguistik* 11.166–182.

————. 1984. "Sechs Prinzipien für die Genuszuweisung im Deutschen: Ein Beitrag zur natürlichen Klassifikation." *Linguistische Berichte* 93.26–50.

MacWhinney, Brian. 1978. "The Acquisition of Morphophonology." *Monographs of the Society for Research in Child Development* 43, 1.

Mills, Anne E. 1986. "Acquisition of the Natural-Gender Rule in English and German." *Linguistics* 24.31–45.

Müller, Natascha. 1990. "Developing two Gender Assignment Systems Simultaneously." *Two First Languages: Early grammatical development in bilingual children,* ed. by Jürgen M. Meisel, 193–234. Dordrecht: Foris.

Mugdan, Joachim. 1977. *Flexionsmorphologie und Natürlichkeit.* Tübingen: Narr.

Nouveau Petit Larousse. 1969. Paris.

Peters, Ann M. 1983. *The Units of Language Acquisition.* Cambridge: Cambridge University Press.

Tucker, G. Richard, Wallace E. Lambert & André A. Rigault. 1977. *The French Speaker's Skill with Grammatical Gender: An example of rule-governed behavior.* Mouton: The Hague.

Zubin, David A. & Klaus-Michael Köpcke. 1984. "Affect Classification in the German Gender System." *Lingua* 63.41–96.

Gender and Number Agreement within DP

Natascha Müller
University of Hamburg

1. Introduction

The following paper discusses the issue of the emergence of the grammatical features "gender" and "number" in the grammar of two bilingual children (German/French). The focus will be on the syntactic consequences of choices made with respect to the lexical specifications of heads.

I start from the assumption that noun phrases in adult German and in adult French contain at least one functional projection above NP which is the position of the inflectional features of nominals. There hardly seems to be any doubt that these features are not available in early child grammar. This relates to the hypothesis made by researchers like e.g. Clahsen, Eisenbeiß & Vainikka (1994), Guilfoyle & Noonan (1988), and Radford (1990) which states that the nominal functional category is not available from the very beginning of language development. I will try to argue, among other things on the basis of distributional facts, that this assumption is plausible for the early grammar of the two bilingual children I studied. Furthermore, I will outline the process by which the grammatical features number and gender are integrated into child grammar and how the child arrives at a near-target-like representation of noun phrases.

2. Gender and Number as AGR-Features of DET

Researchers like Abney (1986), Bhatt (1990), Felix (1990), Löbel (1990a,b), Olsen (1991) and others argue, in what has been labelled the DP-hypothesis, that determiners should be identified as the lexical realization of the nominal counterpart of INFL, DET(eterminer). DET contains the inflectional features of the noun phrase, i.e. it serves the same role INFL plays at the sentential level. In German and in French, the functional category DET minimally contains the features definiteness, case, number, and gender.

In what follows, I will focus on number and gender markings on definite and indefinite articles. Markings on pronouns will not be investigated.

Before I turn to the structure of nominals containing one of the elements mentioned above in the adult system, I will summarize the basic facts of the two gender and number systems which are relevant for the discussion of the acquisition data.

2.1. Gender and Number Markings in Adult German and French

French has two genders, masculine (le_{def}/un_{indef}) and feminine (la_{def}/une_{indef}). Gender is marked in the singular and in the plural. For the different forms of determiners and adjectives cf. Koehn (this volume) and Stenzel (this volume).

Number is marked on determiners (les_{def}/des_{indef}) and (mostly not in speech) on nouns and adjectives in French. One peculiarity of the French number system is that if a plural determiner precedes a noun beginning with a vowel, the final plural -s of the determiner fuses with that vowel, e.g. *[le] [zanimo]* (=les animaux) 'the animals'. For the different forms of determiners and number markings on nouns cf. Koehn (this volume).

German has three genders, masculine (der_{def}/ein_{indef} – nominative), feminine ($die_{def}/eine_{indef}$ – nominative), and neuter (das_{def}/ein_{indef} – nominative). Gender is marked only in the singular. Most determiner forms are plurifunctional, e.g. *die* 'the' is used to indicate singular and feminine gender on the one hand and plural on the other. For the different forms cf. Koehn (this volume).

As in French, number is marked on determiners (die_{def}/ϕ_{indef}) and on nouns in German. Again, one finds plurifunctional markings. One example of this is -e which may function as a plural allomorph, e.g. in *tiere* 'animals', and as an integrated part of the lexical item, e.g. in *tasche* 'bag'. For number markings cf. Koehn (this volume).

2.2. The DP-Hypothesis

Following the DP-hypothesis, German and French noun phrases contain at least one nominal functional category above NP which is the position of the inflectional features of the noun phrase. One thus obtains a structure as in (1).[1]

(1)

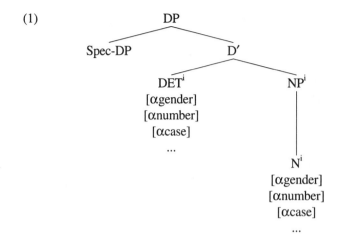

The grammatical features of DET percolate from DET up to DP. Thus, if DET contains the feature [+sg], the whole DP will be characterized as [+sg]. There are at least two kinds of grammatical features discussed in the literature, AGR-features and inherent features which are not mutually exclusive. Gender, for instance, is an inherent feature of N and an AGR-feature of DET (cf. further below). There must be an agreement relation between the AGR-features of DET and the lexical features of N.

> This agreement cannot arise through percolation since DET, D′ and NP are different syntactic categories. It arises by virtue of the functional selection relation between DET and NP. (Olsen 1989:41)

This agreement is encoded by identical superscripts in structure (1). With respect to definiteness, Löbel (1990b) argues that in German, it is an inherent feature of DET and not an AGR-feature, since it obviously does not have any consequences for agreement within the noun phrase; cf. structure (2) overleaf. This is also plausible for French.

It seems to be uncontroversial that definite articles are positioned in DET. In the recent literature, many proposals have been advanced for the syntactic position and the categorial status of indefinite articles.

Among others, Olsen (1986) suggests that indefinite articles are located in DET in German. The observation that definite and indefinite articles are mutually exclusive indicates that this assumption is plausible.

(2)

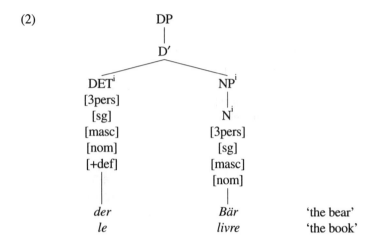

der	*Bär*	'the bear'
le	*livre*	'the book'

Bhatt (1990) argues that German *ein-* is a homonym which may function as an indefinite determiner and as a quantifying adjective. Among other things, this is lent support by the observation that there are languages such as English where the indefinite article is *a* and the numeral *one*; cf. also nominals like *das eine buch* 'the one book' where the form *eine* is interpreted as a quantifying adjective. As an indefinite article, *ein* is positioned in DET, as a quantifying adjective in the position where the adjective is base-generated.[2]

The issues of how many nominal functional categories one needs and how they are specified as well as the categorial status of elements like indefinite articles are far from being settled.[3] It seems to be impossible to make a final decision for one analysis at this point of time, since the arguments the researchers advance in favor of their analyses are based on quite different properties of the respective languages, i.e. on distributional and on inflectional facts, to name just two criteria. Note that the existence of competing (perhaps also complementary) analyses may also reflect the fact that noun phrases are not structured similarly across all natural languages (cf. e.g. Fukui & Speas 1986). Much research still has to be done in this domain of the grammar.

The grammatical feature "gender" is a feature which is part of the lexical entry of nouns. One has to distinguish nouns that have gender as an inherent feature and words that get gender by agreement, such as adjectives, for instance. The inherent, invariable characteristic of nominals will be called gender-attribution, in contrast to the variable characteristic of modifiers which is defined as gender-agreement (cf. Carroll 1989). It has been argued that the process by which a particular gender feature is paired with a particular noun in gender attribution is subject to restrictions (cf. Köpcke 1982; Köpcke & Zubin 1983; Tucker, Lambert & Rigault 1977), i.e. we are not dealing with a completely arbitrary process. Those regularities which underlie gender-attribution are discussed in Koehn (this volume); cf. also Müller (1990c). Within the DP-framework, gender-agreement is accounted for in the following way. The gender feature is inserted as part of the particular noun from the lexicon into syntax, triggering agreement among the different modifying elements (the masculine noun *hund* 'dog' triggers the appearance of the masculine form of the definite article *der* under DET for example). This amounts to saying that DET agrees with the gender feature of N.[4]

In contrast to gender, number may be chosen freely by the speaker. The grammatical feature "number" is similar to gender in that it depends on a semantic feature of N, namely [αcountable] which has to be listed for every N in the lexicon. Those nouns which have the feature [−countable] are inherently specified for [+singular].

Since nouns with the feature [−countable] behave like nouns in the singular, Löbel (1990a) assumes that [+singular] represents the unmarked realization of the feature "number" in German. The same is valid for French.

The source of the grammatical feature "number" is far from being clear. To my knowledge, the question has not even been raised in the recent literature. There are at least two possibilities: DET or N.[5] If singular and plural nouns are stored separately in the lexicon, then number is a lexical property of N, similar to gender; cf. Koehn (this volume) for a discussion of this assumption for adult and early child grammar. Since number is marked among other things on determiners, DET agrees with the number feature of N. Again, one needs to distinguish number as an inherent feature and as an AGR-feature.

3.   The Availability of Functional Categories in Child Grammar

Noun phrases used by very young children differ in crucial ways from their respective adult counterparts. They lack number, gender and case markings and they do not consist of more than two elements. A plausible assumption would be that nominal functional categories are not available in early grammar, i.e. functional categories undergo some development (for further discussion of this issue with respect to the category COMP, cf. the contributions in Meisel (ed.) (1992) and Müller, this volume, chap. 9).

Researchers like Clahsen (1990), Gawlitzek-Maiwald, Tracy & Fritzenschaft

(1992), Meisel & Müller (1992), Penner (1990) and Roeper (1992) argue that child grammar may contain underspecified functional categories during some developmental phases. This amounts to saying that even at the point of development where there is evidence for functional categories in child grammar, these differ from their adult counterpart (cf. Müller this volume, chap. 9 for further discussion).[6]

In what follows, I will present evidence in support of the claim that the nominal functional category DET undergoes some development. More specifically, DET does not seem to be available from the onset of language acquisition (cf. Clahsen, Eisenbeiß & Vainikka 1994). Furthermore, I want to show that DET in early child grammar differs from DET in adult language.

4. The Analysis

The subjects of this study are a boy — Ivar — and a girl — Caroline. The language use of both children has been analyzed for the acquisition of number by Koehn (1989a,b; 1991) and for gender by myself (Müller 1990a,b,c) for the age range from 1;5 to 5;0 (Caroline) and 1;6 to 5;10 (Ivar). The acquisition of gender and number is much intertwined. It is possible to treat the topics separately if one assumes a morphological and a syntactic perspective, respectively. In what follows, I will present the results of Koehn's and my studies under a syntactic perspective. The age period investigated in this paper covers the age span from 1;6 to 3;0 in Caroline and from 1;5 to 3;0 in Ivar (for a description of the research project, MLU-values and further information about the children see Köppe, this volume, chap. 2).

5. Early Grammars without DET

In what follows, I will argue that both children pass through a developmental stage where the relevance of the grammatical features "gender" and "number" has not been discovered yet. In Caroline, this phase covers the age range from 1;5 to 2;0 in German and from 1;5 to 1;9 in French. In Ivar, this phase lasts from 1;6 to 2;4 in both languages. Meisel (1986; on Caroline), Parodi (1990; on Ivar) and Stenzel (this volume; on two other children) conclude that case markings do not show up either during this developmental phase. Berkele's (1983) study of Caroline's data indicates that the feature "definiteness" is not available. As these features are assumed to be generated under the nominal functional category DET in adult grammar (cf. structure (1)), it is conceivable that this category has not yet been developed in child grammar.

5.1. *The Non-Availability of the Grammatical Features "Number" and "Gender"*

The most important observation during this developmental phase is that Caroline and Ivar do not make productive use of adult-like determiners in either language, except for *un* and *ein* 'one' in Ivar (cf. Koehn 1989a) which are analyzed as being numerals.[7]

A first possible reason for the absence of determiners could be the complexity of the underlying semantic concepts. However, this is not a satisfactory explanation.

With respect to number, Koehn (1989a) observes that from 1;10 onwards, Ivar uses the forms *un/un autre* 'one'/'another' and *ein* 'one' in order to refer to a single object and *deux* and *zwei* 'two' in order to refer to more than one object in the respective language, which indicates that the underlying semantic concept "singularity vs. plurality" has been discovered by that time.

With respect to gender, the corresponding semantic concept would be "female vs. male". In the data from both children, there is no evidence that this concept has been discovered. Interestingly enough, Ivar begins to use *[aman]* (=ein Mann) 'a man' from 1;8,8 onwards to refer to animate beings such as a man, a woman, Ivar's mother, a cowboy, a snake. Caroline uses *das* 'this' in order to refer to non-animates. Although the children do not seem to distinguish female and male sex, they apparently have discovered the relevance of one prerequisite concept for natural gender, namely animacy (cf. Mills 1986 for the importance of the features [αanimate] and [αhuman] in gender attribution; "animacy and personal rule").[8]

A second possible reason for the absence of determiners expressing gender and number distinctions could be the supposedly very complex structure of noun phrases which contain more than one element. The problem with this approach is that both children do use presyntactic forms like [ə], [də], [a] already in combination with nouns at this early age (cf. Dolitsky 1983) which, however, do not seem to encode grammatical distinctions such as gender, number, definiteness, or case. In addition, Ivar uses noun phrases which contain an adjective and a noun. Since the children are able to use nominal constructions consisting of two items, one has reason to believe that formal complexity is not responsible for the absence of determiners.

I want to suggest that the absence of adult-like determiners to encode grammatical number and gender distinctions is due to the unavailability of the corresponding grammatical features. The hypothesis is that if the relevance of the grammatical features has not yet been discovered, then it is plausible to assume that the nominal functional category DET is not available in the children's grammar either.

It is immediately clear that from the mere absence of adult-like determiners to express grammatical gender and number distinctions in child grammar it does not necessarily follow that the grammatical features are not available. Rather, the children might express these distinctions with other forms they have acquired which are, however, target-deviant. I will show that this alternative is untenable.

The first point, then, is that the presyntactic forms the children use are combined with masculine as well as with feminine nouns on the one hand and with singular and plural nouns on the other hand. One would expect this to be the case if these forms were not used in order to express grammatical gender and number distinctions.[9]

(3)   *[ə] [dede]* (=Teddy) 'teddy' MASC   (Iv;1;8,8)
(4)   *[ə] b[o]me* (=Blume) 'flower' FEM   (Iv;1;10,30)
(5)   *[a] mama* 'mummy' FEM   (Ca;1;6,26)
(6)   *[a] papa* 'daddy' MASC   (Ca;1;6,26)
(7)   *[ə] ba[du]* (=bateau) 'boat' SG   (Iv;1;9,28)
(8)   *[ə] [z]oeufs* 'eggs' PL   (Iv;1;10,30)

The second observation is that adjectives appear without inflectional markings during this first phase and thus do not reflect an understanding of the gender and number systems. Some examples for this usage are:

(9)   *gu bum* (=große Blume) 'big flower' FEM   (Iv;1;10,30)
(10)   *gu haus* (=groß) 'big house' NEUT   (Iv;1;11,7)
(11)   *gan pubi* (=kleine Puppe) 'small doll' SG   (Iv;1;11,17)
(12)   *gran[t] schuhe* (=grand) 'big shoes' PL   (Iv;2;2,7)
(13)   *petit nounours* 'small teddy' MASC   (Iv;2;3,5)
(14)   *petit vache* 'small cow' FEM   (Iv;2;3,5)

Again, one would expect formally invariable adjectives, if the grammatical features have not yet been discovered.

Another observation is that the elements *ein, un* and *un autre* are used irrespective of the gender and number specification of the co-occurring nouns. These forms are combined with masculine and feminine nouns and with formally plural nouns.

(15)	*un [zyni]* (=soleil) 'a sun' MASC	(Iv;1;10,12)
(16)	*un dame* 'a woman' FEM	(Iv;2;0,29)
(17)	*ein a-anas* (=Ananas) 'a pine-apple' FEM	(Iv;1;10,30)
(18)	*ein deddi* (=Teddy) 'a teddy' MASC	(Iv;2;3,5)
(19)	*un autre dame* 'another woman' FEM	(Iv;2;0,29)
(20)	*un autre cahar* (=canard) 'another duck' MASC	(Iv;2;0,29)
(21)	*un aut(re) [zamono]* (=animaux) 'another animals'	(Iv;2;1,27)
(22)	*un aut mal* (=animal) 'another animal'	(Iv;2;3,5)
(23)	*[anot] schuhe* (=un autre) 'another shoes'	(Iv;2;2,7)
(24)	*un autre [zu]* (=Schuh) 'another shoe'	(Iv;2;2,7)

The numerals *zwei* and *deux* are combined with formally singular as well as with plural nouns.

(25)	*deux [zamono]* 'two animals'	(Iv;2;2,21)
(26)	*deux schuhe* 'two shoes'	(Iv;2;2,21)
(27)	*[sai] [aus]* (=zwei Haus) 'two house'	(Iv;2;3,5)
(28)	*deux paket* 'two parcel'	(Iv;2;3,19)

Note that Ivar already produces the respective formally correct singular nouns *mal* 'animal' and *schuh* 'shoe' on the one hand and the plural noun *häuse*[10] (=Häuser) 'houses' on the other. The crucial observation is that in examples (21) to (28), the *numerals* are referentially adequate (cf. Koehn 1989a). In contrast, nouns which already vary formally are used in an unsystematic way in combination with these numerals, i.e. formally singular and formally plural nouns occur with both singular and plural numerals.

Again, one would expect examples such as (21) to (28) to show up in the data if the children have not recognized the importance of the AGR-features gender and number and have not classified the respective nouns according to their gender and number specification. Number which is clearly marked during this developmental phase seems to be a semantic feature of numerals.

A last point refers to Koehn's (1989a) observation that, although Ivar already makes use of bare nouns like *schuh* 'shoe' and *schuhe* 'shoes' (these nouns show up without a numeral, a presyntactic form, or an adjective), this morphological variation does not serve to express number distinctions, i.e. plural and singular forms may have both plural and singular reference.[11]

(29)	*kind* 'child'	RSg	(Iv;1;9,28)
		RPl	(Iv;1;9,28)
(30)	*oma* 'grand-ma'	RSg	(Ca;1;11,4)
		RPl	(Ca;1;11,4)
(31)	*kinder* 'children'	RSg	(Iv;1;9,28)
		RPl	(Iv;1;9,28)
(32)	*schuhe* 'shoes'	RSg	(Ca;1;11,4)
		RPl	(Ca;1;7,9)

These observations confirm that the grammatical features "number" and "gender" are not available in child grammar during this developmental phase.

5.2. *The Structure of Early Noun Phrases*

The question arises how to account for the nominal constructions which the children use during this early stage. A possible structure would be the one in (33) where XP is realized as a numeral (*un, deux, ein, zwei, un autre*), as an adjective (*petit, grand, klein, groß*) or as a presyntactic element.

(33)

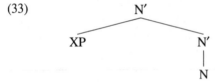

By assuming (33), one can account for the observation that the choice of the numeral and of the adjective is dependent on properties of the object referred to but not on properties of the syntactic category N. If the grammatical features gender and number (and case; cf. Stenzel this volume) are not available, then there is nothing to agree with.

One prediction that follows from a structure like the one in (33) is that examples for constructions such as *ein groß haus* 'a big house', *un petit garçon* 'a little boy' where both a numeral and an adjective are realized should not be attested in the children's speech, which is also the case, i.e. they do not occur (cf. also Clahsen, Eisenbeiß & Vainikka 1994 and Mills 1985). The reason for the absence of such constructions may be that the prenominal elements used are generated in the same syntactic position and thus are mutually exclusive.

It is not clear whether numerals and adjectives are lexical realizations of the same syntactic category, Adj, or whether they belong to different categories, Q and Adj respectively. Note that the numerals *ein* and *un* for instance may be

compared with the adjectives *groß/grand* and *klein/petit*, in that they do not have
a grammatical but a referential meaning in the children's grammars. I want to
leave open the question of the categorial status of these elements, because it does
not directly bear on the issue under discussion. Crucially, the children position
these elements in the same syntactic position.

Another question which arises with the structure (33) is whether early
nominal constructions conform to X-bar theory. Related to this is the question
as to why numerals and adjectives are located in a Chomsky-adjoined position
to N′ and not in the specifier position. Since these issues are far from being
settled (cf. the contributions in Meisel (ed.) 1992), the structure given in (33) is
rather preliminary.

6.   The Integration of DET into Child Grammar

In the course of further development, i.e. at approximately 1;10/2;0
(Caroline) and 2;4 (Ivar) (MLU approximately 2,0) respectively, both children
start using grammatical gender and number markings. They make productive use
of definite, indefinite, and possessive articles.[12] In addition, they make number
distinctions on nouns (cf. Koehn 1989a,b). In view of these observations, it
seems reasonable to assume that the corresponding grammatical features are now
part of the children's structure of noun phrases.

Another observation, which may indicate that the children have reached a
new developmental stage, is that Ivar and to a lesser extent also Caroline start
using complex nominal expressions like *ein gro siff* 'a big boat' (Iv;2;5,7), *un
petite fille* 'a small girl' (Iv;2;5,7), *'ne rala* (=leere) *flasche* 'an empty bottle'
(Ca;2;4,8), *un petit auto* 'a small car' (Ca;2;3,11) where the determiner appears
in front of an adjective, followed by a noun. On the basis of this distributional
fact it may be argued that the children's structure of noun phrases now contains
more than two positions, according to my analysis the nominal functional
category DET. The specification of the different syntactic positions will be
explored in the following paragraphs.

6.1. *The Emergence of the Grammatical Features "Number" and "Gender"*

I will start with a survey of the relevant observations concerning number
and gender markings in the children's noun phrases until about age 3;0. The
acquisition data suggest that both adult grammatical features "number" and
"gender" emerge step-by-step in child grammar. They are first interpreted as

inherent properties of N, based solely on the phonological shape of nouns in the case of number and on both phonological and semantic properties of nouns in the case of gender. It will be shown that number and gender agreement are first restricted to noun phrases which contain a definite article in the children's grammar of German and French. It is argued that the agreement relation does not extend to those nominals which contain an indefinite article, since indefinite articles are analyzed as being numerals. The target-like categorization of indefinite articles is taken to be the trigger for the emergence of the adult grammatical features "number" and "gender".

6.1.1. Number

With respect to number, one has to distinguish between number specification, i.e. the process of determining the reference of nominals, and number agreement. The terms "plural noun" and "singular noun" refer to formally singular and plural nouns respectively, independently of their reference.

6.1.1.1. Number Specification

As for number, Koehn (1989a,b; 1991) shows that Ivar uses numerals, which were already target-like during the preceding developmental phase, and quantifying expressions such as *alle/tou(s/tes)* 'all', *viel/beaucoup* 'many', *beide* 'both' correctly with respect to the number of objects referred to. This is also the case for the possessive *unser* 'our' which is used to indicate more than one possessor.[13] Although these forms are infrequent[14] in Caroline's data,[15] they are always referentially correct as well. A similar restriction holds of singular forms like *der* 'the' (later *das* 'the'), *le/la* 'the' and *ein/eine/un/une* 'a' (*un autre*) which are always used in a referentially correct way, i.e. in order to refer to a single object. *mein/dein/mon/ton* 'my', 'your' etc. always indicate one possessor. The plural definite articles *die* and *les*, on the other hand, show up in combination with plural nouns[16] to refer to a single object as well as to more than one object; e.g. *die tiere* 'the animals' may refer to a single animal or to more than one animal. This can be observed in Ivar until the age of 2;11 in both languages (cf. Koehn 1989a) and in Caroline until the age of 2;6 in French and 2;10 in German (cf. Berkele 1983). The complete lists of examples are given in (1) to (4) in the appendix. If one considers types only, then the following picture emerges:

Table 1. Reference of die/les+*plural noun combinations*

die/les+plural noun		RPl	RSg
Ivar	German (2;4–2;11)	5	6
	French (2;4–2;11)	10	7
Caroline	German (2;0–2;10)	3	6
	French (1;10–2;6)	9	7

The following episode at 2;5,4 is an illustrative example for the use of *die+plural nominalized adjective* in order to refer to a single object.

(34)   Ca: *wo ist die bäbär?* *bäbär* (fetches a teddy)
         'where is teddy? teddy'
         Ca: *wo ist die andere?* (searches for a second teddy)
         'where is the other (one)'
         A: *wo ist die andere?*
         'where is the other (one)'
         Ca: ... *wo ist die anderen?* da aah (fetches the second teddy)
         'where is the others? there'

Usage of plural noun phrases for singular reference can also be observed with demonstratives; cf. Ivar 2;7,17 *ces [zamono]*[17] (=animaux) (RSg) 'these animals', Caroline 2;9,29 *diese deckel* (RSg) 'these covers'. The observations made for definite articles seem to extend to demonstratives. Since demonstratives are very rare in the data from both children, however, this has to remain speculative.

Koehn (1989a) argues that target-deviant usages occur until the corresponding contrastive form has been acquired for most nouns (i.e. at 2;6,27 in Ivar). The usage of both the adult singular and the plural form is interpreted as an intermediate stage during which the child makes productive use of both nominal forms without knowing the target-like number specification. If the lack of the corresponding contrastive form was the only reason for target-deviant uses, then one would expect singular nominals to be used with plural reference as well which is not the case (cf. below).

So far, I have only considered the German plural definite article *die* in combination with plural nouns, such as *tiere*. Since the article *die* is plurifunctional in the German article system, i.e. it serves to express plural and singular (feminine gender), the question arises whether *die+singular noun* may refer to more than one object. The most interesting cases are *die sandale* 'the sandal', *die puppe* 'the doll', *die küche* 'the kitchen', where *-e* does not have the status of a plural allomorph in adult German. The shape of singular nouns like *tasche, puppe, küche* (cf. the plural nouns *schuhe* 'shoes', *tiere* 'animals', *kühe* 'cows') may lead the child to the assumption that these nouns are plural forms. Interestingly enough, neither child ever uses singular noun phrases with a plural shape like *die sandale* in order to refer to more than one object. The child will make use of the plural noun phrase *die sandalen* in this case. This is true for other *die+singular noun* combinations as well such as *die uhr* 'the watch', *die polizei* 'the police' which always have singular reference.

In sum then, singular forms as well as elements determining plural, i.e. quantifying expressions and possessives, are always referentially correct, with the exception of *die/les* in combination with plural nouns which are used in order to refer to a single object and to more than one object. Thus, number (singular vs. plural) is marked on determining elements in an adult-like way, except for the plural definite articles *die/les*. The observation that the combination *die+singular noun*, but not *die+plural noun* is always referentially correct may be accounted for by assuming that [+singular] represents the unmarked feature, as opposed to [−singular]. This amounts to saying that *die+N* and *les+N* seem to be analyzed as a singular noun phrase in the first place, until evidence suggests that this analysis is wrong. Under this approach, errors in reference should occur in one direction only which in fact seems to be the case. I will elaborate this last point further below.

Koehn (1989a) shows that the choice of nominal forms which are used without determiners does not always correspond to the target-language.[18] Caroline uses *tonne* 'cask' and *tonnen* 'casks' at 2;5,18 in order to refer to one cask, for instance. Ivar refers to one arm with the forms *arm* 'arm' and *arme* 'arms' and to one boat with the forms *schiff* 'boat' and *schiffe* 'boats'.[19] The use of bare nominal forms (these nouns are used without determining and without modifying elements) seems to be subject to the same restrictions that have already been observed with *die+singular noun*, as opposed to *die+plural noun*.[20] Plural nouns may refer to more than one object as well as to a single object. The complete lists of examples are found in (5) to (8) in the appendix.

Table 2. Reference of bare plural nouns

bare plural nouns (types)		RPl	RSg
Ivar	German (2;4–2;11)	24	8
	French (2;4–2;11)	4	1
Caroline	German (2;0–2;6)	2	2
	French	——	——

The reference of bare singular nouns, on the other hand, is nearly always target-like. In Caroline's data, the last example for the use of a singular noun for plural reference is at 2;0,09 *schuh* 'shoe' which, however, may also be a self-correction: *schuh schuhe de de da* 'shoe shoes there'. Ivar uses *buntstift* 'crayon' at 2;6,6 in order to refer to more than one object. Note that these are the only exceptions. The systematic usage of singular nouns for singular reference represents a further step in the children's development, since these nouns had singular and plural reference during the preceding developmental stage, as compared to plural nouns. One may account for this new step in development by claiming that nouns are now specified for number and that [+singular] is the unmarked specification (cf. further below).

Apart from the observation that referentially inadequate usage is restricted to *die/les+plural noun* combinations and to bare plural nouns, there is more evidence to suggest that noun phrases such as *die pferde* 'the horses' which have singular reference are syntactically specified for number, namely for [+singular]. For those referentially inadequate nominals which are subjects of finite clauses, the verb shows up with singular morphology. Examples for this are *(des) männer kommt* (RSg) 'the men comes' (Iv;2;4,9), *und eh schiffe paßt* (RSg) 'and eh boats fits' (Iv;2;6,27), *die hasen die will gucken* (RSg) 'the bunnies they wants to look' (Iv;2;11,7), *macht da die tiere* (RSg) 'does there the animals' (Iv;2;11,21), *da's die sessel* (=ist) 'there's the arm-chairs' (Ca;2;10), *où l'est les poussettes* (RSg) 'where they is the baby carriages' (Ca;2;1,26).

Meisel's (1986, 1990) analysis of subject–verb agreement in Caroline and in Ivar clearly shows that the verbal functional category INFL is available in the grammar of both children during this developmental stage. In addition, he concludes that subject–verb agreement with respect to the feature [αperson] is target-like almost from the very beginning, i.e. when the children start using finite verb forms (at approximately 2;4 in Ivar and at approximately 2;1 in Caroline). Koehn (1989a) observes some agreement errors with respect to the feature [αnumber]. The comparison of these studies shows that, again, errors are systematic. Those noun phrases which contain an element that has been identified as having singular reference by the child, e.g. *der/le/la+noun* and *ein/un+noun*, show up with a singular verb form. In contrast to this, referentially adequate plural nominals are sometimes used with a singular verb form, although the corresponding contrastive verb form has already been acquired; *und [he] schiffe paßt* 'and boats fits' (Iv;2;6,27), *wir macht ein haus* 'we makes a house' (Iv;2;6,27), *les poupées va pas man[z]er...* (=manger) 'the dolls will+SG not eat' (Iv;2;8,15), *da is noch noch no viele noch viele noch* 'there is still still many still many still' (Ca;2;6,8), *regarde il fait pipi tous les trois* 'look he/they[21] pees all three of them' (Ca;2;10) where *schiffe, wir, les poupées, viele,* and *tous les trois* are referentially correct.[22] Note that referentially correct plural nominals also show up with a plural verb form; *a[n]e männer könn' runterfalln* (=alle) 'all men can-SG fall down' (Iv;2;8,15), *wolln wir nich* 'want-SG we not' (Iv;2;6,6), *oui les poupées elles arrivent* 'the dolls they arrive' (Iv;2;8,15), *wir schaukeln* 'we swing' (Ca;2;5,18), *die schlafen erst* (die=two dolls) 'they sleep first' (Ca;2;6,8). These observations suggest that nominals such as *die pferde* (RSg) 'the horses', *les cacaos* (RSg) 'the chocolats', as well as *der teddy, le nounours,* 'the teddy' are not unspecified for number, but instead have the feature [+singular]. They also indicate that the verb agrees in cases where the subject has the feature [+singular]. On the other hand, the verb does not always seem to agree with a referentially plural nominal in subject position.[23]

To conclude, number specification on nouns and determiners is nearly target-like in both languages, except for *les/die+plural noun* and bare plural nouns, which are used for both singular and plural reference. As for plural nouns, Koehn (1989a) argues that schemas play a decisive role in the process of how plural nouns are associated with their correct number specification in the lexicon. I argued in support of the assumption that plural nominals used for singular reference are specified as [+singular], until evidence suggests that this choice is wrong.

The plurifunctionality of *die* and most of the nominal endings in adult German (cf. above) which serve the function of a plural allomorph indicating plural and that of an integrated part of the lexical item may be the reason for the use of *die+plural noun* with singular reference in child language use. If plurifunctionality were a plausible explanation, then it would remain an open question how target-deviant usages of *les+plural noun* can be accounted for. Here, plurifunctionality may only explain why plural nouns have singular reference in child speech (cf. *chev[o]* (=chevaux) 'horses' — *bat[o]* (=bateau) 'boat'; *[z]animaux*[24] (=animaux) 'animals' — *[z]èbre* 'zebra'). Note that in adult French, the majority of nouns are not even marked (in speech) for number. The French article system, however, provides different forms for the singular (*le/la*) and for the plural (*les*). Why should it be then that the children use *les+plural noun* for singular reference?

I want to suggest that definite articles are analyzed as functional elements by the children (Ca at 2;0, Iv at 2;4) and that the grammatical feature "number" is treated as an inherent property of N, which is based on the phonological shape of the noun, excluding *le [zamono]* and *der schweine,* for example. The child does not seem to know that there is a plural form for each singular form. I will discuss this issue further below.

6.1.1.2. *Number Agreement*

I now come to the description of the syntactic relations within noun phrases. An interesting observation is that neither child ever uses the singular definite articles *der* and (later) *das* in combination with plural nouns. The same restriction is valid for French. Combinations such as *le/la [zamono]* (=animaux) 'the+SG animals' and *le/la chevaux* 'the+SG horses' do not show up in the data. Thus, not only *der* (*das*) and *le/la* always have singular reference, they are also consistently combined with singular nouns. Although the children sometimes use *die/les+plural noun* combinations in order to refer to a single object, definite nominals are formally target-like with respect to number marking (where this exists in spoken French). This amounts to saying that singular nouns appear with singular definite articles and plural nouns with the plural definite article. This is also valid for demonstratives, which are rare, however; Ivar (2;7,17) uses *ces [zamono]* (RSg) (=animaux) 'these animals' but never *ce [zamono]* 'this animals'.

These observations are even more striking if one considers that at least in Ivar's data, one finds examples where *ein/un* are used in combination with plural nouns. The referent of *ein/un* (and *eine/une*) is always a single object. Examples for this usage mostly occur until the age of 2;11 in Ivar.[25, 26] There are no examples in the data from Caroline.[27]

(35)	*ein schweine* 'a pigs'	(Iv;2;5,21)
(36)	*ein häse* 'a bunnies'	(Iv;2;5,21)
(37)	*ein vögel* 'a birds'	(Iv;2;6,6)
(38)	*ein gro vögel* 'a big birds'	(Iv;2;6,6)
(39)	*ein kühe* 'a cows'	(Iv;2;6,6)
(40)	*ein füßen* 'a feet'	(Iv;2;6,6)
(41)	*ein füge* 'a birds'	(Iv;2;6,6)
(42)	*ein jünge* 'a boys'	(Iv;2;6,6)
(43)	*ein affen* 'a monkeys'	(Iv;2;7,17)
(44)	*ein [zamo]* (=animaux) 'an animals'	(Iv;2;7,17)
(45)	*[a] menschen* (=ein) 'a people'	(Iv;2;7,17)
(46)	*eine kinder* 'a children'	(Iv;2;8,1)
(47)	*ein sitze* 'a seats'	(Iv;2;10,24)
(48)	*eine klötzer* 'a bricks'	(Iv;2;11,7)
(49)	*ein räder* 'a wheels'	(Iv;2;11,21)
(50)	*un autre [z]enfant* 'another children'	(Iv;2;11,21)

Note that the corresponding contrastive singular form is already used by Ivar;
e.g. *vogel* 'bird', *kuh* 'cow', *fuß* 'foot', *afflaffe* 'monkey', *klotz* 'brick', *enfant*
'child'. More importantly, most of these singular forms are combined with
ein/eine as well during the age period from 2;5 to 2;11,[28, 29] even within one
recording and sometimes in episodes such as the following:

(51)   A: *is das ein kleiner oder ein großer vogel?*
          'is this a small or a big bird?'
          I: *ein (grau) vogel/ ein gro vögel*
          'a grey bird/ a big birds'

(52)	*ein schwein* 'a pig' — *ein schweine* 'a pigs'	(Iv;2;5,21)
(53)	*ein hase* 'a bunny' — *ein häse* 'a bunnies'	(Iv;2;5,21)
(54)	*ein junge* 'a boy'	(Iv;2;5,21)
	— *ein jünge* 'a boys'	(Iv;2;6,6)
(55)	*ein vogel* 'a bird' — *ein vögel* 'a birds'	(Iv;2;6,6)
(56)	*ein kuh* 'a cow' — *ein kühe* 'a cows'	(Iv;2;6,6)
(57)	*ein fuß* 'a foot' — *ein füßen* 'a feet'	(Iv;2;6,6)
(58)	*ein graf vogel* (=groß) 'a big bird'	
	— *ein gro vögel* 'a big birds'	(Iv;2;6,6)
(59)	*ein affe* 'a monkey' — *ein affen* 'a monkeys'	(Iv;2;7,17)
(60)	*ein klotz* 'a brick'	(Iv;2;9,5)
	— *eine klötzer* 'a bricks'	(Iv;2;11,7)

The same type of variation that can be observed with *ein/eine+N* obtains in
cases where a referentially plural noun phrase contains a quantifying expression
such as *alle* 'all' or *zwei* 'two'.[30] Note that these expressions always refer to
more than one object.[31] There are no examples for this usage in the data from
Caroline (she does not use these elements prenominally).

(61)	*zwei freunde* 'two friends'	(Iv;2;5,21)
(62)	*zwei kindern* 'two children'	(Iv;2;6,6)
(63)	*zwei kind* 'two child'	(Iv;2;6,6)
(64)	*zwei kinder* 'two children'	(Iv;2;6,6)
(65)	*alle kinder* 'all children'	(Iv;2;8,1)
(66)	*alle männer* 'all men'	(Iv;2;8,15)
(67)	*zwei kanal* 'two channel'	(Iv;2;11,7)
(68)	*alles tiere* 'all animals'	(Iv;2;11,21)
(69)	*drei töcker* (=Stöcker) 'three sticks'	(Iv;2;11,21)

(70)   *zwei aff* 'two monkey'   (Iv;2;11,21)
(71)   *zwei affe* 'two monkey/s'   (Iv;2;11,21)

With respect to noun phrases containing a quantifying expression, Ivar obviously has not made progress yet. On the basis of the observation that adult indefinite articles behave like quantifying expressions in Ivar's language use, I want to suggest that he still analyzes these elements as numerals having a referential but no grammatical meaning. As a consequence of this, numerals do not agree with N.[32] In contrast to numerals, definite articles are analyzed as functional elements which enter into an agreement[33] relation with N.[34] More interestingly, the same kind of variation that has been observed for number markings also shows up with gender markings.

6.1.2. *Gender*

One needs to distinguish between gender as an inherent feature of nouns (gender-attribution) and as a variable characteristic of modifiers (gender-agreement). As both properties, i.e the feature and its syntactic consequences, are intertwined, it is not possible to treat them separately.

6.1.2.1. *Gender-Attribution and Gender Agreement*
With respect to gender in child language one has to distinguish markings on definite articles on the one hand from those on the other determining elements on the other hand. Definite articles are used mostly target-like from the very beginning in both languages, except for neuter nouns. Ivar and Caroline begin to discover neuter at the age of approximately 2;8 and 2;7 respectively. Nearly all neuter nouns are initially combined with the wrong form of the determiner, as far as the choice of definite articles is concerned. This seems to indicate that until after age 3;0, neuter gender does not represent a separate noun class in the children's lexicon, but instead, a subgender[35] (cf. Corbett 1989); for a detailed discussion see Müller (1990a,b,c).

As for French, it is remarkable that Ivar chooses the wrong form of the definite article only with 4 nouns (types) up to the age of 2;11 (13 up to 5;10) and Caroline with 6 nouns (types) up to the age of 2;11 (8 up to 5;0).[36] This shows that gender marking with respect to the definite article is not a problem in French. I argued in Müller (1990c) that target-deviant uses of definite articles indicate that the children have discovered gender regularities (for Caroline's data

cf. Müller 1990c; for Ivar's data cf. Müller 1990a,b).[37] The phonological shape
as well as semantic properties of the respective noun influence the choice of the
definite article. Both children, for example, combine nouns ending in a nasal
vowel with the masculine definite article *le*, even in cases where adult French
requires the feminine article, i.e. *main* 'hand' FEM, *dent* 'tooth' FEM, *maison*
'house' FEM, *maman* 'mother' FEM are used with *le*. Other regularities are
discussed in Müller (1987, 1990a,b,c) (cf. also Koehn, this volume).

Patterns in the German data resemble those in French if one considers only
feminine and masculine nouns. Ivar chooses the wrong form of the definite
article with 3 nouns (types) up to the age of 2;11 (9 up to 5;10) and Caroline
with 8 nouns[38] (types) up to the age of 2;11 (15 up to 5;0). Gender marking of
feminine and masculine nouns with respect to definite articles is thus not a
problem in German either. There is evidence that the children have discovered
gender regularities. In Ivar's data, monosyllabicity clearly is associated with the
masculine definite article. Thus, feminine nouns like *zahl* 'number' and *tür*
'door' (and many neuter nouns such as *dach* 'roof', *bett* 'bed', *loch* 'hole', *schiff*
'boat', *boot* 'boat', *brot* 'bread', *bein* 'leg') are combined with the masculine
definite article *der*. The observation that the form *der* never shows up with plural
nouns (cf. above) is also relevant here. Choice of *der* with monosyllabic nouns
may be interpreted as a clear indication of their status as singular nouns. Note
that monosyllabicity is associated with the singular in adult German as well; cf.
Köpcke (1988). Another regularity concerns the ending *-a*. Caroline combines
nouns with this ending with the feminine definite article *die*; *die opa* 'the
grand-pa' MASC, *die papa* 'the daddy' MASC, (later at 4;2,16) *die sofa* 'the sofa,
NEUT'. Following Köpcke (p.c.), this kind of association also exists in adult
German. Another important regularity concerns the very frequent schwa-ending.
Both children associate nouns with this ending with the form *die*. Ivar uses *die
hase* 'the bunny' MASC as a target-deviant noun phrase. Caroline uses French
nouns like *conen[ə]* (=coccinelle) 'ladybug' and *port[ə]* (=porte) 'door' with the
form *die*. Interestingly enough, Ivar leaves out the schwa-ending with the target-like
noun *affe* 'monkey' MASC and then chooses the masculine definite article *der*; *der
aff*.

To conclude, "gender" (or some aspect of adult grammatical gender) has
been discovered by the children. It seems to be interpreted as an inherent
property of N. Gender marking on definite articles is nearly target-like in both
languages. I will discuss the issue of whether we are dealing with adult-like gender
classification at the very beginning of this developmental phase further below.

Unfortunately, demonstratives are used infrequently by both children, making it difficult to draw reliable conclusions with respect to gender marking. Whenever they appear, however, the choice is either target-like or reflects formal regularities which have been observed for definite articles. For instance Caroline uses *diese* (and *die*, cf. above) in combination with nouns ending in schwa. Ivar chooses *dieser* (and *der*, cf. above) with monosyllabic nouns.

A very different pattern emerges with indefinite articles, which do not seem to follow the same regularities as with definite articles.

The observations which I will present in the following paragraphs are summarized in Table (3) below.

Table 3. Usage of un/une *and* ein/eine

un/une+noun (types)		*un*	*une*
Ivar (2;4–2;8)	MASC	55	6
	FEM	18	29
Caroline (1;10–2;11)	MASC	27	7
	FEM	15	16
ein/eine+noun		*ein*	*eine*
Ivar (2;4–2;8)	MASC/NEUT	103	2
	FEM	22	6
Caroline (1;10–2;11)	MASC/NEUT	31	5
	FEM	11	18

Ivar and Caroline use *une* in combination with French nouns ending in a nasal vowel and *ein* with German nouns ending in schwa. Examples of this usage are:

(72)	*une pu[n]* (=pullover) 'a sweater' MASC	(Iv;2;4,23)
(73)	*une pont* 'a bridge' MASC	(Iv;2;6,27)
(74)	*ein puppe* 'a doll' FEM	(Iv;2;5,21)
(75)	*ein katze* 'a cat' FEM	(Iv;2;6,6)
(76)	*une avion* 'a plane' MASC	(Ca;2;2,23)
(77)	*une gens* 'a person' MASC	(Ca;2;7,20)
(78)	*ein tonne* 'a cask' FEM	(Ca;2;5,18)
(79)	*ein katze* 'a cat' FEM	(Ca;2;7,20)

It would, however, be premature to conclude that Ivar and Caroline wrongly associate *le* with *une* and *die* with *ein*. Note that it is not evident why the child should make wrong associations, for they never occur in the child's input. Interestingly enough, mostly up to the age of 2;8 in Ivar's data and up to 2;11

in Caroline's data, French nouns ending in a nasal vowel and German nouns ending in schwa occur with both forms of the indefinite article. Many instances of the use of both indefinite articles in combination with the same noun are found in both children within the same recording.

(80)	*un dame — une dame* 'a woman' FEM	(Iv;2;6;6)
(81)	*un pont — une pont* 'a bridge' MASC	(Iv;2;6,27)
(82)	*eine rage*	(Iv;2;6,6)
	— ein garage 'a garage' FEM	(Iv;2;6,27)
(83)	*ein affe*	(Iv;2;7,17)
	— eine affe 'a monkey' MASC	(Iv;2;11,21)
(84)	*une avion*	(Ca;2;2,23)
	— un avion 'a plane' MASC	(Ca;2;3,11)
(85)	*un gens*	(Ca;2;7,20)
	— une gens 'a person' MASC	(Ca;2;8,19)
(86)	*eine katze*	(Ca;2;5,4)
	— ein katze 'a cat' FEM	(Ca;2;7,20)
(87)	*eine brille — ein brille* 'glasses' FEM	(Ca;2;8,5)

Furthermore, the wrong form of the indefinite article is used not only in combination with nouns ending in a nasal vowel or schwa, but also with other nouns which systematically show up with the correct form of the definite article in both languages, e.g. (Ivar) *le nounours — une nounours* 'teddy' MASC, *la poupée — un poupée* 'doll' FEM; *die eisebahn — ein eisebahne* 'train' FEM, *der schiff*[39] *— eine schiff* 'boat' NEUT; (Caroline) *le pied — une pied* 'foot' MASC, *la tête — un tête* 'head' FEM; *die ampel — ein ampel* 'traffic light' FEM, *der bär — eine bär* 'bear' MASC.

The variation of both forms of the indefinite article occurs with nouns other than those ending in a nasal vowel or schwa as well. Some examples for this kind of variation are:

(88)	*un chèvre*	(Iv;2;5,21)
	— une chèvre 'a goat' FEM	(Iv;2;6,6)
(89)	*une nounours*	(Iv;2;6,6)
	— un nounours 'a teddy' MASC	(Iv;2;9,5)
(90)	*ein lego — eine lego* 'a lego' MASC	(Iv;2;6,6)
(91)	*ein schiff — eine segelschiff* 'a boat' NEUT	(Iv;2;6,27)
(92)	*une abeille — un abeille* 'a bee' FEM	(Ca;2;2,9)

(93)	*une bateau*	(Ca;2;6,8)
	— *un bateau* 'a boat' MASC	(Ca;2;7,6)
(94)	*eine schiff* — *ein schiff* 'a boat' NEUT	(Ca;2;6,8)
(95)	*ein elefant* — *eine elefant* 'an elephant' MASC	(Ca;2;8,5)

One peculiarity in Caroline's development is that she uses indefinite articles in a systematic way with respect to nouns ending in a nasal (*un*) and nouns ending in schwa (*eine*) at the beginning of the developmental phase, beginning at 1;10 in French and at 2;0 in German. I hypothesized in Müller (1990c) that the appearance of these forms is due to surface rhyming (cf. Levy 1983). These usages, however, do not seem to reflect insights into the respective gender systems since it is with those nouns mentioned that Caroline makes the most errors from approximately 2;2 in French and 2;5 in German onwards.

An interesting phenomenon is the case of self-corrections with indefinite articles in both languages. They indicate the insecurity in the use of indefinite articles; e.g. un *une une aillette* (=alouette) 'a lark' FEM, *un su-une sucette* 'a lollypop' FEM, *une-un légo* 'a lego' MASC, *eine ein wagen* 'a car' MASC, *eine ei-ein mann* 'a man' MASC.

As has already been observed for number marking in noun phrases which contain a quantifying expression, the child does not seem to have made progress yet with respect to gender marking on indefinite articles. The choice of the indefinite article does not depend on formal properties of the co-occurring noun, as opposed to definite articles. If one assumes that indefinite articles initially are analyzed as numerals by the children, having a referential but no grammatical meaning, as opposed to definite articles which are functional elements (cf. below), we are able to explain why indefinite articles do not enter into an agreement relation with N like definite articles.

6.2. *The Nature of the Grammatical Features "Number" and "Gender" in Child Grammar*

I want to suggest the following structure for the children's noun phrases during the developmental phase under discussion.[40]

(96)

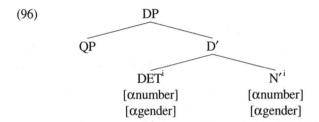

With respect to number, the child seems to interpret the grammatical feature "number" as an inherent and formal property of N, as compared to gender-attribution based on phonological properties of nouns. S/he has to learn that it depends on the number of the objects referred to. Furthermore, the child seems to determine the number specification for each nominal separately. I have suggested that all nominals are (inherently) specified as [+singular] in the first place. The children then have to learn whether nominals are specified as [−singular]. Thus, the reference for each plural N is determined in an item-by-item fashion. These observations indicate that the adult grammatical feature "number" (or plural) emerges step-by-step.

With respect to the grammatical feature "gender", I have argued that it is interpreted as well as an inherent property of N (based on phonological shape and semantic properties) by the children. It is difficult to draw a clear line between the inherent gender feature and gender agreement. In adult language, having masculine, feminine, or neuter gender means that the noun may be combined with several particular function words which are related in gender paradigms, e.g. masculine nouns occur with both *un* and *le* in French. In Müller (1990c) I tried to show that Caroline starts out with word-specific paradigms from approximately 2;6/2;7 onwards in both languages.[41] She associates, among other things, *die tasche* 'the bag' with *eine tasche* 'a bag' and *le champignon* 'the mushroom' with *un champignon* 'a mushroom', for instance, without knowing that all nouns which are used with *le* are used with *un* as well. First word-specific gender paradigms can be observed in Ivar at the age of approximately 2;6/2;7 in both languages as well. It seems to be the case that the adult gender feature also emerges step-by-step. It is first learned in combination with particular lexical items.

In structure (96), definite articles are positioned in DET, which is specified for the grammatical features "number" and "gender". The formal regularities that have been observed with definite articles may be interpreted as the morphological reflex of the agreement relation between DET and N′ encoded by identical superscripts. Definite articles are analyzed as functional elements by the children which enter into an agreement relation with N. This is valid for *le/la*, *der/das* as well as for *les* and *die*. The agreement relation is interpreted by the children as a purely formal relationship between DET and N. In French, it is hard to tell whether the usage of *les* depends on formal properties of N, since number is mostly not marked on N in spoken French. The observation that plural but not singular determiners are used with *[zamono]* 'animals' may suggest that formal properties of N determine the choice of the article in French as well. *les* may also function as a default-form. Note that *les* is a possible choice for most nouns in the child's input (except for singular nouns where the plural differs from the singular). It follows from the assumption that the adult grammatical features "number" (or plural) and "gender" emerge step-by-step, that number and gender agreement in child grammar are different from that in adult grammar with respect to the shared features. I have argued in support of the assumption that in cases where *die/les+plural noun* have singular reference, the nominal is specified as [+singular]. DET and N would share the feature [+singular] then, where choice of the form of the definite article depends on formal properties of N. Gender agreement has to be accounted for in terms of sharing abstract features until the children begin to build up word-specific paradigms.

I hypothesized that indefinite articles are initially analyzed as numerals, i.e they are treated as elements serving a referential but no grammatical function. Number is a semantic feature of these elements, gender is not marked at all. One consequence of this categorization is that they do not agree with N. This explains why errors occur in both directions, namely why singular and plural numerals are combined with both singular and plural nouns, for instance. Furthermore, I want to suggest that numerals are positioned in a position different from DET. Note that the children sometimes use constructions where both positions are lexically realized: Ivar uses nominals like 2;7,17 *ein der teddy* 'a the teddy', 2;8,1 *ein der zoo* 'a the zoo', 2;9,5 *(deux) les oreilles* 'two the ears', 2;11,7 *deux [n]argent* 'two the money', and Caroline uses *une la poule* 'a the hen' at 2;0,9. There are at least two possible positions for numerals in structure (96): a position adjoined to D' or SpecDP. The choice for one of these positions depends on the status of the category DET as a functional or as a lexical category in child grammar. Under the approach presented so far, DET should be a functional head and as a consequence it projects a specifier. Numerals are then positioned in SpecDP.[42]

One consequence of the claim that indefinite articles are initially analyzed as being numerals is that [−definite] is not marked at all or in a target-deviant way. Berkele's study (1983) shows that definite articles encode [+definite] (or

[+specific reference]) in the children's grammars. A possible assumption would be that [−definite] (or [−specific reference]) is marked by Ø, and [+definite] by elements like definite articles and quantifying expressions respectively. Similar claims have been advanced by Bickerton (1981) for Creole languages. It may also be suggested that nouns (except for proper names) are inherently specified as [−definite] and that [−definite] is not marked at all. It is important to look at the acquisition data in more detail with respect to the role of definiteness.

The important question is which changes in child grammar cause the emergence of the adult grammatical features "number" and "gender". I suggest that the categorization of *ein/eine* and *un/une* as indefinite articles, i.e. as functional elements like the definite articles plays a decisive role in the emergence of the adult grammatical features. As far as number is concerned, the child recognizes from then on that the grammatical feature "number" is related to the semantic feature "number" (encoded by numerals). With respect to gender, the child begins to recognize that *le* and *un* for instance are related in a paradigm which corresponds to saying that the adult feature [masc] emerges.

One prediction that follows from the categorization of *ein/eine* and *un/une* as indefinite articles is that target-deviant zero-markings of nouns should no longer occur. Berkele (1983) finds that in Caroline, zero-markings completely disappear from the age of approximately 2;11 onwards in both languages. The absolute number of zero-markings already drops below 50% at the age of approximately 2;6. This suggests that the integration of the indefinite article is a gradual process. Note that at the age of approximately 2;6, target-deviant references with *die/les+plural noun* begin to disappear in French and in German. In addition, first word-specific gender paradigms are attested (cf. Müller 1990c). The gradual emergence of the adult grammatical features "gender" and "number" is reflected then in the gradual process of the integration of indefinite articles. Since Ivar's language use has not been analyzed for zero-markings yet, it is impossible to draw reliable conclusions. My analysis shows that future research has to take into account the development of the grammatical feature "definiteness" in child grammar.

Appendix

IVAR

(1) Singular Reference

die [zamono] (=animaux) 'the animals'	(2;4,23)
die tiere 'the animals'	(2;8,1)
die vögel 'the birds'	(2;8,15)
die hasen 'the bunnies'	(2;11,7)
die puppen 'the dolls'	(2;11,7)
die tiere 'the animals'	(2;11,21)
les cacaos 'the chocolats'	(2;5,21)
les poupées 'the dolls'	(2;9,18)
les tables 'the tables'	(2;9,18)
les sacs 'the bags'	(2;9,18)
les dos 'the backs'	(2;9,18)
les trains 'the trains'	(2;11,7)
les jambes 'the legs'	(2;11,21)

(2) Plural Reference

die füße 'the feet'	(2;8,15)
die kinder 'the children'	(2;8,15)
die sandalen 'the sandals'	(2;8,15)
die füße 'the feet'	(2;9,5)
die tiere 'the animals'	(2;11,21)
les pieds 'the feet'	(2;6,27)
les légos 'the legos'	(2;7,17)
les ma[n]s (=mains) 'the hands'	(2;7,17)
les chaussons 'the socks'	(2;8,1)
les poupées 'the dolls'	(2;8,15)
(deux) les oreilles 'two the ears'	(2;9,5)
les pieds 'the feet'	(2;9,5)
les tasses 'the cups'	(2;9,5)
les chiens 'the dogs'	(2;9,18)
les bras 'the arms'	(2;10,24)

CAROLINE

(3) Singular Reference

die schuhe 'the shoes'	(2;0,9)
die pferde 'the horses'	(2;0,9)
die poussetten 'the baby carriages'	(2;1,26)
die carolines 'the carolines'	(2;3,11)
die pullover 'the pullovers'[43]	(2;7,6)
die sessel 'the arm-chairs'	(2;10)
les couches 'the diapers'	(2;0,9)
les poussettes 'the baby carriages'	(2;1,26)
les mémés 'the grand-mas'	(2;1,26)
les tables 'the tables'	(2;1,26)
les feuilles 'the leaves'	(2;2,23)
les chaussures 'the shoes'	(2;5,18)
les tomommes 'the bonhommes'=name of a doll	(2;6,8)

(4) Plural Reference

die boote 'the boats'	(2;4,20)
die trünfen (=Strümpfe) 'the stockings'	(2;5,18)
die toffen 'the stockings'	(2;5,18)
les oreilles 'the ears'	(1;10)
les mains 'the hands'	(1;10)
les pieds 'the feet'	(1;10)
les pieds 'the feet'	(2;0,9)
les bäbärs 'the teddies'	(2;0,9)
les enfants 'the children'	(2;1,26)
les oreilles 'the ears'	(2;4,8)
les enfants 'the children'	(2;6,8)
les queues de cheval 'the pigtails'	(2;6,8)
les cartes 'the cards'	(2;6,22)
les boules 'the balls'	(2;6,22)
les schlumpfs 'the smurfs'	(2;9,29)
les mains 'the hands'	(2;10,28)

IVAR

(5) Singular Reference

cub[ə] (=cubes) 'dice'	(2;4,9)
männer 'men'[44]	(2;4,9)
freunde 'friends'	(2;5,21)
kinder 'children'	(2;6,6)
füßen 'feet'	(2;6,6)
arme 'arms'	(2;6,6)
schiffe 'boats'	(2;6,27)
clowne 'clowns'	(2;11,7)
[z]oreilles 'ears'	(2;6,6)

(6) Plural Reference

ti[j]e (=tiere) 'animals'	(2;4,9)
füße 'feet'	(2;4,9)
kinder 'children'	(2;4,9)
zähne 'teeth'	(2;4,23)
füße 'feet'	(2;5,21)
klötzer 'bricks'	(2;6,6)
füßen 'feet'	(2;6,6)
handschuhe 'gloves'	(2;6,6)
haare 'hair'	(2;6,6)
strümpfe 'stockings'	(2;6,6)
schiffe 'boats'	(2;6,27)
tage 'days'	(2;6,27)
tiere 'animals'	(2;7,17)
kinder 'children'	(2;7,17)
autos 'cars'	(2;8,1)
tiere 'animals'	(2;8,1)
kinder 'children'	(2;8,15)
ohren 'ears'	(2;9,5)
füße 'feet'	(2;10,24)
bauklötzer 'bricks'	(2;11,7)
legos 'legos'	(2;11,7)
boote 'boats'	(2;11,7)
löcher 'holes'	(2;11,7)
tie[j]e (=tiere) 'animals'	(2;11,21)

[zamono] (=animaux) 'animals'   (2;4,9)
[z]oreilles 'ears'   (2;4,23)
[zamono] 'animals'   (2;5,21)
[zɸ] (=yeux) 'eyes'   (2;6,6)

CAROLINE

(7) Singular Reference

schuhe 'shoes'   (2;0,9)
tonnen 'casks'   (2;5,18)

(8) Plural Reference

schuhe 'shoes'   (2;0,9)
haare 'hair'   (2;4,8)

Acknowledgements

I am grateful to Roger W. Andersen, Susanne Carroll, Sonja Eisenbeiß, Peter Jordens, Georg Kaiser, Caroline Koehn, Regina Köppe, Elisabeth Löbel, Jürgen Meisel, Zvi Penner, Julia Philippi, Tom Roeper, and Achim Stenzel for comments on an earlier draft of this paper.

Notes

1. I want to leave open the question of whether N projects maximally.

2. This position modifies N.

3. Ritter (1990, 1991) argues that number projects a separate category in syntax, namely NUMP. Löbel (1990a) and Giusti (1991) assume the existence of a projection called QP. The categorial status of indefinite nominals is discussed further in Diesing (1992) and Vater (1986).

4. In possessive nominals like *seine tasche* 'his$_{FEM}$ bag$_{FEM}$', the choice of the stem *sein* (=possessor) depends on the context.

5. A third possible source of the grammatical feature "number", which has been pointed out to me by Peter Jordens, is DP.

6. Cf. Demuth (1992) for the assumption that null elements are replaced by phonological material.

7. There are five instances of the spontaneous use of adult-like determiners other than *ein/un* during this phase: *le lait* 'the milk' (Ca;1;8,6), *'ne oma* 'a grand-ma' (Ca;1;11,4), *la moto* 'the motorbike' (Iv;1;10,12), *la gi* (=guitarre) 'the guitar' (Iv;2;2,7), *l'eau* 'the water' (Iv;2;3,5). I refer to productive usage of a particular form in cases where it appears with some regularity in the data, i.e. more than only once per recording and/or in subsequent recordings.

8. As young children are likely to think of moving objects as animates, this conclusion is very preliminary.

9. MASC denotes masculine gender, FEM feminine gender, NEUT neuter gender in the adult language. SG denotes singular, PL plural.

10. *häuse* is an imitation. Ivar's mother uses this target-deviant form as the plural of *haus*.

11. RSg denotes singular reference, RPl plural reference.

12. The demonstrative is infrequent in the data from both children in both languages.

13. Other plural possessives do not appear. French *nos* 'our' begins to be used at 3;2,14 by Ivar. It is referentially adequate (cf. Koehn 1989a).

14. Caroline does not use these elements prenominally. Pronominal usage is not as frequent as in Ivar, but it occurs in subsequent recordings and more than once per recording.

15. She does not use plural possessives such as *unser* 'our' yet.

16. Since plural marking on nouns is very rare in French, this mainly relates to the German data.

17. The usage of "liaison" -*s* as part of the noun indicates that Ivar has wrongly segmented adult French *les animaux* 'the animals' into *[le] [z]animaux*.

18. Koehn (1989a) observes that the French data from Ivar contain only very few examples of the use of bare plural nouns. Caroline does not use bare plural nouns in French at all. However, the same restrictions that can be found in German with respect to the reference of bare plural and singular nouns can be observed in Ivar's French. Therefore, I want to suggest very tentatively that the generalizations made for German are also valid for French.

19. Cf. also *[zamono]* (=animaux) which is used for singular and plural reference by Ivar (cf. Koehn 1989a).

20. This also applies to Ivar's French.

21. The pronouns *il* 'he' and *ils* 'they' are phonetically non-distinct.

22. Cf. also the following example from Caroline at a later age (3;3,17): *nee die kinder darfen nur, das die kinder, die kinder, [n] darf das nur* 'no the children are allowed only, this the children, is allowed only this'.

23. For the exact number of agreement errors, see Koehn (1989a) and Meisel (1990).

24. This refers to the language use of the children under investigation.

25. The following list of examples is exhaustive.

26. The only examples after 2;11 are: 3;2,14 *ein balle* 'a balls', 3;3,12 *ein [z]omme* 'a men', 3;8,1 *an katzen* 'a cats', 4;0,4 *ein bücher* 'a books'.

27. The forms *häse, jünge, füge* do not exist in the target language. As they have a plural shape and Ivar also knows the corresponding singular forms, he may have analyzed them as plural nouns.

28. There is only one example for this type of variation after 2;11, namely 3;8,1 *eine katze* 'a cat' — 3;8,1 *an katzen* (=ein) 'a cats'.

29. The list of examples is exhaustive.

30. The list of examples is exhaustive.

31. This type of variation does not completely disappear after 2;11: 3;2,14 *drei gabel(n)* 'three forks', 3;2,14 *drei gabel* 'three fork', 3;2,14 *drei krokodil* 'three crocodile', 3;3,12 *drei cowboy* 'three cowboy', 3;4,23 *alle käfig* 'all cage', 3;4,23 *viele löwe* 'many lion', 4;0,4 *alle kerze* 'all candle', 5;0,25 *zwei stuhl* 'two chair', 5;1,8 *zwei gefängnis* 'two prison', 5;2,28 *zwei flugzeug* 'two plane'; cf. also the self-correction at 4;1,15 *unser drei [s]iff-segel[s]iffe* 'our three boat-sail-boats'.

32. Roger Andersen pointed out to me that many natural languages do not mark number on nouns which are preceded by a numeral or a plural quantifier. Quechua and Papiamento are two such languages.

33. Below I will discuss the issue whether we are actually dealing with adult-like agreement, i.e. feature sharing.

34. It may also be suggested that number agreement is sensitive to the feature definiteness. Then, we would be able to explain why noun phrases containing a demonstrative behave in the same way as those with a definite article. As demonstratives are very rare in the data, this assumption clearly is speculative.

35. "Subgenders are agreement classes which control minimally different sets of agreements, that is, agreements differing for a small proportion of the morphosyntactic forms of the controller (typically a single one), not including the most basic form (usually the nominative singular)" (Corbett 1989).

36. For Caroline's difficulties with the article *la* up to the age of 2;2, cf. Berkele (1983).

37. For a discussion of the notion of gender rule cf. Koehn (this volume).

38. I included those uses of definite articles which I think are due to other factors than wrong association on the basis of formal properties of nouns. Caroline chooses the form *die* irrespective of formal properties of the noun, if the noun phrase occurs in a syntactic environment requiring a non-nominative determiner, i.e. if preceded by a preposition. If we exclude these assignments, we are left with 5 nouns which are combined with the non-adult-like form of the definite article.

39. Neuter nouns initially are used with masculine definite articles (e.g. *der, den*) by Ivar.

40. I want to leave open the question of whether AP is adjoined to N′ or whether it is positioned in SpecNP since the focus of this paper is not the development of the agreement relation between adjectives and nouns.

41. The first noun which is combined with a definite and with an indefinite article form is at 2;2,23 *mouton* 'sheep' and at 2;0 *bär* 'bear' in Caroline.

42. Note that adjectives do not seem to be allowed in this position. Constructions similar to *ein der teddy* do not occur with adjectives. This suggests that the children distinguish adjectives and numerals on the one hand and that they locate them in different syntactic positions on the other. These positions modify N and DET respectively. Since the children also use noun phrases such as *les deux poupées* 'the two dolls' and *der ein schlumpf* 'the one smurf' at the end of the developmental phase under discussion, it is conceivable that quantifying expressions (except for the universal quantifier *all*) are also allowed in a position modifying N. Evidence for the assumption that QP agrees with N at later stages are examples from Ivar like 4;0,4 *allem teilem* 'all parts', 4;0,18 *alle teile* 'all parts', 4;5 *alles mögliches* 'all possible', 3;5,7 *viele luft* 'much air' FEM, 4;4,14 *viele kraft* 'much power' FEM, 4;8,17 *viele arbeit* 'much work' FEM.

43. Errors such as *die pullover* and *die sessel* (cf. also in the data from Caroline at 3;6,16 *die puppenkarren* 'the doll carriage' and in the data from Ivar at 3;0,19 *die führer* 'the driver') where the shape of the plural noun does not vary from the singular form in adult German, may also be interpreted as plural noun phrases with singular reference.

44   Ivar uses the form *des* in front of the noun *männer*. However, it is not clear whether *des* is a determiner in this case.

References

Abney, Stephen. 1986. "Functional Elements and Licensing." Manuscript, Massachusetts Institute of Technology, Cambridge, Mass.

Berkele, Gisela. 1983. *Die Entwicklung des Ausdrucks von Objektreferenz am Beispiel der Determinanten. Eine empirische Untersuchung zum Spracherwerb bilingualer Kinder (Französisch/ Deutsch)*. Masters thesis, University of Hamburg.

Bhatt, Christa. 1990. *Die syntaktische Struktur der Nominalphrase im Deutschen* (=*Studien zur deutschen Grammatik*, 38). Tübingen: Narr.

Bickerton, Derek. 1981. *Roots of Language*. Ann Arbor: Karoma.

Carroll, Susanne E. 1989. "Language Acquisition Studies and a Feasible Theory of Grammar." *Canadian Journal of Linguistics* 34.399–418.

Clahsen, Harald. 1990. "Constraints on Parameter Setting: A grammatical analysis of some acquisition stages in German child language." *Language Acquisition* 1.361–391.

Clahsen, Harald, Sonja Eisenbeiß & Anne Vainikka. 1994. "The Seeds of Structure: A syntactic analysis of the acquisition of Case marking." *Language Acquisition Studies in generative Grammar*(=*Language Acquisition and Language Disorders*, 8), ed. by Teun Hoekstra & Bonnie D. Schwartz, 85–118. Amsterdam: John Benjamins.

Corbett, Greville G. 1989. "An Approach to the Description of Gender Systems." *Essays on Grammatical Theory and Universal Grammar*, ed. by Doug Arnold, Martin Atkinson, Jacques Durand, Claire Grover & Louisa Sadler, 53–89. Clarendon Press: Oxford.

Demuth, Katherine. 1992. "Accessing Functional Categories in Sesotho: Interactions at the morpho-syntax interface." Meisel 1992, 83–107.

Diesing, Molly. 1992. *Indefinites* (=*Linguistic Inquiry Monographs*, 20). Cambridge, Mass.: MIT Press.

Dolitsky, Marlene. 1983. "The Birth of Grammatical Morphemes." *Journal of Psycholinguistic Research* 12.352–360.

Felix, Sascha W. 1990. "The Structure of Functional Categories." *Linguistische Berichte* 125.46–71.

Fukui, Naoki & Margaret Speas. 1986. "Specifiers and Projections." *MIT Working Papers in Theoretical Linguistics* 8.128–172.

Gawlitzek-Maiwald, Ira, Rosemary Tracy & Agnes Fritzenschaft. 1992. "Language Acquisition and Competing Linguistic Representations: The child as arbiter." Meisel 1992, 139–179.

Giusti, Giuliana. 1991. "The Categorial Status of Quantified Nominals." *Linguistische Berichte* 136.438–454.

Guilfoyle, Eithne & Máire Noonan. 1988. "Functional Categories and Language Acquisition." Paper presented at the B.U. Conference on Language Development, Boston University, October 1988.

Koehn, Caroline. 1989a. *Der Erwerb der Pluralmarkierungen durch bilinguale Kinder (Französisch/Deutsch). Eine empirische Untersuchung*. Masters thesis, University of Hamburg.

———. 1989b. "Zum Numeruserwerb bei Caroline." Manuscript, University of Hamburg.

———. 1991. "Zum Numerus- und Genuserwerb bei Ivar, Caroline und Pascal." Manuscript, University of Hamburg.

Köpcke, Klaus-Michael. 1982. *Untersuchungen zum Genussystem der deutschen Gegenwartssprache* (=*Linguistische Arbeiten*, 122.). Tübingen: Niemeyer.

———. 1988. "Schemas in German Plural Formation." *Lingua* 74.303–335.

Köpcke, Klaus-Michael & David A. Zubin 1983. "Die kognitive Organisation der Genuszuweisung zu den einsilbigen Nomen der deutschen Gegenwartssprache." *Zeitschrift für germanistischen Linguistik* 11.166–182.

Levy, Yonata. 1983. "The Acquisition of Hebrew Plurals: The case of the missing gender category." *Journal of Child Language* 10.107–121.

Löbel, Elisabeth. 1990a. "D und Q als funktionale Kategorien in der Nominalphrase." *Linguistische Berichte* 127.232–264.

―――. 1990b. "Zur kategorialen Bestimmung der Possessiva in der NP/DP: Possessiva als adjektive." *Arbeiten des Sonderforschungsbereichs 282: Theorie des Lexikons*, University of Düsseldorf.

Meisel, Jürgen M. 1986. "Word Order and Case Marking in Early Child Language. Evidence from simultaneous acquisition of two first languages." *Linguistics* 24.123–183.

―――. 1990. "INFL-ection: Subjects and Subject-Verb Agreement." Meisel 1990, 237–298.

――― ed. 1990. *Two First Languages: Early grammatical development in bilingual children* (=*Studies on Language Acquisition*, 10.). Dordrecht: Foris.

―――. 1991. "Early Grammatical Development: Verbal functional categories." Manuscript, University of Hamburg.

―――. ed. 1992. *The Acquisition of Verb Placement: Functional categories and V2 phenomena in language development* (=*Studies in Theoretical Psycholinguistics*, 16.). Dordrecht: Kluwer.

Meisel, Jürgen M. & Natascha Müller. 1992. "Finiteness and Verb Placement in Early Child Grammars: Evidence from simultaneous acquisition of French and German in bilinguals." Meisel 1992, 109–138.

Mills, Anne. 1985. "Acquisition of German." *The Crosslinguistic Study of Language Acquisition*. Vol. I: *The Data*, ed. by Dan I. Slobin, 141–254. Hillsdale, N.J.: Erlbaum.

―――. 1986. *The Acquisition of Gender: A study of English and German*. Berlin: Springer.

Müller, Natascha. 1987. "Der Genuserwerb im Französischen und Deutschen: Eine empirische Untersuchung eines bilingualen Kindes." Masters thesis, University of Hamburg.

―――. 1990a. "Der Genuserwerb bei Ivar I (Determinanten und Adjektive)." Manuscript, University of Hamburg.

―――. 1990b. "Der Genuserwerb bei Ivar II (Determinanten und Adjektive)." Manuscript, University of Hamburg.

―――. 1990c. "Developing two Gender Assignment Systems Simultaneously." Meisel 1990, 193–294.

Olsen, Susan. 1986. "Zum substantivierten Adjektiv im Deutschen: Deutsch als eine pro-drop Sprache." *Studium Linguistik* 21.1–35.

―――. 1989. "Das Possessivum." *Linguistische Berichte* 120.133–153.

————. 1991. "Die deutsche Nominalphrase als Determinansphrase." *DET, COMP und INFL: Zur Syntax funktionaler Kategorien und grammatischer Funktionen* (=*Linguistische Arbeiten,* 263.), ed. by Gisbert Fanselow & Susan Olsen, 35–56. Tübingen: Niemeyer.

Parodi, Teresa. 1990. "The Acquisition of Word Order Regularities and Case Morphology." Meisel 1990, 158–190.

Penner, Zvi. 1990. "On the Acquisition of Verb Placement and Verb Projection Raising in Bernese Swiss German." *Spracherwerb und Grammatik: Linguistische Untersuchungen zum Erwerb von Syntax und Morphologie* (= *Linguistische Berichte, Sonderheft 3*) ed. by Monika Rothweiler, 166–189.

Radford, Andrew. 1990. *Syntactic Theory and the Acquisition of English Syntax: The nature of early child grammars of English.* Oxford: Blackwell.

Ritter, Elizabeth. 1990. "Evidence for Number as a Nominal Head." Paper presented at GLOW, Leiden, March 1991.

————. 1991. "Two Functional Categories in Noun Phrases: Evidence from Modern Hebrew." *Perspectives on Phrase Structure: Heads and licensing* (= *Syntax and Semantics,* 25.), ed. by Susan Rothstein, 37–62. New York: Academic Press.

Roeper, Thomas. 1992. "From the Initial State to V2: Acquisition principles in action." Meisel 1992, 333–370.

Tucker, G. Richard, Lambert, Wallace E. & André A. Rigault 1977. *The French Speaker's Skill with Grammatical Gender: An example of rule-governed behavior.* The Hague: Mouton.

Vater, Heinz. 1986. "Zur Abgrenzung der Determinantien und Quantoren." *Zur Syntax der Determinantien* (=*Studien zur deutschen Grammatik,* 31.), ed. by Heinz Vater, 13–31. Tübingen: Narr.

Getting FAT
Finiteness, Agreement and Tense in Early Grammars

Jürgen M. Meisel
University of Hamburg

1. Introduction

Language acquisition studies, in as far as they are committed to theoretical endeavors, may be expected to contribute in significant ways not only to a better understanding of the development of linguistic knowledge and language use, but also to a theory of grammar which aims at exploring the mental reality of language. This presupposes, however, that one adopts the grammatical "continuity-assumption" (Pinker 1984:7) which postulates that

> in the absence of compelling evidence to the contrary, the child's grammatical rules should be drawn from the same basic rule types, and be composed of primitive symbols from the same class, as the grammatical rules attributed to adults.

Yet whereas the continuity assumption establishes the potential relevance of findings concerning developing grammars for our understanding of mature grammars, it appears to be in contradiction with the obvious fact that child language differs in substantial ways from adult language. The question thus arises whether these differences can be explained without recourse to different kinds of grammatical knowledge.

A possible solution to this problem is offered by the theory of parameters in grammatical theory. It allows one to distinguish between those phenomena which result from non-parameterized universal principles, as opposed to those which depend on parameters of universal grammar (UG) and those which are language-specific properties of grammar. Perhaps the most interesting ones, from an acquisitional perspective, are those related to parameterized principles of UG, for the children need to find out how the values of the parameters are set in the language(s) they are acquiring. And since, in these cases, UG allows for different solutions, one can, in fact, expect the child to explore the range of variation defined by parameterized options of UG. These parameters, however, relate primarily to the non-substantive elements of the lexicon, see Chomsky (1989), and this is the reason why it is particularly fascinating to study the development of functional categories. As has been suggested by Radford (1986, 1987, 1990), Guilfoyle & Noonan (1988), and others, they may initially be lacking altogether, and the children have to discover which functional categories need to be implemented and what their position is in the grammar of the language they are acquiring.

In what follows, I explore some of the options which can be derived from assumptions of this kind, focusing on the category INFL and categories which, more recently, have been argued to replace it, i.e. AGR, TENSE, and FINITE-NESS. I will show that of these three grammatical notions, agreement is the earliest to develop, tense coming in significantly later; my suggestion is that developmental order reflects the hierarchical order of the respective phrases in sentence structures. I will further argue that "finiteness" should be defined as depending on the presence of agreement and tense and that, in child as well as in mature grammars, one of these two may be sufficient to count as an instantiation of finiteness. Finally, this analysis raises the question whether AGR should be analyzed as the head of an independent maximal projection AGRP.

2. Some Properties of the Mature Grammars

Before turning to the analysis of developing grammatical systems, let me briefly summarize some of the relevant facts of the corresponding adult grammars. It is generally agreed that French adheres rather strictly to SVO order, whereas German is a "verb-second" (V2) language with underlying SOV order. Non-finite verbal elements occupy final position in both main and subordinate clauses in German. According to the usual analyses, see (1) and (2) below, both are verb-raising languages, i.e. the finite verb moves to INFL. This is normally also the surface position of the finite verb in French, as well as in German subordinate clauses which exhibit verb-final order. The V2 phenomenon of German main clauses is derived by further movement of the verb into COMP, the head of CP, together with movement of a maximal projection (X^{max}), e.g. the subject NP, into Spec-CP. In German subordinate clauses, the verb remains in INFL because the COMP position is occupied by a complementizer. As for

French, the finite verb can only be moved to COMP in exceptional cases, i.e. in so-called inversion constructions (see Rizzi & Roberts 1989).

(1)   German

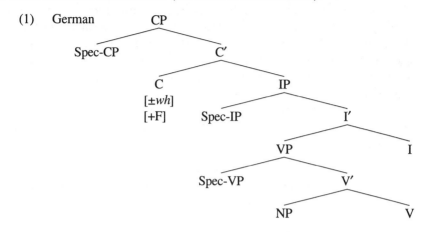

(2)   French

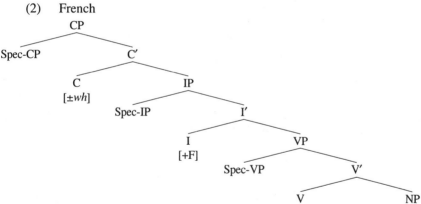

Note that two features are largely responsible for the differences between the two languages. One is that *headedness* is specified differently for INFL in French (head-initial) and in German (head-final). Another difference concerns the position of [±finite]. Platzack & Holmberg (1989) suggest a *finiteness parameter* which specifies the placement of the operator [+F], either in INFL, as in French and English, or in COMP, as in German. According to their analysis, it is the position of this operator which determines whether a language exhibits V2 phenomena or not.

The theory of grammar predicts that important aspects of the necessary knowledge need not be learned, in the usual meaning of the word. Rather, this knowledge has to be triggered by the input data; see Carroll (1989) for a useful discussion of the difference between learning and triggering. Crucial parts of X-bar grammar and the existence of Move-α, probably also its instantiations as WH-movement, NP-movement, head-to-head movement, etc. are, indeed, not learned, if these assumptions are correct. But our brief description of the adult system refers to a number of other notions, some of which, at least, need to be learned; for others, the parameterized options of UG, input data must trigger their implementation into the particular grammar to be acquired. Leaving other problems aside, we may say that the following issues are part of the developmental problems the child faces:

(3)   a.   The existence of notions like agreement and finiteness.
       b.   The presence of functional categories (e.g. I, C) in the particular grammar.
       c.   The setting of the finiteness parameter.
       d.   The choice between the headedness options for all projections of X-bar structure.
       e.   Language-specific overt markings for agreement, finiteness, etc.

In what follows, I will address these issues in inverse order, beginning with the phenomena which are most easily accessible in the input, i.e. overt markings.

3.   The Emergence of Grammar

It is obvious from structures like (1) and (2), above, that sentences are VPs dominated by a set of functional categories. Although the main goal of the present study is to analyze the emergence of these functional categories, it is useful to begin with a sketch of the linguistic knowledge available to the child during the phases preceding these developments. My hypothesis is that the category verb is the cornerstone of first grammatical structures; its identification by the child should therefore be of crucial importance for early grammars. I will restrict this to a short exposition of the most crucial hypotheses, illustrating them with some empirical findings, mostly from *one* child, Ivar; for more details and further empirical evidence, see Meisel (1991).

The first question, in searching for syntactic properties of child speech, concerns the appearance of multiword utterances. In the case of Ivar, there already exist a few of these during the first recording, at age 1;6 (years;months).

But it is only at around age 1;10, in French, that the *first predicate+argument constructions*[1] appear. At the same time, multiword utterances become more frequent and more productive. Iv, for example, uses *[le]* 'it is', *cassE* 'broken', *ça cassé* 'that one broken', *c'est cassé* 'this is broken', *maman est là* 'mommy is there'.[2] The situation is similar in German where Iv starts using combinations of "subjects" with verbs and adjectives at age 1;10,30. But the types of combinations are still limited. For example, only proper names like *mama, papa* and *teddy* are combined with verbs. All other multiword utterances up to age 2;0 show the pattern S+O or S+Adj. It is, therefore, not justifiable to qualify these as "subjects" or "objects" at this point of time, since these patterns only consist of predicates, mostly particles, and adjectives, combined with nominals which do not yet, however, function as subjects in the technical sense of the term. This is to say that their morphological form and their placement are not governed by grammatical principles. Instead, the sequencing appears to be determined to a large extent by theme–rheme ordering in both languages. Language-specific patterns can nevertheless already be observed; in German, for instance, predicates appear consistently in final position, whereas in French, ordering is somewhat more variable. But these approximations to patterns of the target languages can be accounted for in terms of the influence the respective input is likely to exert.

Note that this account of very early multiword utterances is not in contradiction with our assumptions about the role of UG in language acquisition or with the continuity assumption, mentioned in the Introduction, above. Knowledge about surface order and even that about certain D-structure ordering regularities, see (3d), needs to be extracted from the input, as is obviously also the case for morphological forms. With respect to the continuity of grammatical development, the quote from Pinker (1984), above, states quite clearly that it refers to the nature of the child's grammatical rules, which are claimed to be of the same type as those of adult grammars. This leaves open the possibility that during an early phase children may not have access to grammar at all, although they are clearly able to use semantic–pragmatic principles to organize the form of their speech. This is, indeed, what I believe is happening here, i.e. early multiword combinations do not exhibit syntactic properties. To the extent that one finds a preferred word order, e.g. "V-final" for Ivar, this order varies from child to child, even with the same lexical elements. Where the children deviate from the preferred order, this seems to depend on pragmatic factors.[3] To mention one example, the element on which the child is focusing is placed in final position by Iv. Context and intonation suggest, for example, that in *teddy donne* 'teddy give' Iv insists that he be given the toy, whereas in *donne+X* 'give X' he focuses on the particular object; see Meisel (1991) for further details.

My claim is that early multiword utterances represent what Bickerton (1990a, b) calls "protolanguage", that is, they are not organized according to morphosyntactic principles; in fact, at this stage, no structure at all can be detected beyond what is evidenced by linear sequences. According to Bickerton, neurological maturation makes UG available to the child, and this happens around age 2;0, approximately. This is, I want to argue, where the principle of grammatical continuity comes into play: once grammar is accessible, categories and rules of child grammars are of the same type as those in their mature counterparts. The emergence of these categories and rules is an autonomous process, independent of the child's pragmatic competence; grammatical development thus does not rely crucially on the grammaticization of semantic–pragmatic principles.

One way to decide from which point onwards grammatical principles determine the use of child language is to determine when the child is capable of identifying syntactic categories. According to current linguistic theory, X-bar structure is not learned. Consequently, if the child is able to recognize specific syntactic categories, e.g. verbs, s/he should also be able to project them to the X″ level, i.e. to VP.

As far as Iv's linguistic development is concerned, it is important to note that no finite forms appear in his early multiword utterances. In fact, N+Adj sequences are significantly more frequent at this time than S+V or V+O constructions. More precisely, except for *dodo* 'sleep', only adjectives are combined with "subjects" before age 2;0, and forms like *parti* 'gone', *cassé* 'broken', *collé* 'glued', are also adjectival elements; see Meisel (1985). At around 2;0, more productively as of 2;2, present tense forms begin to emerge in French. Looking for finite verb forms combined with nominal elements in subject position, one finds that "subjects" are still extremely rare. The first unambiguous subject–verb constructions appear at age 2;0,2, with the same French verb, *dort* 'sleeps'.

(4)   a.   *nounours dort*   (Iv 2;00,02)
           'teddy sleeps'
      b.   *dort bébé*   (Iv 2;00,02)
           'sleeps baby'

At the same time, one also finds a number of probably formulaic constructions with *est*, e.g. *c'est, l'est* =il est and *maman est là* (2x). At age 2;2,7, [*jepa*] (répare) '(I) fix (it)', *dort* 'sleeps', *coule* 'runs' are combined with nominal subjects. Note that the subject has been placed in final as well as in initial position, with a certain preference for the latter; as of 2;2, however, it appears consistently in preverbal position.

In sum, then, before age 2;0, I find no reasons to assume that the child has access to a grammar which assigns hierarchical syntactic structures to concatenations of predicates and nominal arguments. Only after 2;0 or 2;2 do we have empirical justification for the claim that grammatical knowledge is indeed available. A crucial fact is that finite forms emerge. Assuming that formal properties of this type enable the learner to identify verbal elements and to distinguish them from other predicates (adjectives, particles), and supposing that properties of X-bar structure need not be learned by experience, one may conclude that the discovery of syntactic categories now makes structures like (6) (for French) available where nominal categories function as verbal arguments.

In German, similar developments can be observed at roughly the same time. Early verb forms which are not yet marked for agreement often also lack subjects preceding them. At age 2;0,2, presentative *das ist* 'this/that is' sequences appear. Simultaneously, uses of presentative *das*+Adj/N are frequently attested, but *das* is not yet combined with main verbs.

(5) a. *das gita*   (Iv 2;0,2)
         'that guitar'
     b. *das kaputt*   (Iv 2;0,2)
         'that broken'
     c. *das is [bozu]*   (Iv 2;0,2)
         'that is bonjour'
     d. *das ist [a] mann*   (Iv 2;0,2)
         'that is a man'

The first finite verb form of a main verb (*passiert, ne* 'happened, uh?') is recorded at age 2;0,29, but it is possibly an imitation of an adult utterance. There are two more examples in the same transcript, but they cannot be interpreted unambiguously, either. Early structures in German thus do not differ significantly from those in French, with the exception of the position of V, German VPs normally being head-final. This gives a structure as in (7) for early German sentences.

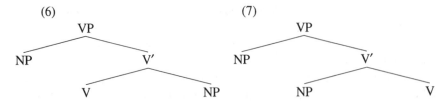

Note that it is hardly possible to decide whether the children have set the headedness parameter correctly in German as soon as such structures emerge. The reason for this uncertainty is that normally only one of the verbal arguments is realized, yielding mostly SV or OV patterns. Yet since in the majority of the utterances verbs are placed in final position, see Clahsen (1982), it is very likely that structures like (7) are discovered quite early. The few precocious SVO-patterned utterances are probably rote-learned expressions since they are usually of the type *das ist N(P)* 'that's N(P)'. But because of the scant empirical basis for these assumptions, the possibility cannot be ruled out that early German structures resemble those in French, as in (6) or that children oscillate, for some time, between (6) and (7); of the children studied here, this applies at least to Iv.

Early sentence structures are thus VPs, with the subject originating in Spec-VP position. This is, indeed, a solution offered by UG; see Kuroda (1988) and others who argue that sentential subjects are base-generated as external arguments of the verb, that is in Spec-VP. According to Kuroda (1988:10), languages are parameterized as to whether agreement is forced or not. "Agreement" here refers primarily to Case assignment, but it also includes gender/number agreement between nouns and their specifiers as well as subject-verb agreement. These assumptions lead to a number of consequences, one being that, in languages like English, the external argument of VP in finite clauses has to move to Spec-IP position to be assigned Case by AGR in INFL; in contrast, in unforced agreement languages like Japanese, mechanisms independent of Case Theory license the Spec-IP position.[4] Kuroda's proposal has a number of interesting implications for the role of functional categories in early grammars. One is that children, led by principles of UG, can assume that agreement is optional; hence, they may initially construe a grammar without any kind of verbal functional category, analyzing the sentence as a projection of the verb, with the subject in Spec-VP position.

4. The Emergence of Agreement

The question now is when and how verbal functional categories come in and whether they all appear simultaneously or in a specific chronological order. If the order of emergence reflects the hierarchical order in sentence structures, one should expect INFL to appear first. The split-INFL hypothesis leads to the further problem of the developmental order of agreement, finiteness, and tense. In a Pollock (1989) framework, AGR is the first candidate. This also follows from Kuroda's (1988) claims about forced and non-forced agreement as crucial distinctions between languages like English and Japanese. And this is precisely what happens. In other words, I want to claim that agreement is acquired before tense. In what follows, I will first summarize some facts about the acquisition of agreement and then address briefly the question of what the role of tense could be. This will lead to a discussion of how to define "finiteness" in developing and in mature grammars. Finally, I will consider some of the consequences of the findings of this study for the architecture of sentence structure.

4.1. *Subject–Verb Agreement in German*

Person and number agreement markings in German are coded as verbal affixes. The paradigm for modals differs slightly from that of main verbs. See Table 1 for a brief overview of the target forms.

Table 1. Morphological markings on main verbs and on modals

	to say			*want*	
	sagen	inf	-n	*wollen*	-n
ich	*sag(e)*	1st sg	-0/(-e)	*will*	-0
du	*sagst*	2nd sg	-st	*willst*	-st
es/sie/es	*sagt*	3rd sg	-t	*will*	-0
wir	*sagen*	1st pl	-n	*wollen*	-n
ihr	*sagt*	2nd pl	-t	*wollt*	-t
sie	*sagen*	3rd pl	-n	*wollen*	-n
	gesagt	p.part	ge- -t/-n		-t

Forms to be learned: { -0, -n, -t, -st }

In Table 2, adapted from Meisel (1990), I summarize the developmental pattern evidenced in the language use of three of the children studied. It shows that one can distinguish between two phases in the appearance of verb forms.[5]

Table 2. *Developmental sequence of finite verb forms in German*

		C 1;11–2;4	Iv 2;0–2;3	P 2;7–2;10
-t	3rd sg	1;11	2;0	2;9
is'	3rd sg	2;1	2;0	2;7
-0	3rd sg mod	2;4	2;3	2;10
-0	1st sg mod	2;5	2;3	2;8

		C 2;5–2;8	Iv 2;5–2;8	P 2;11–3;3
-0	1st sg	2;5	2;7	2;10
-e	1st sg	2;10	2;8	2;9
bin	1st sg	*	2;7	3;3
-st	2nd sg	2;4	2;5	2;11
bist	2nd sg	*	2;8	*
-en	3rd pl	2;5	2;8	2;11
sind	3rd pl	2;6	2;8	3;10
-en	1st pl	2;9	2;6	3;3
sind	1st pl	2;8	*	3;11

During a first phase, all the target forms which code the 3rd sg (i.e., *0*, and -*t*) appear within approximately three months. Towards the end of this period, one also encounters forms of the 1st sg modal; it is difficult to decide whether these already represent productive[6] uses since they are identical to 3rd sg modals, both being zero markings. All other suffixes (i.e., markings for 1st sg, 2nd sg, and 1st and 3rd pl: -*0, -st, -e* and -*en*) emerge during the next phase, which also lasts for about three months. Some so-called irregular forms tend to make their appearance later, and forms of the 2nd pl are not attested at all during the period under investigation.[7] Leaving details aside, one can say that all suffixes are acquired within a rather short period of time:[8] C 1;11–2;5, Iv 2;0–2;8, and P 2;7–3;3. This period is really even shorter since the first occurrences, usually some isolated examples of 3rd sg forms, cannot be regarded as productive uses; see Meisel (1990, 258ff.). Productive uses emerge at ages 1;11 for C, 2;1 for Iv, and 2;9 for P. Verbal inflection markings for person and number thus make their appearance in the children's speech within the following periods: C 1;11–2;5; Iv 2;1–2;8; P 2;9–3;3. In other words, a period of approximately six months is sufficient for the whole inventory of forms to be acquired.

It may be useful to remember that more forms than those just mentioned have been acquired by the children at this point of development since they also use non-finite forms (i.e., infinitives and past participles) which are morphologically marked, as well. In addition, the children also make appropriate use of the imperative. In sum, then, I conclude that inflectional markings on verbs are acquired during a limited period of time, lasting for approximately six months, early in the children's grammatical development. Consistent with this conclusion is the fact that MLU values rise from 1.75–2.25 during our phase I, and from 2.25 to approximately 3.5 during our phase II.

The question now is whether these forms do indeed represent agreement markings. In order to decide on this, it will be necessary to look briefly at the use of subjects. My assumption here is that if the verb agrees with the subject correctly in form and if the respective verb form is used productively, one can argue that the children are able to encode an abstract grammatical relation by means of agreement markers. Following these guidelines, the analysis of our data in Meisel (1990) leads to the conclusion that the children are using the 3rd sg form productively as of ages 1;11 (C), 2;1 (Iv), 2;9 (P); this corresponds in all three cases to the period when the utterances reach an MLU value of approximately 1.75–2.0. The fact that these utterances normally also contain a subject with which this verb form agrees is a clear indication that a grammatical phenomenon is emerging. The most crucial fact here is that agreement errors are virtually non-existent. To be more precise, I have shown (Meisel 1990) that one may find a few examples which might be interpreted as errors in number agreement but errors in person agreement do not exist. This observation is theoretically relevant. Platzack & Holmberg (1989) have demonstrated that whereas the loss of number agreement in historical change does not affect other grammatical properties of the language, losing person agreement entails significant reorganization in other areas of grammar. Consequently, agreement should primarily be understood in terms of person agreement; number agreement may be added to this, but it is apparently not a necessary criterion in defining this grammatical relation.

Facts concerning agreement of forms thus confirm our claim according to which verb inflection is already used by the children during this early phase to code grammatical agreement. This hypothesis[9] is further corroborated by findings concerning the use of elements in subject position. First of all, subject-like elements begin to be placed in the position preceding the verb as soon as finite verb forms are attested. Secondly, null subjects disappear almost instantaneously. With finite verb forms, subjects are only rarely lacking as of C 1;11, Iv 2;0, P 2;8, even though subject+finite verb sequences are not yet frequent.

To sum up, I tentatively conclude: the grammatical concept of agreement is accessible as soon as the child is able to use grammatical knowledge, perhaps as soon as s/he can parse the relevant markings. The markings are then immediately used productively, even though the necessary inventory of inflectional forms takes more time to be acquired. This happens subsequently, over a period of several months. A further finding, yet to be explained, is that, when agreement markings begin to appear, first only those of the 3rd sg are used; markings for other grammatical persons surface somewhat later. I will discuss the relevance of this observation below.

Table 3. Subject–verb agreement in German

3rd sg	C 1;11	Iv 2;1	P 2;9
1st/2nd sg	C 2;4	Iv 2;5	P 2;11

4.2. *Subject–Verb Agreement in French*

The range of overt inflectional markings on verbs in spoken French is extremely limited. With few exceptions, no such markings are phonetically realized in the singular. As for the plural, only 2nd pl forms are consistently marked (*-ez*), but, just as in German, such forms are not used by the children during the period studied. The 1st pl, *-ons*, rarely appears in colloquial speech; it is replaced by the 3rd sg, as in *on mange* 'one eats = we eat'. The 3rd pl is phonetically identical to singular forms for *-er* verbs, the most frequent inflectional class. Other verbs mark 3rd pl by a final consonant, as in *ils finissent* [il finis] or *ils partent* [il part]. It should be remembered that plurals do not occur frequently, neither in French nor in German.

As should be apparent from these remarks, subject clitics (SCL), rather then verbal suffixes, play the crucial role in marking grammatical person and number. They may, in fact, be regarded as agreement markings, that is, as phonetic realizations of AGR (see Roberge & Vinet 1989 and Kaiser & Meisel 1991). It also follows from the above observations that in analyzing verb forms one has to rely more heavily on those verbs which do mark person and number overtly (a limited number of so-called irregular verbs such as *aller* 'to go', *savoir* 'to know') and on auxiliaries. Let me add that because of the scarcity of overt markings, the finite/non-finite distinction is particularly important, since infinitives and participles are marked unambiguously in most cases. But although these two forms differ phonetically from finite forms[10] with -*er* verbs as well, they cannot, in this case, be distinguished from each other. The first examples of verb forms appear at ages 1;3 (P), 1;4 (C), and 1;5 (Iv), but it is obvious that they cannot be classified as productive uses yet. I interpret them as rote-learned forms.

From the observations made above, it follows that variation of verb forms will be rather limited in French. In analyzing the German data, a major criterion had been that at least two forms of the same verb should be present in the data. This may be too strong a requirement in French. As an example, let us briefly look at C again. The first verb of which two forms are documented in the data shows up at age 1;10: monte–montE. At 2;0, *va* and *allez* 'go' appear, but these might still be rote-learned forms. A little later, at 2;1, there can be no doubt that C uses different verb forms productively, e.g. *tombe, tomber, tombé*. If, however, one looks at the total range of different forms, across various types, it becomes clear that the child makes use of verbs and of verb inflection earlier than that. At age 2;0, the following forms have been recorded:

(8)   (C 2;0)
       Infinitives: *à boire, coucher*
       Imperatives: *attends, tourne, allez, assieds-toi, écoute.*
                        ferme, descends, couchE, regarde
       participles: *parti, fini, ouvé (=ouvert), tombé, cassé, monté*
       present tense: *va, est, a/as, met, monte, ferme, pique, saute*

The variety of forms as well as the fact that some of them are used creatively (*ouvé*, 'opened'), suggest quite strongly that C has begun to use verbs and verb inflection productively.

Applying the same criteria to P's data yields the following result: he starts using various verb forms at age 2;7; finite as well as non-finite forms are present then. If one applies the more rigid criterion of formal variation, however, one will have to conclude that verb inflection emerges at around age 2;9–2;10. As of 2;11, P already uses various irregular verbs in the present tense and with the infinitive (3;0).

As far as Ivar is concerned, one finds that present tense forms begin to appear at age 2;0, more regularly at age 2;2. It is difficult to decide whether during the following period, age 2;2–2;4, verb inflection is already used productively. On the one hand, no verb appears in more than one form. On the other hand, the same verb is used together with what looks like a subject, and also in isolation, that is, the elements in preverbal position are not chunked together with the verb. And infinitival forms are not combined with a nominal element in subject position, except for three instances where the infinitive serves to express an imperative.

(9) a. *mouton sautE!*   (2;02,07)
         'sheep jump'
     b. *Connie retirE!*   (2;03,05)
     c. *Natascha manger brot!*   (2;04,23)
         'Natascha eat bread'

At age 2;5, Iv has definitely acquired verb inflection. Subject clitics of 1st–3rd person are combined with verbs; modal verbs make their appearance, usually in combination with infinitival forms of main verbs; past participles begin to be preceded by auxiliaries; and irregular forms are present from now on (e.g. *il va* 'he goes').

Note that, in French too, virtually no errors in agreement markings for person exist. If a subject is present, the verb correctly agrees with it, and if the child uses an inflectional suffix, it does not violate the rules of subject–verb agreement. Number agreement apparently emerges somewhat later than agreement for person, towards the end of the developmental phase discussed above, and one occasionally finds errors in number agreement. All this, in sum, indicates that subject–verb agreement has been acquired during this phase.

This becomes even more evident looking at subject clitics. The picture which emerges here is that, much as in German, the various forms of subject pronouns in French are acquired within a short period of time. Table 4 shows from what point on they are used productively by the three children. Note that those children who refer to themselves by means of their proper names, use *je* later and less frequently than one might expect.

Discussing verbal forms, I argued above that verb inflection in French is attested approximately one or two months later than in German. The earliest examples show up at the following ages: C 1;10, P 2;7, Iv 2;0. It is only some time later that one finds conclusive evidence indicating that the children use inflection markings productively, i.e. at ages C 2;0–2;1, Iv 2;4–2;5, and P 2;9–2;10. Taking the results on verb inflection and on clitics together, one can

Table 4. Use of subject clitics in French

	C	Iv	P
il	1;11	2;3	2;9
elle	1;11	2;5	2;9
on	2;0	2;5	3;0
tu	2;0	2;5	2;11
je	2;3	2;5	3;0

Table 5. Subject–verb agreement in French

3rd sg	C 1;11-2;0	Iv 2;3	P 2;9
1st/2nd sg	C 2;3	Iv 2;5	P 2;11-3;0

conclude that subject–verb agreement emerges at approximately the ages given in Table 5.

To sum up, the empirical evidence discussed here suggests that, as in German, agreement develops quite early in French. And again, one can observe that, once agreement is available, it still takes some time until the various forms of the target system are acquired. But this does not seem to represent a major acquisitional problem, and they all emerge within a few months. Note that, just as in German, 3rd sg markings precede other markings, in this case by 2–4 months.

5. And What about Tense?

As outlined above, the aim of this paper is to study the development of those grammatical categories associated INFL, i.e. AGR, TENSE, and FINITE-NESS. In the preceding section, I have shown that agreement is present in the children's grammars from very early on. It is, in fact, the first of the grammatical concepts which serve to distinguish finite from non-finite verb forms. The question which immediately arises at this point is: When, in the course of grammatical development, does TENSE come in, the other crucial component of finiteness, commonly defined in terms [+AGR] and [+T]. Note that in asking this question, I am referring to the syntactic feature and its morphological encodings, as opposed to the semantic operator. This distinction is unfortunately not always maintained in the linguistic literature, a failure which leads to further confusion in the already complicated discussion of these issues.

In the context of the present discussion, the crucial issue at stake is the developmental chronology in which AGR and TENSE make their appearance in child grammars. The necessary empirical information, as far as the latter is concerned, can be drawn from an earlier study on the acquisition of tense and aspect in two of the children, C and P; see Meisel (1985).[11] A brief summary of the relevant results reveals the following picture. The first uses of apparently tensed verbs appearing in the two children's speech (at age C 1;9, P 2;6 in German; C 1;4, P 1;11 in French) are invariant rote-learned forms, rather than being the result of productive use. More specifically, it can be demonstrated that the different forms depend on semantic properties of the lexical items. This is to say that one encounters a strong correlation between semantically defined verb classes and the respective forms in which specific verbs belonging to these classes appear. Following the usual distinction between change-of-state, action, and stative verbs, it can be observed that, initially, only change-of-state verbs are used as past participles; in fact, up to ages 2;7 (C) and 3;0 (P), all elements of this class, with the exception of a few imperatives, exhibit past participle forms. Stative verbs, on the other hand, are almost exclusively used as present tense forms. Action verbs, finally, appear initially as imperatives and as infinitives which are used in imperative function. It is with action verbs that the form-funct-ion ties begin to loosen. As of ages 2;1 (French) and 2;3 (German), for C, and 2;9–2;10, for P, they begin to surface as present tense forms.

This analysis of the acquisition of verb forms and of their initial dependence on semantic properties led to the conclusion that a new developmental phase begins at this point (C 2;1 and P 2:9). It is best described as a transitional phase (Meisel 1985:353), because it is characterized by an increasing variety of verb forms, largely independent of the semantic values of these lexical elements but still not encoding temporal notions of the kind found in the adult target language. Rather, they serve to mark the opposition between [±perfectivity] of action; similar facts have been observed by Jordens (1990:1423) for the acquisition of Dutch. Remember that the study of subject–verb agreement revealed that the period corresponding to this transitional phase is precisely the one when the children, having developed the notion of agreement, begin to use morphological markings, i.e. 3rd sg forms. In other words, the observed increasing formal variation is due to the development of agreement markings — whereas tense markers resembling those of the adult grammar begin to surface only later, at a time when the markings for person agreement and most of the number agreement suffixes have already been acquired successfully, except for so-called "irregular forms".

In German, the acquisition of TENSE seems to be related to the emergence of perfect tense constructions. At first, the only "finite" elements in the data are present tense forms. Since these do not stand in opposition to other tensed forms, they can hardly be interpreted as representing a morphosyntactic tense system. The same conclusion is inevitable from a semantic point of view, since these verb forms do not yet express temporal notions; see Meisel (1985). When the children finally begin to use forms of the perfect tense, the notions expressed are semantically still not equivalent to the corresponding tenses in adult grammar, but they do allow the expression of temporal reference [+anterior], and they make available a second form class. As of this point, it appears to be plausible to speak of grammatical tense being part of the children's grammars. This amounts to saying that TENSE begins to appear around age C 2;7-8 and P 3;1-3, at the earliest. Note that it is somewhat difficult to determine more precisely when this happens. C, for example, uses one auxiliary+past participle construction in German at age 2;6, and then again at age 2;8. Even more strikingly, Iv never uses perfect tense in German during the period investigated, i.e. up to age 3;0.

There is, however, another possible clue for when TENSE is acquired in German, namely the use of *war* 'was'. During the period under consideration, it appears once during the recordings with C at age 1;11 and then again at 2;7; P uses it as of 3;1, albeit very rarely. If one is ready to accept an argument based on such infrequent occurrences and if one also ignores the isolated example at C 1;11, these data do support the hypothesis concerning the time of acquisition of TENSE.

Table 6. German verb forms

Forms	Age		MLU	
	C	P	C	P
present tense	1;11	2;9	2.0	2.3
aux+part.part	2;8	3;3	3.0	3.3
war	2;7?	3;1	3.0	3.3
mod+V	2;6	3;0	?	3.0

Two further comments seem to be appropriate at this point. The first is that during the period analyzed, up to age 3;6, no other verbal tense markings emerge in the data of the two children. This includes the observation that no future tense form is attested, although they do use temporal adverbials referring to future events in both languages, e.g. *demain* 'tomorrow', *après, später* 'later', *jetzt* 'now' = in this instant' = [+posterior], all referring to the immediate future. The second point is that the interpretation suggested here is in conflict with most of what one normally finds in the literature on time and tense in early child language. Usually a much later age is given.

The acquisition of tense and aspect in French is, again, more difficult to evaluate because of the scarcity of inflectional markings. As far as TENSE is concerned, one has to rely on the form of the verb itself. Past participle forms are precocious in French, but they do not serve to encode the [±tense] distinction. Instead, they are used much like adjectives in the adult language. This claim is supported by the fact that early uses of aux+participle constructions only contain *être* 'to be', not *avoir* 'to have', indicating that one still has to do with adjectival uses. In sum, then, there is no conclusive evidence for when TENSE emerges in early French grammar. But the available data suffice to show that, as in German, the [±tense] distinction comes in later than subject–verb agreement.

The findings for both languages thus support the hypothesis that agreement precedes tense in the children's developmental chronology. In the following section, I want to address the problem of how to define finiteness in view of these results, and what its role in early grammars might be.

6.   The Role of Finiteness in Developing Grammars

Grammatical theory predicts that with the acquisition of finiteness, children should also acquire certain other syntactic properties of the respective language, e.g. verb placement phenomena such as verb raising to INFL. The position of finite verbal elements thus represents strong evidence as to whether IP or an equivalent functional category subcategorizing VP has been implemented in the child's grammar. Since finiteness is defined in terms of agreement as well as of tense, the results of the two preceding sections raise the question whether agreement alone is sufficient or whether tense also needs to be part of the grammar in order to trigger such syntactic consequences. In other words, one might ask: Do verbs move as soon as agreement is acquired? In view of the findings reported on in above, the question, in fact, can be formulated more specifically, asking whether third person markings are already an indication of finiteness, or whether a richer system is required. In what follows, I will briefly look at data from both languages in order to determine when verb movement phenomena of this type begin to show up.

6.1. *German*

The first piece of evidence is of an indirect kind. Given the assumption of grammatical theory that only finite verbs can appear in a position other than the one they occupy at D-structure level, the logical connection between finiteness and verb placement is demonstrated by the fact that non-finite verbs appear consistently in final position. In other words, non-finite verbs *never* appear in second position in German. In spite of its indirect nature, this is an empirically strong and a theoretically important fact. Note, however, that there do exist violations of the required placement of finite verbs in second position in German; in other words, verbs carrying agreement markings are occasionally left in final position; see examples (10) and (11).

(10) a. *(x Ivar) buch buch liest* (Iv 2;04;07)
 Ivar book reads
 'Ivar reads [the] book'
 b. *(var) ein [s]iff macht* (Iv 2;05,21)
 Ivar a boat builds
 'Ivar builds a boat'
(11) *diese da drauf is* (C 2;10,00)
 this one there on top is
 'this one is there on top'

On the positive side, one will have to look for evidence for the V2-effect, that is, that the verb appears in second position, preceded by either the subject or by some other topicalized constituent. In Iv's language use, for example, V2-constructions begin to appear at age 2;4–2;5. This is an indication that a category subcategorizing VP, e.g. IP, can be assumed to have been implemented in the child's grammar at about this age. See the examples in (12) and (13).

(12) a. *wo is' teddy?* (Iv 2;04,09)
 'where is (the) teddy?'
 b. *kaputt is der* (Iv 2;04,09)
 'broken is it (this one)'

(13) a.   *ein grüner is das*   (C 2;04,22)
            a green one is this
            'this is a green one'
      b.   *da fährt die Caroline*   (C 2;03,11)
            'There goes [the] Caro'

Another crucial bit of evidence is the position of verbs in relation to the negative elements *pas* and *nicht*. Following Pollock (1989) and Weissenborn & Verrips (1989), one can use the position of verbs with respect to the negative element as an indicator of finiteness, since finite verbs, in French and in German, precede the negator, and infinitival verbal elements normally follow it. In German, finite verbs precede the negator *nicht* in main clauses. This is exactly the pattern one finds in Iv's speech as of age 2;4; see (14).

(14) a.   *de-de-des geht   nich*   (Iv 2;04,09)
            that   works not
            'that doesn't work'
      b.   *Ivar darf nich tee*   (Iv 2;04,23)
            Ivar may not   tea
            'Ivar may not drink tea'
      c.   *paßt nich auch*   (Iv 2;05,07)
            fits   not also
            'this doesn't fit either'

A small number of utterances, however, turn out to be problematic for they appear before the point at which finiteness is said to be part of the grammar, but they exhibit SVX (X = object or adverbial) order. According to the standard analysis of adult German, constructions of this type should be derived by means of verb movement, and although some of them are certainly rote-learned forms, especially the *da(s) ist (N)P* 'there/that is (N)P' type mentioned above, others are less easily accounted for. Iv, for example, uses several such constructions, one at age 2;00,29, and a few (7 with 4 different verbs) at age 2;03,05; see (15).

(15) a.   *der sucht das*   (Iv 2;03,05)
            'this one is looking for that'
      b.   *das [simt](=schwimmt) wasser*   (Iv 2;03,05)
            'that one swims on the water'

At least three reasons can be given against a movement analysis for these cases. First, only a very limited number of such cases exist; second, these are

SVX patterns, i.e. not XVS sequences with the verb preposed before the subject; third, one does not yet find constructions with the verb preceding the negative element. The second and the third point refer to the most reliable criteria indicating whether or not movement has taken place. Another observation points in the same direction: one also finds a few VO utterances, i.e. where the subject has been omitted, some with non-finite verb forms. Since not a single un-ambiguous case of movement of non-finite verbal forms is attested, neither in our data nor in the literature on child German, it is safe to conclude that verbs preceding objects or adverbials cannot have been moved into this position. Without assuming verb movement, and if one does not want to regard them as rote-learned patterns, these examples seem to indicate that the headedness parameter has not yet been set and VO and OV orders are still both possible. This is, in fact, exactly what Ouhalla (1991) predicts. Developing in some detail the research program suggested by Chomsky (1989) and others, he argues that parameterization is restricted to functional categories. Consequently, determining head-direction is impossible before the implementation of functional categories in the child's grammar; see the next section below. Assuming that functional categories are still lacking during the period of development under discussion, see structures (6) and (7) above, the order of elements within non-functional phrases like VP is not fixed by syntactic principles.[12]

Let me add that the emergence of modals in the children's speech may also serve as evidence indicating the existence of a category dominating VP, since modals inevitably have to be placed in this position, with the infinitival form of the main verb remaining in VP. In Ivar's data modals appear at the age of 2;5.[13] The use of mod+V constructions in the data of the other children is attested at age C 2;5-6 and P 3;0, respectively; see Table 6, above.

It thus appears that in developing grammars of German, effects of finiteness emerge at more or less the same age[14] (C 2;3-4, Iv 2;4-5, P 2;11–3;0) namely the time at which children begin to use agreement markings other than those of the 3rd person. They appear, in fact, slightly earlier for C and Iv; see Table 3, above. This confirms that the estimations given above have been quite conservative. I therefore want to claim, answering the question raised at the beginning of this section, that agreement alone is sufficient as an instantiation of finiteness, tense clearly coming in later than the phenomena discussed here. Yet agreement only produces these effects once it involves more than one grammatical person. It is at this point of development, I want to conclude further, that a category subcategorizing VP, e.g. IP, must be present in the children's grammars.

(16)   Emergence of finiteness effects in German

C 2;3–2;4   Iv 2;4–2;5   P 2;11–3;0

6.2. French

Similar conclusions can be drawn about the development of French grammar. Remember that in the case of Ivar, the data do not allow one to decide unambiguously whether during the period from 2;2 to 2;4 he is already using verb inflection for agreement. Note, however, that subject clitics begin to be used productively at this point, starting at age 2;4, and more frequently at age 2;5; only the forms of the 3rd person have already emerged at age 2;3. At age 2;5, agreement is also clearly marked on verbs.

It is precisely during this period that negative *pas* is also used, with finite verbs preceding it and non-finite verbs following: *das boit pas* 'that (one) doesn't drink', *pas facile* 'not easy', *a pas trouvé* 'hasn't found'; see also Dieck (1989). As has been pointed out above, one can argue, following Pollock (1989) and Weissenborn & Verrips (1989), that constructions of this type represent evidence that verbs are raised to INFL.

(17)   a.   *Maman veut pas*   (Iv 2;04,23)
            Mummy wants not
            'Mummy doesn't want to'

       b.   *c'est pas euh chaud*   (Iv 2;04,23)
            'it is not hot'

       c.   *a pas trouvé*   (Iv 2;05,07)
            has not found
            '(he) has not found (it)'

Equally important is the observation that auxiliary *avoir* 'have' and modals also make their appearance at age 2;5. And at the same point of development, one finds the first dislocations to the left.

In sum, then, there is abundant evidence that at around the same age when children show evidence of grammatical agreement in their language use, they also have access to the notion of "finiteness". In the case of C and of Iv, this happens around age 2;4–2;5. They are (i) combining subjects with finite verbs, with only very few omissions of the subject, (ii) using subject clitics, (iii) using negative *pas*, placing finite verbs correctly in pre-negative position, (iv) combining the auxiliary *avoir* with past participles and modals with infinitives. It may also be worthwhile to note that during the period before agreement develops, MLU values oscillate between 1.6 and 1.8, whereas they jump to 2.93 at age 2;5, and they stay well over 3.0 from then on. And this is also the case with the other children; i.e. soon after the acquisition of agreement, a dramatic increase of MLU values, rapidly exceeding 3.0, can be observed.

6.3. *Defining Finiteness in Terms of Person Agreement*

The analysis of child language data thus reveals that, in German as well as in French, syntactic phenomena normally attributed to finiteness are present in early grammars as soon as person agreement has been developed. To be more precise, these acquisitional achievements seem to require the ability to distinguish formally between grammatical persons, whereas a differentiation between singular and plural, as far as subject–verb agreement is concerned, is not a necessary prerequisite. This amounts to saying that [+AGR] is the crucial property defining finiteness.

It is appropriate, I believe, to comment on this in a little more detail, for in recent debates on related issues, e.g. the role of verbal inflection for the licensing of null subjects, or the split-INFL hypothesis, a number of alternative and also conflicting suggestions have been put forward. Some authors indeed view AGR as the essential defining property of finiteness, whereas others attribute a similar importance to TENSE. Although this is obviously not the place to try to disentangle the confusion, I want to argue that the contradiction is, to a large extent, due to differences in terminology rather than reflecting truly opposing views. What seems to be uncontroversial is that finite verbs, at least in languages like French, German, and also English, contain the features [+AGR,+T]; see von Stechow & Sternefeld (1988:389). In addition to the fact that finite verbs are usually agreeing elements as well as tensed ones, the morphological encodings of these two syntactic properties are frequently conflated. Thus, German *-t* and English *-s* express 3rd person singular as well as present tense. For these languages, tense is the more salient syntactic property: in tensed clauses of non-pro drop languages empty subjects are not allowed, in non-tensed clauses they are PRO; tensed clauses are not accessible to grammatical operations in the same way as non-tensed clauses are,[15] etc. Summarizing current generative treatments of this problem, von Stechow & Sternefeld (1988:115) suggest a generalization which postulates that INFL must contain AGR if it contains [+T], but not vice versa. This, I suspect, is the reason why finiteness is sometimes identified with TENSE; Chomsky (1989), for example, equates INFL = Tense = [+finite].

Yet although syntactic properties usually attributed to finite verbs, or, to be precise, to INFL (in a pre-Pollock analysis), normally require that both TENSE and AGR be present, this is not necessarily the case. Nor is it generally true that the defining properties of finiteness depend on the presence of TENSE. Even among Indo-European languages, one finds evidence against such assumptions. In Celtic languages, for example, TENSE without AGR seems to serve similar purposes as [+AGR,+T] in most other Indo-European languages. According to Stenson (1989), INFL in Irish contains T, but not AGR; and Stump (1989) argues that [+T,−AGR] is a governing category. In Portuguese, on the other hand, the opposite is true: infinitives can even be marked overtly for subject-agreement, and only these "personal infinitives" license nominative subjects, as opposed to bare infinitives (see Raposo 1987).

I thus conclude that "finiteness" may be defined in terms of agreement and/or TENSE. In other words, although it may be characterized as mentioned above, i.e. as [+AGR,+T], its featural composition is a parameterized option of UG. In other words, UG allows for the possibility that one of the two features suffices to characterize verbs as "±finite".[16] As a consequence, the finiteness operator, [+F], see Platzack & Holmberg (1989), attracts an element specified as either [+Agr,+T],[+Agr], or [+T], depending on how the parameter is set in a given language. This, in turn, means that developing grammars may operate in the same fashion, i.e. the child may work on the assumption that verbs containing only one of these features behave syntactically like finite elements.

I would like to add a few remarks on two language acquisition studies which arrive at apparently contradicting conclusions. The first is one by Aldridge (1986). She found that modals in early English only occur in finite clauses whereas to occurs exclusively in non-finite clauses. She (1986:50) concludes that "I(NFL) contains the feature [±FINITE], with a finite I being filled by a modal, and a non-finite I being filled by infinitival to." She further claims that, at the same time, tense and agreement markings are still lacking. As far as agreement is concerned, this conclusion seems to be unwarranted. The motivation for her claim is that 3rd sg -s is systematically lacking at this age, indicating that the children have not yet acquired agreement. Yet it seems that this result only reflects particularities of English where overt agreement markings are limited to this one form. The analysis of German child language, where the target system exhibits a richer morphological repertoire, shows that agreement is indeed crucial for the definition of finiteness in developing grammars. As far as tense is concerned, however, the present study corroborates the claims put forth by Aldridge (1986).

Verrips & Weissenborn (1990), on the other hand, regard "finite AGR as an innate category." Studying German and French monolingual children, they argue that "the category 'finite' is present in the child's grammatical system from the beginnings." Note, however, that, following general practice, they do not distinguish between [+finite] and [+Tense], nor between finiteness and agreement. In other words, their definitions of the terms lead them to the conclusion that the systematic use of agreement markings is evidence for finiteness. More precisely, agreement morphology together with the word order phenomena mentioned above are interpreted as indicating the presence of finiteness in grammars. I therefore believe that the differences between their conclusions and the hypotheses presented here are largely the consequence of differences in terminology. Both studies concur that agreement is part of developing grammars from very early on.

7.   The Architecture of Early Grammars

In the remainder of this paper, I want to discuss the consequences of the findings of this study for the development of grammar as well as for syntactic theory. In so doing, I will assume that developmental chronology reflects the hierarchical positions of functional categories in sentence structures, i.e. the order of acquisition reveals crucial information about the architecture of X-bar grammar. This is obviously not necessarily true, but it can be plausibly argued to be the null hypothesis. For if one does not share this assumption, one needs to explain the acquisition of these hierarchies independently.

The question now is what the child's grammar may look like during the period under consideration in order for it to account for the facts outlined in the previous sections. Remember that I want to claim that, following a period of protolanguage use during which speech is not yet organized according to underlying grammatical principles, earliest sentence structures are basically VPs; see structures (6) and (7) above. Subjects, at this point, remain in their D-structure position in Spec-VP. What we are looking for now is evidence indicating that a functional category has been implemented in the grammar. One finding has been that early grammars are first capable of handling agreement relationships, earlier than TENSE, probably as early as ages C 1;11, Iv 2;1, and P 2;9. But a number of other syntactic properties do not show up until somewhat later, albeit still clearly before TENSE. Most importantly, verbs then move out of VP, but subjects still precede them in surface order; see Köppe (this volume, chap. 8). It is this kind of evidence which unambiguously argues in favor of the existence of the projection of a functional category above VP. Consequently, at least two questions need to be answered: 1) How can one account for the earliest indications of the presence of grammatical agreement? 2) What is the nature of the first functional category — AGR, INFL, F?

7.1. *VP-internal Agreement?*

The analysis presented in the section on the emergence of agreement, above, led to the conclusion that the three children studied initially used only 3rd sg markings for a few months, in both languages. These forms could nevertheless be identified as being grammatical in nature. Yet, as has been shown in the preceding section, subjects and verbs are not moved out of VP until some time after the emergence of these first agreement markings, i.e. only when 1st/2nd sg forms are also available. What I take to be an empirically important finding of this study is that the period during which only 3rd sg markings are found in both languages, corresponds, in all three children, to the period of VP-only structure. This seems to suggest that it is a restriction on the structural configuration, i.e. that it is a relation holding only within the VP, which results in a limited set of markings (3rd sg). If this is correct, it obviously requires a theoretical explanation, for it is hardly plausible that such a clear developmental pattern in both languages of the three children could be an accidental result of contingent factors.

Interestingly enough, although not based on developmental data, a similar observation has been made by Koopman & Sportiche (1991:221). They find that in Standard Arabic, where both VSO and SVO orders are possible, the verb exhibits only 3rd sg agreement in VSO patterns, whereas in SVO patterns it agrees fully with the subject. The explanation they offer suggests that surface VSO patterns are derived from an underlying INFL-S-V-O order by verb movement to INFL; "If nothing further takes place, INFL has a silent expletive specifier ... (or no specifier position at all) and agreement gets the default value, namely 3rd person singular." SVO order thus requires that the subject be moved to Spec-IP. They further state that "[a]greement is the morphological reflex of a relation between INFL and its specifier, or more generally, between a head and its specifier. This property of INFL is realized on the verb because the verb moves into INFL."

With respect to the child data, arguing along the same lines, one finds that although the specifier is present (subject-NP within VP), what is still lacking is "agreement as a property of INFL". As a consequence, the relation between the verb and its specifier gets marked by the default value, 3rd sg. This corresponds to the analysis of Scandinavian languages proposed by Platzack & Holmberg (1989:70). They distinguish between languages with and without AGR. According to their approach, some languages, for example the Norwegian dialect of Hallingdalen, have neither AGR nor V-movement, yet the verb carries overt inflection, restricted, however, to number agreement. They argue that this is a result of Spec–head agreement in VP.

One can thus hypothesize that a similar situation is evidenced in developing grammars. The first grammatical notion which surfaces in early grammars as morphological encoding on the verb is the specifier-head relation within the VP, marked by the default value. That 3rd sg forms do indeed represent the default value is generally accepted, e.g. Platzack & Holmberg (1989:58). Grammars usually resort to it if no thematic nominal element is available in the specifier position, e.g. with expletive or with empty (pro) subjects, but also with impersonals; or if the element in this position is not a nominative thematic NP, e.g. German *ihrer wurde gedacht* 'of them+GEN was+3rd sg thought = they were remembered', rather than *ihrer wurden gedacht* 'of them+GEN were+3rd pl thought'.

These observations raise the question whether default markings may indeed be regarded as instances of agreement. In order to be able to address this problem, it is helpful to clarify the meaning of this concept. Syntactically, agreement can be understood as a process or as the result of a process by which two elements come to share a number of syntactic features. Feature sharing is possible if the two elements stand in a specifier–head relation or if they are coindexable.[17] Subject–verb agreement indeed requires both conditions to be met, since the element in subject position and the verb need to be coindexable by superscripting. In early child grammars, the structural configuration is already present, namely as a specifier-head relation within VP. The fact, however, that only default markings are used is a strong indication that feature sharing is not yet possible. This would also explain why some children, e.g. Iv and P, occasionally use "stem forms", i.e. forms lacking any kind of inflection; see below. What is not yet available, I suspect, is the mechanism which executes co-superscription. Exactly how superscripting works, however, is not clear,[18] except for the fact that it happens at D-structure level (Chomsky 1981:259). Without a more elaborate theory of agreement it is difficult to gain a deeper understanding of the developments observed here. But it is reasonable to assume, I believe, that the relation between two elements which is marked by superscripted indices, whatever its true nature may be, is the essential prerequisite for feature sharing processes like subject–verb agreement and nominative Case assignment to be possible.[19] It is also a plausible assumption that one of the two elements possesses the capacity of triggering the process which results in feature sharing. In the case of subject–verb agreement, this seems to be verb+agr, in spite of the fact that it is the subject which passes its features on to the verb, and not vice versa. The triggering capacity may be indicated by [+agr]. By phrasing it in this fashion, I am avoiding, for the moment, having to decide on the exact nature of [+agr] — a property of INFL, or the head of an independent category.

This view of the problem suggests that the answer to my question has to be that "VP-internal agreement" represents an elementary version of a grammatical agreement system. In developmental terms, one can say that a first and crucial step has been taken, for the specific syntactic relation between the two elements is recognized and marked. What is lacking is that the two elements in question do not yet share features. Instead, the verb form is selected by default. This situation very much resembles the one described by Platzack & Holmberg (1989), i.e. [+agr] is not present and no verb movement occurs. This amounts to saying that using the default value means that this form is inserted as a whole into syntactic structure from the morphological component, much like suppletive forms in the adult grammar. A similar treatment of the problem has been suggested, by the way, by Clahsen (1986, 1988) for some forms of main verbs and for modals.[20]

I would like to remark, in passing, that the account of early cases of 3rd sg markings suggested here might help to bridge the gap between conflicting hypotheses put forth in the controversial debate on this issue. Clahsen (1986), for example, claims that these inflectional forms do not encode syntactic notions at all; rather, he speculates, they serve to encode a semantic–pragmatic function, i.e. low transitivity. In Meisel (1990), on the other hand, I argued that they are true agreement markers. If the hypothesis developed here can be maintained, it might indicate a way out of the controversy, for it states, on the one hand, that early inflectional markings are indeed syntactic in nature, but on the other hand, it admits that they do not mark agreement in so far as they are not the result of a feature sharing process.

A last point I want to bring up concerning early 3rd sg markings relates to what might be perceived as a contradiction in the claims I have been defending. If these forms are indeed instantiations of a morphological default value rather than resulting from a feature sharing process, how can it be that there are no agreement errors in early speech? Put differently, why do we not find 1st and 2nd sg subject pronouns in combination with verbs marked for 3rd sg?[21] The following observations may help to shed some light on this problem. First of all, third person markings are more frequent in the input than those for 1st and 2nd person since all non-pronominal subjects — in addition to 3rd sg pronouns — require this type of agreement. Secondly, it is conceivable that during a period when only a few subject–verb constructions are used, less frequent items may be missed during one-hour recordings. Remember that the second person pronoun is used rather infrequently; as has been mentioned before, the plural form is never attested during the period under investigation, and the singular form is quite rare in the children's speech in both languages. As for the 1st sg pronoun, some children initially refer to themselves by using their proper names, and this further reduces the number of occurrences of 1st sg pronouns during an early phase. Thirdly, the possibility cannot be excluded that the preference for 3rd person subjects is, to a certain degree, enhanced by general constraints on what children of that age are able and willing to communicate about and also by the specific play situations created during the recordings. Two-year olds tend to accompany verbally the actions performed during the game, telling what someone is doing or should be doing; third person is most likely to appear here. They also tell their interlocutors what to do, using imperatives or infinitives. And they state their own intentions, wishes and needs; in these instances, however, modals show up in the vast majority of cases: *ich will.../je veux...* 'I want...'; see Table 2 above, which reveals that these uses emerge more or less simultaneously with 3rd sg on main verbs. In sum, then, for reasons like the ones alluded to here, 1st and 2nd person pronouns are less likely to occur, and low frequency items may not be caught during the recording sessions.

But this cannot be the whole truth. One finds, for example, that infinitives or imperatives are used in contexts where one would expect pronouns other than 3rd sg to appear, e.g. C at age 2;0 *Alfred gucken* 'Alfred look at/watch+inf', probably meaning that C is watching or wants to watch what Alfred, the cat, is doing. Note that C already uses the imperative of the same verb, *guck*, as of age 1;9. Furthermore, it is probably not an accident that it is precisely the 1st sg pronoun which is omitted most frequently at a time when the number of null subjects of other types has decreased dramatically; see Meisel (1990). A last observations concerns the so-called "stem forms". Iv, during a period ranging from age 1;11–2;3, normally omits the subject in utterances where these forms surface. The four verbs (types, not tokens) used in this way are *mach* 'make', *nimm* 'take', *giess* 'pour', and *schwimm* 'swim'. An example from C's speech is *nein, Oma setz* (=OV) 'no, granny seat (=put)', at age 2;2, after the adult interlocutor had suggested putting the mouse into the car. What these uses indicate, it appears to me, is that the lack of 1st and 2nd person subjects, together with finite verb forms, cannot be explained by means of the above mentioned external factors alone. There clearly exist contexts where they could have been employed, but in these cases, the subject is frequently omitted and/or the verb appears as a non-finite form, i.e. as an imperative, infinitive, or not inflected at all.

In sum then, there are reasons to believe that the default option is used because other ones are not available yet. The empirical evidence, however, is not conclusive. It would be more convincing if one found 1st and 2nd person subjects in constructions with verbs marked for the 3rd sg. Such cases are not attested in our data, but following my hypothesis, I expect them to be possible.[22]

7.2. *The Emergence of Functional Categories*

Let me now turn to the second of the questions raised above: What is the nature of the first functional category implemented in child grammars? The answer will, once more, be a tentative one, and this is again due to the insufficiency of the knowledge available about corresponding features of mature grammars. In the preceding section, I argued that with the appearance of phenomena related to finiteness, there is abundant evidence that a functional category above VP must now exist in the children's grammars, i.e. soon after the emergence of agreement, structural positions must be available to which heads (e.g. verbs), topicalized maximal projections, etc. can be moved. But this only constitutes evidence in favor of the claim that some kind of (functional) X^{max} must be part of the child's grammar; it does not tell us which one it is. Following the definition of finiteness in terms of [+AGR] and/ or [+T], and given that agreement appears first, the most likely candidate for the category in question appears to be AGRP. Yet there exist serious doubts whether it is at all possible to justify the existence of a category AGR with its own prosection AGRP. This is, quite obviously, a problem which cannot be solved, *en passant*, in a study on early grammars. I will therefore limit the following remarks to a brief review of those aspects for which developmental facts could possibly provide evidence helping to decide in favor or against the existence of AGRP.

Remember that the standard assumption, before Pollock (1989) suggested the split-INFL hypothesis, had been that INFL consists of AUX and (optionally)

AGR; see, for example Chomsky (1986). According to this hypothesis, AUX contains minimally Tense, possibly also Aspect and Modality; AGR had been assumed to contain the so-called phi-features. The appeal of the split-INFL hypothesis, as far as I can see, is mainly due to two of its properties: it creates an additional landing site for verb movement and it "eliminates the odd dual-headedness of INFL in earlier treatments" (Chomsky 1989).

The former, however, does not adequately motivate the need for a separate X^{max}. This has been demonstrated quite convincingly by Iatridou (1990), even though she does not offer satisfactory alternative solutions herself for the problems in question, i.e. the position of adverbials. And again: even if one wanted to retain a landing site for "short movement", it is by no means clear that this would have to be AGRP. Note that AGR is claimed to contain infinitives with "generally vacuous" agreement and that it is deletable at LF since it does not play any role there; see Chomsky (1989). This contrasts sharply with the properties of the elements formerly contained in INFL's twin head AUX: Tense is needed at LF, and although Aspect and Modality have not, in the recent literature, received the attention they deserve, there can be no doubt that this is true for them, as well. What I want to say is that the "movement" argument at best demonstrates the need for more than one verbal functional category above VP. But AGR need not be one of them. In fact, Tense, Modality, Aspect, and of course COMP, are more likely candidates.

As for the dual-headedness of INFL, one may wonder whether AGR ever had to be interpreted as a head, in the first place. Remember that INFL, the head of IP, used to be rewritten as "(AGR) AUX". The oddity of this treatment of INFL consists in the non-justified assumption that a syntactic head should dominate other syntactic categories, i.e. elements other than those which are part of its morphological structure. Yet if the picture outlined above is correct, the so-called phi-features are assigned to INFL, rather than being contained in an element base-generated in INFL. At any rate, I do not see any justification for the claim that the presence of the "phi-features" or of their morphological spell-outs should justify the existence of an additional X^{max}. What seems to be uncontroversial is that an element is needed which assigns nominative Case and which triggers subject verb agreement, i.e. [+agr], see above. The problem of its precise nature cannot be pursued any further in the context of the present paper. Suffice it to say that it could be part of the featural composition of INFL, and its phonological realization will have to be affixed or cliticized to a verbal head moved into INFL.

Adopting a strategy suggested by Occam's razor, one should try to avoid a proliferation of functional categories, i.e. a possible candidate will be rejected unless empirical or theoretical evidence obliges us to do otherwise. As far as I can see, this has not yet been achieved in the case of AGR. I will therefore work on the assumption that neither mature nor developing grammars contain an AGRP. The same kind of decision will have to be taken with respect to a number of other grammaticizable notions which may surface in the grammars of individual languages as free morphemes, clitics or affixes, typically combined with verbal heads. At least three such notions, Tense, Modality, Aspect, may indeed have to be analyzed as heading their respective maximal projections. Yet for the time being, following the strategy just mentioned, a single functional category in between VP and CP will be assumed to exist.[23] In view of the fact that one of its crucial properties is that only finite elements can be positioned in its head, "FP" might be an adequate label for this X^{max}. But given that the finiteness operator is located either in this category or in COMP, depending on how the finiteness parameter is set in the respective language, and since "finiteness" is defined differently in various languages, this might be problematic. I therefore suggest we retain the traditional label "IP".

Returning to the analysis of the acquisition data, the question to be asked now is whether the empirical findings reported earlier in this paper are compatible with the ideas about the architecture of grammars just outlined. At least two observations are relevant here. The first one, concerning the developmental precedence of agreement markings, as compared to other grammatical encodings on the verb, has already been covered, for the most part, by the preceding discussions: The earliest instances of 3rd sg forms are explained as default markings on verbal elements in VP. Encodings for other grammatical persons appear simultaneously with verb movement. If one accepts the claims made above, this results from the verb being moved to the head of IP, and subject verb agreement can be accounted for by the properties of INFL containing [+agr]. "Finiteness" of the verb, at this point of grammatical development, means that it has been combined with [+agr]. I believe it is appropriate to say that agreement, in a technical sense of grammatical theory, has now been acquired, even though it may still take a few months before the whole repertoire of verbal forms is mastered by the child.

This claim is in conflict with approaches attempting to define successful acquisition of agreement in terms of completeness of the set of morphological forms available. Clahsen (1986, 1988), for example argues that, in German, the presence of 2nd sg -st indicates that the child is using grammatical agreement and is, from then on, able to move the verb out of VP. Although he does not make explicit why just this form should be the crucial one, completeness of the repertoire of forms is apparently meant to be the explanation since, according to Clahsen (1986, 1988), 2nd sg is the last agreement affix to be learned. Yet this is empirically not correct. Table 2 shows that both C and Iv use 2nd sg before 1st forms. This is why, throughout the present paper, I have argued that availability of forms for two of the three grammatical persons appears to be sufficient as a criterion for successful acquisition.

Verrips & Weissenborn (1990), studying French and German monolingual children, arrive at a similar conclusion. They demonstrate quite convincingly that verbs are moved out of VP before 2nd sg markings are acquired, contradicting explicitly the claims by Clahsen (1986). My interpretation of these developments differs from the position taken by Verrips & Weissenborn (1990), however, in so far as I explain the earliest forms as default markings on verbs still placed in VP, whereas they contend that IP is present right from the beginning. Note that Verrips & Weisssenborn (1990) find that two of the three French children who they studied already use "finite verbs" at a point of development when verbs do not yet move into the head of IP. They suggest that this indicates that the children are having problems with verb movement in French because it's effects are frequently invisible in surface word order. Although this is certainly a possibility, a conjecture of this kind would require additional supporting evidence. It may turn out to be rather difficult to distinguish empirically between a hypothesis claiming the non-existence of IP and one according to which IP is existent but cannot be used. The analysis suggested in this paper, i.e. that early "finite" verb forms are default markings during a phase when IP has not yet been implemented in the children's grammars, would have to be preferred for reasons of parsimony.

The second empirical observation which needs to be matched against the claims about the architecture of grammatical structures concerns verb placement. Note that our claim that the finite verb is moved to INFL yields adult-like structures for French but not for German, as a look at structures (1) and (2) at the beginning of this chapter will easily reveal. German IP exhibits head-final order; consequently, a verb raised to INFL still appears in clause-final position, but this is normally not the case at this point of development in child speech. Note that postulating an AGRP does not solve the problem either, for it would have to be head-final. At first sight, these facts appear to indicate that not only IP but also CP have developed and that the verb is moved to C, as in adult grammar. Alternatively, one might entertain the idea that some other (head-initial) X^{max} has been added to the children's grammar. Yet it can be shown that the observed facts are easily accounted for, assuming that IP in child grammars is ordered head-initially. The finite verb is thus moved to the head position of INFL and remains there, rather than being raised to the head of CP. Both features of developing grammars are explained and justified in Müller (1993) and in Meisel & Müller (1992) and need therefore not be discussed here in more detail.

Consequently, I want to maintain that it is sufficient for early grammars to make two positions available for verbs in German as well as in French; they may remain in VP where they can appear in the 3rd sg (default) form, an option not tolerated by the mature grammar, or they are moved to the head of IP. Interestingly enough, there is some empirical evidence suggesting that these options may indeed exist simultaneously in early grammars. One finds constructions in which the same verb appears twice, in exactly these two positions.

(18) a. *und macht boum macht*   (Iv 2;06,06)
          and goes   bang   goes
          'it goes bang'
     b. *macht [s]eiße der macht*   (Iv 2;09,18)
          makes shit   he makes
          'he makes a mess'

What seems to be happening in such cases is that the children copy the verb where adult grammar requires a trace to be left after movement. Copying of this kind is, in fact, predicted by Roeper (1990).

7.3. *Implementing IP in Early Grammars*

To sum up, then, I have argued that the earliest grammatical structures lack functional categories and resemble, therefore, adult VPs; see (6) and (7), above. With the emergence of subject verb agreement, verb and NP movement out of VP, etc., there can be no doubt that a functional category has been implemented in the children's grammars.

This has been shown to happen at the following ages: C 2;3–2;4, Iv 2;4–2;5, P 2;11–3;0 in German, and C 2;4–2;5, Iv 2;4–2;5, P 2;11–3;0 in French. MLU values, at about this age, increase significantly and stay above 3.0, from then on. Grammatical structures, at this point of development are claimed to be those in (19) and (20), for French and German, respectively.

(19)

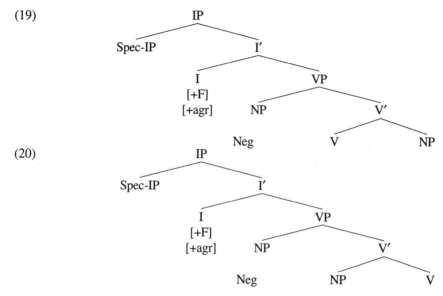

(20)

Note that I do not commit myself to a specific structural position for the negating element. It could be adjoined to VP, but this is not crucial for the present discussion. Subject NPs are raised from Spec-VP to Spec-IP position. This is where they are assigned NOM Case by [+agr] in Infl. Verbs are raised to the head position of IP where they form a unit with [+agr]; the latter will be realized as an affix in German and as a subject clitic in French.

Comparing these structures with those generated by mature grammars, see (1) and (2), one finds that some major differences still prevail. One is that developing grammars at this point still lack a CP. From this it follows that in German, SVO sequences are not yet true V2 structures since these require the placement of finite verbs in the head position of CP, attracted by [+F] which, in adult German, is also placed in C. In addition, IP should be head-final in German. A number of observations suggest that the children's grammars indeed do not yet possess a complementizer system at a point of development where IP is clearly established; see Müller (1993) and Meisel and Müller (1992). In other words, German child grammars still differ in significant ways from their mature counterparts, even though this variation falls within the range of what UG principles and parameters tolerate. The structure of French sentences, on the other hand, is basically the one required by the adult grammar, except for the missing CP. The question what will happen in the course of further developments in German, is studied in detail by Müller (1991, 1993).

8. Conclusion

In conclusion, I believe I have shown that after a kind of "pre-syntactic" beginning during which the children's language is more like "protolanguage" (Bickerton 1990b), child utterances are structured according to grammatical principles following UG. Functional categories, however, emerge consecutively, since the learner has to discover which categories of this type need to be implemented in the grammar of the language being acquired. Early sentences are therefore verb phrases. Agreement is discovered very early, although precocious markings within VP are probably not the result of a grammatical feature sharing process. AGR is however not, I contend, an autonomous syntactic category but a feature of INFL. Finiteness may temporarily be defined in terms of agreement alone, since Tense comes in significantly later. The development of the grammatical notion of "finiteness" triggers the implementation of a category subcategorizing VP, i.e. IP. CP is implemented after some further delay. As a consequence, German as opposed to French sentence structure, must be reanalyzed, once C and its projections have been acquired.

Acknowledgements

This is a revised version of a paper presented at the "Parasession on the Acquisition of Functional Categories", Autumn Meeting of the Linguistics Association of Great Britain, York, September 16–18, 1991. Parts of earlier versions have been presented in talks given during the Winter-Spring period of 1990–1991 at CUNY (Graduate Center), McGill University, the University of Massachusetts, Amherst, and at the University of Hawai'i at Manoa. I am grateful to those who, at these occasions, offered criticisms and comments. I particularly want to thank Susanne E. Carroll, Lynn Eubank, Peter Jordens, Teresa Parodi, Tom Roeper, Maaike Verrips, Jürgen Weissenborn, and the members of the research team DUFDE who all commented on earlier versions of the paper or discussed with me some of the ideas contained in this work. This research has been funded by the Deutsche Forschungsgemeinschaft (DFG) through a grant (1986–1992) to Jürgen M. Meisel. Most of the work on this paper has been carried out during an special sabbatical semester granted by the University of Hamburg. I gratefully acknowledge this support as well as the financial support by the DFG.

Notes

1. The term "predicate" refers to elements which, in adult grammar, are categorized as verbs, adjectives, and verbal particles (e.g. German *ab* 'off, away, gone').

2. The capital -E is used in order to avoid having to decide between infinitive *-er* and past participle *-é*.

3. However, as has been pointed out to me by Susanne Carroll, this might actually be explicable in terms of the phonology of focus, in other words as a grammatical rather than a pragmatic phenomenon.

4. "With the introduction of forced and non-forced Agreement, we have to distinguish between the notions "Agree with a position" and "Agree with a category". ... If the language is a forced Agreement language, the position must be occupied by an appropriately marked ("Agreed with") maximal category, but if the language is not a forced Agreement language, the position may be left vacant or may be occupied by a maximal category devoid of the expected Agreement (Case-marking). This is the meaning of forced Agreement" (Kuroda 1988:11).

5. Note that P is very slow in his linguistic development, following behind by approximately six months the average of the children studied by our research group. He eventually catches up with the others, however, between age 3;0 and 4;0. The slowness of his earlier developments explains perhaps why, in his case, the emergence of some of the forms attributed to the second phase overlap with the appearance of forms of the first phase.

6. A form is regarded as being used productively when it appears with more than one verb (type) and in several subsequent recordings.

7. 2nd pl verb forms are non-existent or extremely rare in other corpora, as well. I suspect that this is due to the fact that the child, during the recording sessions, usually interacts with only one person.

8. I assume that one of the two variants for 1st sg marking may be regarded as sufficient to say that 1st sg marking has been acquired.

9. It will be slightly modified below.

10. The 2nd pl *-ez* = [e] may be ignored, here, since it does not exist in the data.

11. Schlyter (1990) reached similar conclusions studying three other bilingual children, including Iv.

12. Note that even if this explanation failed, the worst case scenario, as far as the time of emergence of finiteness is concerned, would be that finiteness is available earlier than suggested, i.e. at age 2;3 for Iv.

13. Auxiliary+past participle constructions, however, do not appear until much later in Ivar's speech, i.e. not until age 3;2. I have no explanation for this late acquisition.

14. In the case of C and Iv, this seems in fact to happen slightly earlier. Remember, however, that I opted for a "conservative" estimate when discussing agreement; there existed indeed some scattered evidence earlier than at the times mentioned above.

15. Cf. attempts to formulate generalizations of this type as the "tensed S condition".

16. Note that according to this hypothesis, finiteness is a derivative notion, i.e. there is no need for a feature [±finite], since it is defined in terms of [+T] and/or [+AGR],

17. At this point, I am only concerned with subject–verb agreement. Other relations seem to allow for agreement within DPs or between objects and verbs.

18. von Stechow & Sternefeld (1988:300) state that it happens "per conventionem".

19. The fact that both depend on the same condition is captured by the well-known observation that nominative Case assignment is subject to the agreement requirement.

20. As for the latter, however, Clahsen claims that they are inserted directly into the head of INFL and are not subject to movement. I will not go into this, at this point.

21. Note that the same kind of problem arises for every hypothesis trying to explain the chronological precedence of such forms. Clahsen's (1986) account, for example, predicts 1st/2nd sg subjects could occur productively together with 3rd sg verb forms in constructions of "low transitivity".

22. This hypothesis is empirically equivalent to what one would predict to happen if one were to follow Clahsen (1986).

23. Remember that this discussion only refers to categories which have been suggested to replace IP. No claims are made about other functional categories proposed recently, e.g. DP, NumP.

References

Aldridge, Michelle. 1986. "A First Stage in the Acquisition of INFL." *Research Papers in Linguistics* 1.39–58.

Bickerton, Derek. 1990a. *Language and Species*. Chicago: The University of Chicago Press.

———. 1990b. "Syntactic Development: The brain just does it." Manuscript, University of Hawai'i at Manoa.

Carroll, Susanne E. 1989. "Language Acquisition Studies and a Feasible Theory of Grammar." *Canadian Journal of Linguistics* 34.399–418.

Chomsky, Noam. 1981. *Lectures on Government and Binding: The Pisa lectures* (=*Studies in Grammar,* 9.). Dordrecht: Foris (1984³).

———. 1986. *Barriers* (=*Linguistic Inquiry Monographs,* 13.). Cambridge, Mass.: MIT Press.

————. 1989. "Some Notes on Economy of Derivation and Representation." *MIT Working Papers in Linguistics* 10.43–74.

Clahsen, Harald. 1982. *Spracherwerb in der Kindheit: Eine Untersuchung zur Entwicklung der Syntax bei Kleinkindern (=Language Development,* 4.). Tübingen: Narr.

————. 1986. "Verb Inflections in German Child Language: Acquisition of agreement markings and the functions they encode." *Linguistics* 24.79–121.

————. 1988. *Normale und gestörte Kindersprache: Linguistische Untersuchungen zum Erwerb von Syntax und Morphologie.* Amsterdam: John Benjamins.

Dieck, Marianne. 1989. "Zum Erwerb der Negation bei bilingualen Kindern (Französisch–Deutsch): Eine Fallstudie." Masters thesis, University of Hamburg.

Guilfoyle, Eithne & Máire Noonan. 1988. "Functional Categories and Language Acquisition." Paper given at the Boston University Conference on Language Development.

Iatridou, Sabine. 1990. "About Agr(P)." *Linguistic Inquiry* 21.551–577.

Jordens, Peter. 1990. "The Acquisition of Verb Placement in Dutch and German." *Linguistics* 28.1407–1448.

Kaiser, Georg A. & Jürgen M. Meisel. 1991. "Subjekte und Null-Subjekte im Französischen." *'DET, COMP und INFL': Zur Syntax funktionaler Kategorien und grammatischer Funktionen (=Linguistische Arbeiten,* 263.), ed. by Gisbert Fanselow & Susan Olsen, 110–136. Tübingen: Niemeyer.

Koopman, Hilda & Dominique Sportiche. 1991. "The Position of Subjects." *Lingua* 85.211–258.

Kuroda, Sige-Yuki. 1988. "Whether We Agree or Not: A comparative syntax of English and Japanese." *Lingvisticae Investigationes* 12.1–47.

Meisel, Jürgen M. 1985. "Les phases initiales du développement de notions temporelles, aspectuelles et de modes d'action." *Lingua* 66.321–374.

————, ed. 1990. *Two First Languages: Early grammatical development in bilingual children (=Studies in Language Acquisition,* 10.). Dordrecht: Foris.

————. 1990. "INFL-ection: Subjects and subject–verb agreement." *Two First Languages: Early grammatical development in bilingual children (=Studies in Language Acquisition,* 10.), ed. by Jürgen M. Meisel, 237–298. Dordrecht: Foris.

————. 1991." Structure and Development of Functional Categories." Manuscript, University of Hamburg.

Meisel, Jürgen M. & Natascha Müller. 1992. "Verb Placement and the Position of Finiteness in Early Child Grammar." *The Acquisition of Verb Placement: Functional categories and V2 phenomena in language development (=Studies in Theoretical Psycholinguistics,* 16.), ed. by Jürgen M. Meisel, 109–138. Dordrecht: Kluwer.

Müller, Natascha. 1991. "Erwerb der Wortstellung im Französischen und Deutschen: Zur Distribution von Finitheitsmerkmalen in der Grammatik bilingualer Kinder." *Spracherwerb und Grammatik: Linguistische Untersuchungen zum Erwerb von Syntax und Morphologie* (= *Linguistische Berichte Sonderheft*, 3.), ed. by Monika Rothweiler, 127–151. Opladen: Westdeutscher Verlag.

————. 1993. *Komplexe Sätze: Der Erwerb von COMP und von Wortstellungsmustern bei bilingualen Kindern (Französisch–Deutsch)* (=*Language Development*, 16.). Tübingen: Narr.

Ouhalla, Jamal. 1991. *Functional Categories and Parametric Variation* (=*Theoretical Linguistics Series*.). London: Routledge.

Pinker, Steven. 1984. *Language Learnability and Language Development* (=*Cognitive Science Series*, 7.). Cambridge, Mass.: Harvard University Press.

Platzack, Christer & Anders Holmberg. 1989. "The Role of AGR and Finiteness in Germanic VO Languages." *Scandinavian Working Papers in Linguistics* 43.51–76.

Pollock, Jean-Yves. 1989. "Verb Movement, Universal Grammar, and the Structure of IP." *Linguistic Inquiry* 20.365–424.

Radford, Andrew. 1986. "Small Children's Small Clauses." *Bangor Research Papers in Linguistics* 1.1–38.

————. 1987. "The Acquisition of the Complementiser System", *Bangor Research Papers in Linguistics* 2.55–76.

————. 1990. *Syntactic Theory and the Acquisition of Syntax*. Oxford: Basil Blackwell.

Raposo, Eduardo. 1987. "Case Theory and Infl-to-Comp: The inflected infinitive in European Portuguese." *Linguistic Inquiry* 18.85–109.

Rizzi, Luigi & Ian Roberts. 1989. "Complex Inversion in French." *Probus* 1.1–30.

Roberge, Yves & Marie-Thérèse Vinet. 1989. *La variation dialectale en grammaire universelle*. Montréal: Les Presses de l'Université de Montréal.

Roeper, Thomas. 1990. "How the Least Effort Concept Applies to the Acquisition of Head Movement, Copying, and Cyclic WH-Movement." Manuscript, University of Massachusetts, Amherst.

Schlyter, Suzanne. 1990. "The Acquisition of Tense and Aspect." *Two First Languages: Early grammatical development in bilingual children*, ed. by Jürgen M. Meisel, 87–121. Dordrecht: Foris.

von Stechow, Armin & Wolfgang Sternefeld. 1988. *Bausteine syntaktischen Wissens*. Opladen: Westdeutscher Verlag.

Stenson, Nancy. 1989. "Irish Autonomous Impersonals." *Natural Language and Linguistic Theory* 7.379–406.

Stump. Gregory T. 1989. "Further Remarks on Breton Agreement." *Natural Language and Linguistic Theory* 7.429–471.

Verrips, Maaike & Jürgen Weissenborn. 1990. "Finite AGR as an Innate Category." Manuscript, Max Planck Institut für Psycholinguistik, Nijmegen.

Weissenborn, Jürgen & Maaike Verrips. 1989. "Negation as a Window to the Structure of Early Child Language." Manuscript, Max Planck Institut für Psycholinguistik, Nijmegen.

More about INFL-ection and Agreement
The Acquisition of Clitic Pronouns in French

Georg A. Kaiser
University of Hamburg

1. Introduction

The emergence and role of functional categories in child language has been the subject of a number of recent acquisition studies in several languages. While some researchers assume that functional categories are present in child language from the very beginning, others contend that they appear later in children's grammars, probably due to maturational factors.[1]

In the present study, I will deal with agreement phenomena in French child language and with the development of the functional category INFL. To be more precise, I will investigate the acquisition of French clitic pronouns. After considering their very special properties and behavior, I will argue that they are agreement markers. I will assume that subject clitics are generated under the INFL node. Consequently it is predicted that their acquisition should be intimately related to the emergence of INFL. Data from two bilingual boys, Pascal (Pa) and Ivar (Iv), will be analyzed to show that this prediction is correct. The emergence of subject clitics corresponds to what has been found by Meisel (1990) and others concerning the development of INFL. They emerge very early and suddenly in children's speech and precisely at the point when INFL is presumed to become available. In contrast to subject clitics, I will assume that object clitics are base-generated under the V^0-node making them appear to be part of the lexical category verb. Since lexical categories, in particular verbs, are assumed to be present in child grammar from early on, one might expect that object clitics should also appear early and that their acquisition should not depend on the emergence of a functional category. However, the acquisition data show that they occur much later than subject clitics. In addition, like subject clitics, they emerge suddenly and are mastered within a short period of time.

In what follows, I will give a short description of the properties of French clitic pronouns and provide an analysis within the framework of the *Theory of Principles and Parameters* (cf. Chomsky 1981, 1989). I will then demonstrate that the acquisition data are consistent with the proposed analysis of clitic pronouns.

2.   Some Preliminary Assumptions about Adult Grammar: The Status of Clitic Pronouns in French

It is well-known that clitic pronouns, like clitics in general, display very special characteristics. Among other things, they are characterized by the fact that they must always be attached to an independent word. Furthermore, they can not be stressed contrastively nor can they be topicalized. Being bound elements, they share many properties with affixes and may have properties which typically belong to affixes only.[2]

Of all the Romance languages, French has the richest inventory of clitic pronouns. In addition to object clitics, which are common to all Romance languages, it also possesses a full set of subject clitics.[3] Apart from relative and interrogative pronouns, clitic pronouns are the only elements in French exhibiting overt features for case-marking.[4] Whereas 1st and 2nd person clitics can be divided into nominative and non-nominative case forms, the 3rd person clitics display an additional morphological distinction between dative and accusative case. In many descriptions of French, however, these case distinctions are ignored and clitic pronouns are classified according to their general grammatical functions into *subject* and *object* clitics (Grevisse 1986:1007):[5]

Table 1. Clitic pronouns in French[6]

	Subject clitics	Object clitics
1st sg	*je*	*me*
2nd sg	*tu*	*te*
3rd sg	*il, elle*	*le, la, lui; se*
1st pl	*on, nous*	*nous*
2nd pl	*vous*	*vous*
3rd pl	*ils, elles*	*les, leur; se*

In Romance linguistics, the status and function of these clitics, especially of subject clitics, have been discussed at some length. It has been argued that French subject clitics cannot be analyzed in the same way as non-clitic subjects, but must be regarded as verbal affixes replacing the verbal inflectional suffixes which have almost completely disappeared in modern spoken French.[7] Recently, in several analyses of spoken Colloquial French, this claim has been corroborated empirically (e.g., Ashby 1977; Lambrecht 1981; Sankoff 1982; Kaiser 1992). It has been observed that the overwhelming majority of subject nouns or non-clitic subject pronouns are accompanied by a coreferential subject clitic. Such 'clitic doubling constructions' are exemplified in (1a) and (1b):

(1)   a.   *Jean il mange*
            John he eats
            'John is eating.'
       b.   *Lui il mange*
            him he eats
            'He is eating.'

Analyzing data from French Canadians, Sankoff (1982) found that in 55% of all finite sentences containing a subject NP, a subject clitic occurred as well. Data from two women from France, included in the same study, revealed a rate exceeding 80%. In my own empirical analyses of data from Colloquial French, I obtained similar results (Kaiser & Meisel 1991; Kaiser 1992).

Given this frequent use of subject clitics, it is unlikely that such constructions mark any special pragmatic function such as stress or emphasis. It seems, rather, that this emphatic function is expressed by 'double clitic doubling constructions' as in (2) (Auger 1990):

(2)   *Jean lui il mange*
            John him he eats
            'John, he is eating.'

In addition, according to all available empirical studies of Colloquial French it is an uncontroversial fact that sentences like those in (1) are generally pronounced *without* any recognizable pause (see Ashby 1977; Larsson 1979; Ronat 1979). In view of this, it is quite surprising that many researchers maintain the claim that these constructions should be regarded as "instances of Left Dislocations, with a pause between the initial NP and the following subject clitic" (Jaeggli 1982:95). It is more plausible to assume that subject clitics have been *grammaticalized* (Sankoff 1982). This is to say that, in Colloquial French, subject clitics have become obligatory overt grammatical markers of agreement between subject nouns or pronouns and verbs. Therefore, they do not function as full subjects, and, accordingly, are not base-generated in the SpecIP position nor are they moved into this position from within the VP. Following an analysis by Rizzi (1986b) for Trentino, they can presumably be analyzed as a "spell-out of AGR under INFL" (cf. among others Auger 1990; Roberge 1986, 1990; Hulk 1991; Kaiser & Meisel 1991; Kaiser 1992). A consequence of this approach is that the SpecIP position may remain lexically empty. Thus, French, like the other Romance languages, is a *null subject language* which allows the empty category *pro* in the external argument position. According to Rizzi (1986a), the feature-content of *pro* is identified via coindexation with INFL which contains 'rich' AGR-features, namely the clitic.[8]

An additional argument supporting the analysis of French as a null-subject language can be made based on the observation that in Colloquial French subjects can also appear in *post*verbal position, as in (3):

(3)   *Il   mange Jean*
         he eats   John
         'John is eating.'

Note that an utterance like (3) does not necessarily involve a pause before the postverbal subject and that the interpretation of such a sentence does not differ in substantial ways from the interpretation of the same sentence with a *pre*verbal subject. In other words, the sentence in (3) is 'roughly synonymous' with the sentence in (1a) (Safir 1985:172). In addition, the example in (3) shows that a definite subject NP can occur in postverbal position in French and that there is no need for the presence of an 'impersonal verb' in such a construction. This is to say that constructions with a postverbal subject in French are *not* restricted by the so-called 'Definiteness Effect' (Safir 1985). Neither do they depend on the presence of an expletive pronoun (Rizzi 1982). Thus French allows the so-called 'Free Inversion' of subjects which is considered to be one of the essential properties of null subject languages (Chomsky 1981:255).

It seems that object clitics have a status similar to subject clitics. In other words, they can be regarded as agreement markers. A crucial observation supporting this view is that in French there exist constructions such as those in (4) showing unified intonation pattern without any pause (Rothe 1966; Harris 1976:43f.; Larsson 1979:17; Ronat 1979; Lambrecht 1981:86):

(4) a. *Marie l'   a   vu   Jean hier*
         Mary him has seen John yesterday
         'Mary has seen John yesterday.'

     b. *Marie le lui   a   donné le   livre   à Jean*
         Mary it to him has given the book to John
         'Mary has given John the book.'

Interestingly, the word order of the object complements is generally the same as in a sentence lacking object clitics, i.e. object nouns are placed immediately after the verb, with no intervening elements such as adverbs (Carroll 1982:308f.). This indicates that such utterances are *not* instances of right dislocations. Rather, they should be analyzed as clitic doubling constructions where the object clitic functions as an agreement marker (Auger 1990; Roberge 1986, 1990; Kaiser 1992). This hypothesis about the status of French object clitics, however, seems to be weakened by the observation that the frequency of clitic doubling is much lower with objects than with subjects. Empirical studies show that only about 10% of all lexical objects are "doubled" by an object clitic which means that, in contrast to subject clitics, object clitics are far from being *obligatory* agreement markers (Hulk 1991; Kaiser 1992). One crucial argument, however, supports the claim that object clitics are agreement affixes, namely the fact that only *affixes* can be inserted between an affix and its 'host' (Klavans 1982:18; Zwicky & Pullum 1983:507). If one agrees with the assumption that French subject clitics are affixes, it then follows that object clitics also have to be affixes for they generally appear *between* the subject clitic and its host, the finite verb.

On the basis of this analysis French is not only a *null subject* language but also a language which allows *null objects*. In order to describe the special properties of object clitics, I will assume that object clitics are base-generated under V^0. This captures the fact that object clitics are affix-like elements or even affixes and, as such, are attached to the verb (Lapointe 1980).[9] I therefore propose the structure in (5) for finite clauses in French (see next page).

3. Predictions for the Acquisition of Clitic Pronouns in French

In this paper, I will assume that the 'continuity hypothesis', proposed by Pinker (1984), is basically correct. Pinker argues that child grammars are organized in accordance with the same syntactic rules and principles which are attributed to adult grammar by standard linguistic investigations. To be more

(5)

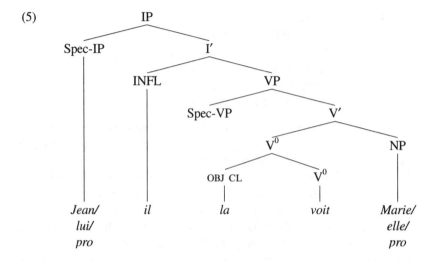

precise, I adopt a 'weak' version of the continuity hypothesis which does not require that children initially have access to all grammatical principles and categories which are part of the adult grammar. On this view, children might lack certain kinds of linguistic knowledge in the early stages. Thus, child grammar is in principle of the same nature as adult grammar, but specific child grammars differ from their respective adult grammars since the child still has to decide which parameterized options of universal grammar are instantiated in the grammar of the language to be acquired.

In accordance with this weak version, it has been argued that functional categories are lacking or underspecified in early grammars (Guilfoyle & Noonan 1988; Radford 1986; Müller 1993, this volume, chap. 9). Under this assumption, the subsequent emergence of elements such as verbal inflectional markers or conjunctions is explained by the fact that children have developed access to functional categories.

If this view is correct, we can then make the following predictions about the acquisition of French clitics. Given the assumption that subject clitics are inflectional prefixes and, as such, generated under INFL, one should expect the appearance of subject clitics in child language only when INFL is available to the child. Prior to this, subject clitics should only appear sporadically or not at all. However, once the functional category INFL has emerged, we should observe a sudden increase in the use of these clitics. Different predictions apply to the acquisition of object clitics. According to the analysis proposed above, object clitics are generated in the VP. Therefore, if early child language is characterized by the absence of functional categories but by the presence of lexical categories, the emergence of object clitics should not correlate with the emergence of functional categories. Instead, nothing should prevent the object clitics from appearing early in child language nor from being mastered rapidly. This account thus predicts a quite different pattern of emergence for subject and object clitics.

4.   Clitics in Child Language

4.1. *Previous Studies*

The acquisition of clitics in French has received little attention so far. There exist several analyses studying the null subject phenomenon in child language where the use of subject clitics, especially in comparison to lexical subjects, has been taken into account (Hulk 1987; Pierce 1989; Meisel 1990).[10] However, the emergence and the development of subject clitics in child language generally has not been examined. The same observation applies to research on the acquisition of object clitics.[11] Studies on this issue mostly deal with the problem of word order (e.g., Nuckle 1981; Haverkort & Weissenborn 1991) and merely report that object clitics are acquired fairly late (Clark 1985:714).[12] They generally agree that the placement of object clitics presents few problems for young children; preverbal object clitics normally appear in their appropriate position. Only in positive imperatives, where object clitics have to appear postverbally in French, do children make mistakes, during a first stage, by using object clitics in preverbal position (Haverkort & Weissenborn 1991). Problems also arise when more than one object clitic occurs. In this case, the order of the clitics is sometimes reversed, or one clitic is simply dropped (Nuckle 1981).

In the following analysis of the acquisition data of the two bilingual boys, Pa and Iv, I focus on the question of emergence and development of subject and object clitics and discuss related phenomena such as the development of word order and agreement markers and the use of lexical arguments.

4.2. *The Acquisition of Subject Clitics*

The first examples in Pa's and Iv's data containing a possible subject clitic form are utterances with *ce* and with *ça*. Both forms appear from the very beginning in the data of both children. However, there can be no doubt that *ce*

is rote-learned and is not yet analyzed as a clitic since it is always used as part
of the formulaic *c'est* construction (see also Meisel 1990:278):

(6)   a.   *(c'est) mal*   (Pa 1;10)
           'this is bad'
      b.   *c'est kaputt*   (Iv 2;3)
           'it's broken (=Germ.)'

As far as the use of the (subject) pronoun *ça* is concerned, it generally
appears, in adult grammatical form, together with the *c'est* construction:

(7)   a.   *qui c' est ça*   (Pa 1;11)
           who this is this
           'who is this'
      b.   *c' est c' est ça*   (Iv 1;11)
           this is this is this
           'this is so'

In these utterances *ça* does not behave like a clitic but rather like a deictic
pronoun. This holds for all early uses of *ça*. Note that *ça*, also when it directly
precedes the verb, is often accompanied by a pointing gesture, as shown in the
following examples:

(8)   a.   *(ç)a pique*   (Pa 2;0)
           'it pricks'
      b.   *ça cassé*   (Iv 1;10)
           'this (is) broken'

During this early acquisition phase, i.e. until 2;1 (for Pa) and 2;2 (for Iv),
the only subject clitic forms other than *ce* or *ça* are found in utterances which are
imitations of adult speech, as shown in (9):

(9)   a   Ad.: *où elle est*
           Pa: *où elle est*   (Pa 1;11)
           'where is she?'
      b.   Ad.: *je le   connais pas encore*
                I him know   not yet
           Iv.: *(je) connais pas*   (Iv 2;1)
           'I don't know'

Thus, both such imitated forms and the early *ce* and *ça* cannot count as evidence for the beginning of productive use of subject clitics since they must be interpreted as initially representing unanalyzed forms (see also Meisel 1990:279).

Tables 2a and 2b display the emergence of subject clitics in the speech of the two children:[13]

Table 2a. The emergence of subject clitics (Pascal)

subj. clitic	1;09	1;10	1;11	2;00	2;01	2;02	2;03	2;04	2;05	2;06
je				(1)				3(3)	11	6
tu							1(1)	(1)	5(2)	5
il/elle			(5)	(3)	2(1)	2	12(2)	35	28(2)	7
on	(2)						(1)	2(1)	1	10
nous/vous										
ils/elles							1		(1)	7

subj. clitic	2;07	2;08	2;09	2;10	2;11
je	24	8	30	17	14
tu	3	1	10	3	2
il/elle	28	17	23(1)	43(1)	20
on	7	8	9	8	5
nous/vous					
ils/elles	2	9			1

As can be seen in Table 2a, the first clear examples in Pa's data of subject clitics in non-imitated and non-formulaic utterances are found at the age of 2;1:

(10) a. *maman   elle est là*   (Pa 2;1)
          Mommy she is here
          'Mommy is here'
      b. *où   l'(=elle) est maman*   (Pa 2;1)
          where she   is Mommy
          'where is Mommy?'

Pa continues using these clitic forms, for two months, combining them exclusively with the copula *être* 'be':

Table 2b: The emergence of subject clitics (Ivar)

subj. clitic	1;10	1;11	2;00	2;01	2;02	2;03	2;04	2;05	2;06	2;07
je				(1)			1(3)	2(1)	3	2
tu		(2)					1	1	2	
il/elle				(1)	(2)	2	4(1)	2(4)	12	4(1)
on		(1)		(1)		1		8	3	1
nous/vous										
ils/elles										1

subj. clitic	2;08	2;09	2;10	2;11	3;00
je	1	4	2(1)	10	30
tu		1	1	4	10
il/elle	3(1)	15	6	31	37
on	6	3	13	20	24
nous/vous					
ils/elles	1	15		1	1

(11) a. <u>elle</u> *est là*   (Pa 2;2)
      'she is here'

    b. <u>l'</u>*(=il/elle) est pas là*   (Pa 2;2)
      'he/she is not here'

From the age of 2;3 onwards, one can observe a significant increase in the appearance of these clitics. Moreover, they appear from now on in combination with verbs other than *être*, as shown in (12):

(12) a. <u>il</u> *[pronɛme](=promène)*   (Pa 2;3)
      'he is walking'

    b. <u>il</u> *est pas là*   (Pa 2;3)
      'he isn't here'

    c. *où*   <u>elle</u> *est la* *[kuɛr](=fleur)*   (Pa 2;3)
      where she is the flower
      'where is the flower?'

    d. <u>elles</u>   *sortent la nuit*   (Pa 2;3)
      'theyFEM go out at night'

The fact that they are now combined with different verbs allows one to conclude that they are used *productively* (see also Meisel 1990). Interestingly, these first clitic forms used by Pa are all 3rd person clitics. Until the age of 2;3, only one clear example appears of the use of clitics other than *il(s)* or *elle(s)*, namely the 2nd person clitic *tu*:

(13)   *t'as raison*   (Pa 2;3)
         'you're right'

One month later, one can observe the emergence of 1st person clitics:

(14) a.   *moi j'ai   (tout) mangé (le) fromage*   (Pa 2;4)
           me I have all   eaten   (the) cheese
           'I have eaten the whole cheese'

      b.   *on va voir*   (Pa 2;4)
           'we will see'

      c.   *c'est comme ça qu' on joue*   (Pa 2;4)
           it's so   that we play
           'it's like that that we play'

Note that in adult French, although semantically a 1st person clitic, *on* behaves like a 3rd person clitic and appears exclusively with 3rd person verb forms. From the beginning of its use, Pa employs it *productively* since he already combines it with different verbs. As for *je*, he first uses it only in one utterance — repeated three times — with the auxiliary *avoir* 'have'. Nevertheless one month later, *je* occurs in combination with different verbs:

(15) a.   *je veux ça*   (Pa 2;5)
           'I want this'

      b.   *je vois pas la tête*   (Pa 2;5)
           I see not the head
           'I don't see his head'

At the same age, *tu* also appears and is used with a variety of verbs:

(16) a.   *tu mets*   (Pa 2;5)
           'do you put (it)?'

      b.   *tu veux*   (Pa 2;5)
           'do you want?'

As far as Iv's acquisition of subject clitics is concerned, one can observe a similar development (see Table 2b) (see also Meisel 1990). The first utterances with clearly non-imitated and non-rote-learned subject clitic forms emerge at the age of 2;2:

(17) a.   *(il) dort*   (Iv 2;2)
          'he is sleeping'
     b.   *(elle a) cheveux*   (Iv 2;2)
          'she has hair'

It is questionable whether both these examples represent clear evidence of the use of clitic forms since they are quite unintelligible. However, only one month later, there are clear examples of the use of *il* and *elle* which are consistently used in combination with different verbs from this time on:

(18) a.   *(i)l écoute*   (Iv 2;3)
          he hears
          'it (=alarm clock) is ticking'
     b.   *il sommeille un peu*   (Iv 2;4)
          'he is taking a nap'
     c.   *elle est propre*   (Iv 2;3)
          she is   clean
          'it (=nose) is clean'
     d.   *elle (est) cherchée papier hygiénique*   (Iv 2;6)
          'she (is) looking for toilet-paper'

One can thus conclude that Iv employs these clitics *productively* from the age of 2;3 on. What is interesting is that, like Pa, he starts using 3rd person clitics first. Apart from *il* and *elle*, he uses *on* only once before 2;3 in an incomplete utterance:

(19)   *on va-*   (Iv 2;3)
          'we are going to-'

From the age of 2;5 onwards, Iv employs *on* frequently and in combination with different verbs:

(20) a.   *ça on met*   (Iv 2;5)
          this we put
          'we'll put this (there)'
     b.   *ici on peut dormir*   (Iv 2;5)
          'here we can sleep'

The first clitics other than 3rd person appear at the age of 2;4. Only one month later they are readily used in combination with different verbs:

(21) a.   *non, [z̲]'ai encore (a-) malade*   (Iv 2;4)
          'no, I'm still sick'
     b.   *j̲e veux*   (Iv 2;5)
          'I want'
     c.   *t̲u vois*   (Iv 2;4)
          'you see'
     d.   *t̲'es tombé*   (Iv 2;5)
          'you fell down'

Thus we can see that Pa and Iv acquire subject clitics in a similar way. They begin to acquire them approximately at the same time. Table 3 shows that both children start with 3rd person clitics. Other clitics emerge only one or two months later and, like 3rd person clitics, appear suddenly and are mastered within a short period of time.

Table 3. Productive use of subject clitics

	Pascal	Ivar
il/elle	2;3	2;3
on	2;4	2;5
je	2;5	2;5
tu	2;5	2;5

4.3. *The Acquisition of Object Clitics*

The most striking observation with regard to the acquisition of object clitics is that both children acquire object clitics later than subject clitics. This can be seen in Tables 4a and 4b where the emergence of object clitics is documented.

The first object clitic forms used by Pa appear at the age of 2;4, i.e. three months after he produces subject clitics for the first time:

(22) a.   *on s̲'   déguise*   (Pa 2;4)
          one himself disguise
          'we're going to dress up'
     b.   *veux l̲e rem[ɛ]-(=remettre)*   (Pa 2;4)
          want it back-put
          '(I) want to put it back'

Table 4a. The emergence of object clitics (Pascal)

obj. clitic	2;02	2;03	2;04	2;05	2;06	2;07	2;08	2;09	2;10	2;11
me					(1)					
te			(1)							
le(s)/la			7	3	4	2(2)	3	13	3(2)	8
lui/leur										
nous/vous										
se			1	1				2	2	2

obj. clitic	3;00	3;01	3;02	3;03
me			3	1
te				2
le(s)/la	3	4	10	5(3)
lui/leur				2
nous/vous				1
se			1	3

As can be seen in Table 4a, Pa employs the 3rd person object clitic *le* (and later also *les* and *la*) quite frequently once he begins using it. Right from the beginning, he combines it with different verbs, mostly nonfinite ones. Apart from this clitic, Pa sporadically uses the reflexive *se*. Although quite rare, it seems to be used productively from early on for it occurs with different verbs. As far as other object clitics are concerned, they are totally absent in Pa's data for a long period of time. Only at age 3;2 does Pa begin to employ object clitic forms other than *le(s)/la* or *se*. From their first appearance on he uses them quite regularly and in combination with different (finite and nonfinite) verbs. It seems that by the age of 3;3 Pa has acquired all object clitics in French with the exception of *vous*. Examples are shown in (23):

(23) a. *il(s) me mange(nt)*   (Pa 3;2)
           'he is (/they are) eating me'

        b. *il t'a mordu*   (Pa 3;3)
           'did he bite you?'

        c. *on peut pas le faire*   (Pa 3;2)
           'you cannot do it-MASC'

d.   *et après on la mange*   (Pa 3;2)
     'and later we will eat it-FEM'
e.   *on va lui donner (ça)*   (Pa 3;3)
     'we'll give (it) to him(/her)'
f.   *tu   sais   que- que vient   nous chercher*   (Pa 3;3)
     you know what   comes us   to look for
     'do you know what (=who) is coming looking for us?'
g.   *ils se tapent*   (Pa 3;2)
     'they are slapping each other'

Table 4b. The emergence of object clitics (Ivar)

obj. clitic	2;04	2;05	2;06	2;07	2;08	2;09	2;10	2;11	3;00	3;01
me									1	
te		(1)						(1)	3	4(1)
le(s)/la				(2)		(2)			1	4
lui/leur										
nous/vous									1	
se					(1)	13	(1)	2(1)	3	2

obj. clitic	3;02	3;03	3;04	3;05
me	1		3	
te	2		1	
le(s)/la	11	12(4)	16	11
lui/leur				
nous/vous				
se	6		4	2

In Iv's data, there are no regular uses of object clitics until the age of 3;0. Table 4b indicates that object clitics are almost completely absent up to this age. Only the reflexive *se* appears earlier. Note that, at the age of 2;9, *se* occurs exclusively in a single construction which seems to be rote-learned, see (24a). Two months later, it is used, for the first time, in combination with other verbs, as shown in (24b) and (24c):

(24) a.   *ils se battent*   (Iv 2;9)
           'they are hitting each other'

    b.   *il s' fait mal*   (Iv 2;11)
        'he is hurting himself'

    c.   *elle se lève*   (Iv 2;11)
        'she is standing up'

Apart from *vous* and the dative clitic *lui* (and *leur*), all object clitic forms begin to emerge in Iv's data between the age of 3;0 and 3;1:

  (25) a.   *moi je me tiens*   (Iv 3;0)
          'I'am holding myself'

      b.   *je t'invite avec [n]e(=le) bus*   (Iv 3;0)
          'I invite you with the bus'

      c.   *[z]e(=je) peux [n]e(=le) con(str)uire*   (Iv 3;1)
          'I can build it-MASC'

      d.   *et   [n]a(=la) prends*   (Iv 3;0)
          and it-FEM   take
          'and take it!'

      e.   *et (il) nous voit [n]e(=le) vo[n]eur*   (Iv 3;1)
          and he us   sees the   thief
          'and the thief sees us'

Note that from this moment onwards, Iv employs most of these clitics in a productive way since they occur in combination with different verbs.

    To summarize these results, both children acquire object and subject clitics in a similar way. With the exception of *le(s)/la* and *se* which are used by Pa quite early, object clitic forms show up in both children's data at about the same time. They appear suddenly and are then used in a productive way.

Table 5. Productive use of object clitics

	Pascal	Ivar
le(s)/la	2;4	3;1
se	2;5	2;11
me	3;2	3;2
te	3;3	3;0
lui/leur	3;3	———
nous/vous	3;3(?)	3;1(?)

5.   Discussion of the Results

The results concerning the acquisition of subject clitics confirm the prediction made on the basis of the weak version of the continuity hypothesis. As predicted, subject clitics only appear sporadically in the beginning. Then most of the subject clitics emerge within a short period of time and from this moment onwards are used productively. According to the predictions made above, at this moment one should also expect the functional category INFL to be available in the children's grammars. In other words, one should find evidence for the emergence of elements, such as inflectional markers, which are supposed to be part of INFL.

Unfortunately, when studying the acquisition of verb inflection in French one has to face the problem that in modern spoken French overt verbal inflectional endings have almost completely disappeared. With few exceptions, no such endings are phonetically realized in the singular and, in the plural, only 2nd plural forms are consistently marked.[14] However, one morphological distinction which remains in spoken French with respect to verb forms is the one between finite and non-finite verbs. Therefore, the emergence of finite verb forms in child grammar can be seen as evidence that INFL has emerged. Apart from verb morphology, the position of the verb with respect to the negative marker *pas* reveals whether the children use a finite or a non-finite verb (Verrips & Weissenborn 1992). One crucial observation concerning this distinction is that children begin to distinguish morphologically between finite and non-finite verbs at the same time that they start using subject clitics productively. This is what has been observed by Meisel (1990) studying Iv and two other bilingual children, Pierre (P) and Caroline (C). In addition to this, Meisel finds that, at the age of 2;5, Iv distinguishes between verb forms which precede *pas* and those which follow it, even if overt inflectional markings are often lacking. In other words, as Meisel (1990:269) points out, "finiteness is, at this point, indeed part of the child's grammar," i.e. at the moment when Iv has developed the full system of subject clitics (see also Meisel, this volume).

Although I did not analyze Pa's acquisition data specifically with respect to the distinction between finite and non-finite verbs, it seems that the above conclusion also holds for Pa's language development. One observation supporting this conjecture is that Pa *never* uses a subject clitic in combination with a non-finite verb form. Meisel (1990, this volume) observes that the same is true for Iv and for other children as well.[15]   .

These findings strongly indicate that both children, Iv and Pa, work with the implicit assumption that subject clitics are intimately related to finiteness. This is corroborated by the fact that from very early on, i.e. right from the moment when they start using subject clitics productively, both children combine subject noun phrases or subject pronouns with subject clitics in finite sentences. They employ subject clitics in order to mark morphologically the agreement in number, gender and person between subject and verb. Examples are shown in (26) and (27) (compare also the examples in (10a), (14a), (25a) and (33a)):

(26) a. *la grand-mère   elle est là*   (Pa 2;3)
          the grand-mother she is here
          'the grand-mother is here'

      b. *moi j'ai   malade aussi*   (Pa 2;5)
          me I have sick   too
          'I am sick too'

      c. *toi tu   dors aussi*   (Pa 2;9)
          you you sleep too
          'you are sleeping too'

      d. *les rouges   ils   sont pas les meilleurs*   (Pa 2;10)
          the red ones they are not the best ones
          'the red ones are not the best ones'

      e. *lui il fait   pas caca*   (Pa 2;11)
          him he makes not caca
          'he doesn't do caca'

(27) a. *Ivar i(l) repare*   (Iv 2;5)
          Ivar he repairs
          'Ivar repairs'

      b. *les poupées elles arrivent*   (Iv 2;8)
          the dolls   they arrive
          'the dolls are coming'

      c. *moi je vais manger dans ma bouche*   (Iv 2;10)
          me I will eat   in my mouth
          'I will eat (it) in my mouth'

      d. *lui il va   dans son lit*   (Iv 2;11)
          him he goes in   his bed
          'he goes to his bed'

In addition to utterances of this kind, one also finds sentences in which the subject clitic agrees with a subject in a *post*verbal position, as shown in (28) and (29) (compare also the examples in (12c) and (25e)):

(28) a. *(i)l est pas dans l'eau   le canard*   (Pa 2;4)
　　　　he is not in   the water the duck
　　　　'the duck is not in the water'

　　 b. *tu   (bois) du jus d'orange toi*   (Pa 2;5)
　　　　you drink of orange-juice you
　　　　'you are drinking orange juice'

　　 c. *qu'est-ce qu'il   fait   lui?*   (Pa 2;5)
　　　　what   he does him
　　　　'what is he doing?

　　 d. *ils   peut   la tête dans l'eau   les vaches*   (Pa 2;8)
　　　　they can-IST SG the head in   the water the cows
　　　　'the cows can (put) their heads in the water'

(29) a. *c'est kaputt   nounours*   (Iv 2;4)
　　　　it is broken$_{[Germ.]}$ teddy
　　　　'Teddy is broken'

　　 b. *l'   est pas partie maman*   (Iv 2;6)
　　　　(she) is not gone   mommy
　　　　'Mommy hasn't gone'

　　 c. *[z]'étais à Paris moi*   (Iv 3;2)
　　　　I   was in Paris me
　　　　'I was in Paris'

　　 d. *on a   pas une tour   nous*   (Iv 3;2)
　　　　we have not a   tower we
　　　　'we don't have a tower'

What is interesting is that there is a observable development with respect to utterances with postverbal subjects (see Köppe, this volume). Prior to age 2;5, Iv, for instance, only occasionally uses subjects in postverbal position. He clearly prefers preverbal subjects. Pa, on the other hand, initially employs postverbal subjects more frequently than Iv. However, postverbal subjects often occur in utterances which seem to be rote-learned forms.

Note that, as soon as they start using subject clitics productively, both children make use of postverbal subjects more frequently than before. As far as Pa is concerned, the number of postverbal subjects increases in a quite dramatic way. This development can be accounted for, I believe, within a parameterized theory. As pointed out above, in Colloquial French, utterances with postverbal subjects can be considered to be instances of Free Inversion. As in the adult grammar, the children's utterances with postverbal subjects generally are pronounced without any observable pause. In addition, one finds nearly identical utterances in children's data which differ merely with respect to the position of the subject:

(30) a. *moi je peux abendbrot   essen*   (Pa 2;10)
    me I can supper$_{[Germ.]}$ eat$_{[Germ.]}$
    'I can have supper'

 b. *je peux abendbrot   essen   moi*   (Pa 2;10)
    I can supper$_{[Germ.]}$ eat$_{[Germ.]}$ me
    'I can have supper'

(31) a. *ce[n]ui-[n]à(=celui-là) i[n](=il) est*
    this one here   he   is
    ma[n]ade(=malade)   (Iv 3;4)
    sick
    'this one (here) is sick'

 b. *i[n](=il) est ma[n]ade(=malade) ce[n]ui(=celui)*   (Iv 3;0)
    he   is sick   this one
    'this one is sick'

Note that the meaning of each utterance in (30) and (31) remains the same regardless of whether the subject is in a preverbal or postverbal position. Moreover, both children mostly employ definite postverbal subjects. This is to say that utterances with postverbal subject can be regarded as instances of Free Inversion; the occurrence of postverbal subjects does not involve a semantic change with respect to a sentence with a preverbal subject nor is it restricted by the Definiteness Effect.[16] Both children, thus, display a typical property of null subject languages; it seems that they already have set the null subject parameter to the appropriate value. This is supported by the increase of utterances with postverbal subjects coincident with the acquisition of subject clitics. This strongly suggests that the setting of the null subject parameter takes place as soon as the system of subject clitics has emerged. As shown above, subject clitics are analyzed from early on as inflectional markers. As a consequence, once the children have acquired the subject clitics they possess a system in which INFL is "rich enough" to identify lexically empty subjects. From this moment on, therefore, they should be able to set the null subject parameter by choosing the null subject option. This involves, as predicted by the standard parameter theory, the simultaneous emergence of all typical properties of null subject languages, such as Free Inversion, without further acquisition (see Meisel, to appear).

Note that on the basis of the assumption that subject clitics are agreement markers which are generated in INFL one can account for another striking observation concerning the acquisition of French subject clitics. As has been pointed out, both children start using 3rd person clitics first, clitics other than 3rd person emerge later. Interestingly, this developmental sequence of subject clitics corresponds to what has been found in several studies on the acquisition of verb inflections or agreement markers in languages other than French. For example, studies on the acquisition of German agree in the observation that children acquire verbal inflections of 3rd person before those of other persons (cf. Clahsen 1986; Clahsen & Penke 1992; Meisel 1986, 1990, this volume). Ezeiza-barrena (to appear) reports similar findings from the acquisition of Basque, observing that the first inflectional marker used by children is that of 3rd person. In other words, Pa and Iv acquire subject clitics in a way similar to children acquiring inflectional markers in other languages.

As far as object clitics are concerned, their acquisition also can be explained if one adopts the analysis given above, according to which they are agreement markers. It can be observed that both children, Iv and Pa, employ object clitics in constructions which contain coreferential lexical object nouns as soon as they use object clitics productively:

(32) a. *je vais les   prendre les jaunes*   (Pa 2;8)
          I   will them take   the yellows
          'I will take the yellow ones'

      b. *on peut les   manger les poissons*   (Pa 2;9)
          one can them eat   the fishes
          'we can eat the fish'

(33) a. *moi [z]e(=je) le   prend(re) [n]e(=le) bus*   (Iv 3;1)
          me   I   him take   the bus
          'I'll take the bus'

      b. *main(te)nant [z]e(=je) les   range   mes photos*   (Iv 3;2)
          now   I   them tidy up my photos
          'now I am tidying up my photos'

Although these examples are rather infrequent, their existence indicates that both children have recognized that object clitics function as agreement markers.[17] Another observation which supports this assumption is that there are no cases of errors where clitics occur in the postverbal complement position. This type of error, however, could be expected to show up in child language if object clitics were analyzed as base-generated in postverbal NP-position, and therefore not as agreement markers (see also Weissenborn 1988).

Note that these results correspond to what one might expect if one adopts the analysis that object clitics are agreement markers. Recall, however, that based on this analysis, one might also expect object clitics to emerge earlier than subject clitics. Given the assumption that object clitics are lexical heads, they might emerge quite early in child grammar since lexical categories are supposed to be present in child grammar from early on. The data from language acquisition, however, show that object clitics are a late development. This seems to weaken the analysis given for French object clitics. Interestingly, however, in so-called object agreement languages the acquisition of object agreement markers resembles the acquisition of French object clitics. In other words, in object agreement languages, markers for object–verb agreement display a development similar to French object clitics, i.e. they appear and are mastered later than markers for subject–verb agreement. This is the case, for example, in Basque, a language which possesses different verbal affixes for both overt subject-verb agreement and overt verb agreement with direct and indirect objects. Ezeiza-barrena (to appear) reports that, for a long period of time, children acquiring Basque do not mark object–verb agreement while they already make use of subject–verb agreement markers. The same seems to be true as well for the acquisition of Hungarian where the agreement between verbs and definite objects must be marked overtly. Here too, children take a long time to acquire the relevant agreement markers (MacWhinney 1976). Furthermore, in Romance languages other than French, where object clitic pronouns also function as affixes, they emerge later than inflectional markers which serve to mark subject–verb agreement (see Mahlau, to appear, for Spanish).

This parallelism between French object clitics and object agreement markers in other languages strongly supports, I believe, the analysis of French object clitics as agreement markers. What is not explained within this analysis, however, is their relatively late development. Under the view that object clitics are lexical heads such a development is surprising. Rather, one should expect them to arise quite early in child language. In addition, being lexical heads with a complex morphological paradigm their acquisition should require a long period of time. Interestingly however, most object clitics are acquired rather rapidly and within a short period. Note that this resembles the acquisition of subject clitics. Given the weak version of the continuity hypothesis, this amounts to saying that the acquisition of object clitics is also related to the emergence of a functional category. In Müller, Crysmann & Kaiser (1993) it is argued that this functional category is COMP. Current studies on language acquisition have shown that this functional category is available only late in child grammar. And indeed at least

Iv's acquisition data seem to confirm the relationship between object clitics and COMP. He starts using object clitics productively at the age of 3;0, at the time when he seems to have developed access to the CP-node (see Müller 1993, this volume, chap. 9). Thus, the sudden increase of object clitics could be explained along the same lines as the acquisition of subject clitics for they both depend on the emergence of a functional category.

6. Conclusion

Based on an analysis of clitic pronouns in adult Colloquial French, it has been argued that clitics are agreement markers. It follows from this analysis that Colloquial French is like all other Romance languages with respect to null subject phenomena. It has to be regarded as a null subject language. On the one hand, it allows lexically empty subjects which are identified by subject clitics. On the other hand, it can invert both indefinite and definite subjects without further consequences for the meaning of such sentences. In addition to this, French is a null object language since object clitics are also analyzed as agreement markers, able to identify lexically empty objects.

Based on this analysis, data from French first language acquisition have been analyzed which provide evidence for it. It has been shown that both subject and object clitics can be regarded as agreement markers; as soon as they emerge in child language they are used in combination with nouns or pronouns in order to mark overt agreement. As for subject clitics, their emergence is closely related to the emergence of the functional category INFL. As soon as INFL is available in the child's grammar, subject clitics suddenly emerge and are mastered within a short period. At the same time, there is an observable development of postverbal subjects; namely as soon as subject clitics are used productively, postverbal subjects are employed in a frequent way. It has been argued that this is due to the setting of the null subject parameter. Once the children have developed the system of subject clitics they possess a system which allows them to identify lexically empty subjects, and therefore they are able to set the parameter to the appropriate value.

In contrast to subject clitics, objects clitic are a late development. This parallels with what has been found in acquisition studies in object agreement languages where markers for object-verb agreement also emerge relatively late. Interestingly, object clitics, like subject clitics, are acquired within a short period of time. This amounts to saying that, in contrast to what had been predicted above, their acquisition seems to be triggered by the emergence of a functional category to which object clitics are related.

Acknowledgements

I am indebted to all members of the DUFDE project, Caroline Koehn, Regina Köppe, Jürgen M. Meisel, Natascha Müller and Achim Stenzel, for their stimulating discussions and criticisms of previous versions of this paper. In particular, I would like to express my warmest thanks to Susanne E. Carroll and Howard Nicholas for their helpful comments. Thanks go too to Andolin Eguzkitza, Marijo Ezeizabarrena, Axel Mahlau, Peter Jordens, and an anonymous reviewer for their criticisms.

Notes

1. See Meisel (ed. 1992) for a recent collection of studies on this issue.

2. See Zwicky (1977) and Zwicky & Pullum (1983) for a synopsis of the typical characteristics of clitics; see also Klavans (1982) and Prinz (1991). For a more extensive discussion of the special properties of clitics in Romance languages see Kayne (1975:81–92), Strozer (1976:106–113), Kaiser & Meisel (1991) and Kaiser (1992:29–47).

3. In addition, French has two pronominal clitic adverbs, *y* and *en*, which will be not treated in the present study.

4. In the following discussion of the acquisition of clitic pronouns, I will ignore the problems the children may have with case marking. On this issue, see Meisel (1986), Parodi (1990) and Stenzel (this volume).

5. Note that the case form and grammatical function of a clitic pronoun are not necessarily identical (cf. Hunnius 1991:114; Kaiser 1992).

6. One can add to this table the demonstrative pronouns *ce* and *ça* which share all properties of clitic elements (Morin 1979:22f.; Lambrecht 1981:20).

7. See Hunnius (1977) and Kaiser (1992) for a summary of the debate on the role of French subject clitics in Romance linguistics.

8. Note that under the view that the subject clitics are agreement markers French displays a "uniform morphology" which is purportedly decisive for the licensing of lexically empty subjects (Jaeggli & Safir 1989).

9. In contrast to this, the claim that object clitics are adjoined to V' (Carroll 1982; Di Sciullo 1990) does not capture this relationship between clitic and verb.

10. See also Roberge & Vinet (1989) and Carroll & Roberge (1989) for an overview of some of these studies.

11. There are a few exceptions, e.g., Meisel (1990) who studied the development of subject–verb agreement and subject clitics or, e.g., Weissenborn (1988) who analyzed the development of object clitics.

12. Only Weissenborn (1988) observes an early development of object clitics. Unfortunately he does not provide further details about their frequency or developmental sequences. Therefore, it remains unclear whether object clitics are used *productively* from early on. Thus, it is difficult to compare Weissenborn's results with the results of other studies, including the present one.

13. The numbers in brackets refer either to clitics appearing in constructions which imitate a previous adult utterance or to forms which cannot be identified unambiguously as clitics because they are not clearly audible.

14. Note that 2nd plural forms are scarcely or not used at all in early child language (see also Meisel 1990).

15. See also Pierce (1989:42f.) who makes the same observation in her study.

16. In contrast to my view, researchers studying clitics or word order in French generally regard sentences with postverbal subjects as instances of right dislocations, even when they are analyzing subject clitics as agreement markers (Roberge 1986, 1990; Hulk 1991). As a consequence, in acquisition studies based on this assumption these sentences are treated in a different way than sentences with preverbal subjects which leads to slightly different results (Hulk 1987; Pierce 1989; Roberge & Vinet 1989); see also Köppe, this volume, for a discussion of this problem with respect to the analysis of Pierce (1989).

17. Weissenborn (1988) also finds early examples for this type of construction. Furthermore, he observes that these constructions "show up at the same time in child's language as other agreement processes like subject-verb agreement" (Weissenborn 1988:17). This observation provides, as he points out, an additional argument for the status of object clitics as agreement markers.

References

Ashby, William J. 1977. *Clitic Inflection in French: An historical perspective.* Amsterdam: Rodopi.

Auger, Julie. 1990. "Colloquial French Argument-Markers: Independent words, clitics, or prefixes?" Manuscript, University of Pennsylvania at Philadelphia.

Barnes, Betsy K. 1986. "An Empirical Study of the Syntax and Pragmatics of Left Dislocations in Spoken French." *Studies in Romance Linguistics* (= *Publications in Language Sciences,* 24.), ed. by Osvaldo Jaeggli & Carmen Silva-Corvalán, 207–223. Dordrecht: Foris.

Carroll, Susanne E. 1982. "Redoublement et dislocation en français." *La syntaxe comparée du français standard et populaire: approches formelle et fonctionnelle. Part 1*, ed. by Claire Lefebvre, 291–357. Québec: Editeur officiel du Québec.

Carroll, Susanne E. & Yves Roberge. 1989. "On the Acquisition of Morphosyntactic Systems." Manuscript, OISE and University of Toronto.

Chomsky, Noam. 1981. *Lectures on Government and Binding: The Pisa lectures* (= *Studies in Generative Grammar, 9.*). Dordrecht: Foris, Second revised edition 1982.

––––––. 1989. "Some Notes on Economy of Derivation and Representation." *MIT Working Papers in Linguistics* 10.43–74.

Clahsen, Harald. 1986. "Verb Inflections in German Child Language: Acquisition of agreement markings and the functions they encode." *Linguistics* 24.79–121.

Clahsen, Harald & Martina Penke. 1992. "The Acquisition of Agreement Morphology and its Syntactic Consequences: New evidence on German child language from the Simone-corpus." Meisel 1992, 181–223.

Clark, Eve V. 1985. "The Acquisition of Romance with Special Reference to French." *The Crosslinguistic Study of Language Acquisition.* Vol. 1.: *The Data,* ed. by Dan I. Slobin, 687–782. Hillsdale: Erlbaum.

Di Sciullo, Anna-Maria. 1990. "On the Properties of Clitics." *Binding in Romance. Essays in Honour of Judith McA'Nulty,* ed. by Anna-Maria Di Sciullo & Anne Rochette, 209–232. Ottawa: The Canadian Linguistic Association.

Ezeizabarrena, Maria Jose. To appear. "Adquisición infantil de la triple concordancia verbal en euskera." To appear in *Actas del Coloquio international "Las Lenguas en la Europa Comunitaria",* Amsterdam, 25–28 nov. 1992.

Grevisse, Maurice. 1986. *Le bon usage. Grammaire française.* 12ième édition refondue par André Goosse. Paris — Gembloux: Duculot.

Guilfoyle, Eithne & Máire Noonan. 1988. "Functional Categories and Language Acquisition." Paper presented at the 13th Annual Boston University Conference on Language Development.

Harris, Martin. 1976. "A Typological Approach to Word-Order Change in French." *Romance Syntax: Synchronic and diachronic perspectives,* ed. by Martin Harris, 33–53. Salford: University of Salford, reprinted 1977.

Haverkort, Marco & Jürgen Weissenborn. 1991. "Clitic and Affix Interactions in Early Romance." Paper presented at the 16th Annual Boston University Conference on Language Development.

Hulk, Aafke. 1987. "L'acquisition du français et le paramètre pro-drop." *Études de linguistique française offertes à Robert de Dardel par ses amis et collègues,* ed. by Birgitte Kampers-Mahne & Co Vet, 53–61. Amsterdam: Rodopi.

––––––. 1991. "Les pronoms clitiques sujets et la théorie linguistique." *Actes du XVIIIe congrès international de linguistique et philologie romanes. Université de Trèves (Trier) 1986.* Tome 2: *Linguistique théorique et linguistique synchronique,* 504–513. Tübingen: Niemeyer.

Hunnius, Klaus. 1977. "Frz. *je*: ein präfigiertes Konjugationsmorphem? Ein Forschungsbericht zur Frage der Prädetermination." *Archiv für das Studium der neueren Sprachen und Literaturen* 214.37–48.

————. 1991. "*T'as vu?* — Die Deklination der klitischen Personalpronomina im Französischen." *Zeitschrift für französische Sprache und Literatur* 101.113–124.

Jaeggli, Osvaldo. 1982. *Topics in Romance Syntax* (= *Studies in Generative Grammar,* 12.). Dordrecht: Foris.

Jaeggli, Osvaldo & Kenneth J. Safir. 1989. "The Null Subject Parameter and the Parametric Theory." *The Null Subject Parameter* (= *Studies in Natural Language and Linguistic Theory,* 15.), ed. by Osvaldo Jaeggli & Kenneth J. Safir, 1–44. Dordrecht: Kluwer.

Kaiser, Georg A. 1992. *Die klitischen Personalpronomina im Französischen und Portugiesischen. Eine synchronische und diachronische Analyse* (= *Editionen der Iberoamericana,* Reihe III, 44.). Frankfurt am Main: Vervuert.

Kaiser, Georg A. & Jürgen M. Meisel. 1991. "Subjekte und Null-Subjekte im Französischen." *'DET, COMP und INFL'. Zur Syntax funktionaler Kategorien und grammatischer Funktionen* (= *Linguistische Arbeiten,* 263.), ed. by Susan Olsen & Gisbert Fanselow, 110–136. Tübingen: Niemeyer.

Kayne, Richard S. 1975. *French Syntax: The transformational cycle.* Cambridge, Mass: MIT Press.

Klavans, Judith. 1982. *Some Problems in a Theory of Clitics.* Bloomington: Indiana University Linguistics Club.

Lambrecht, Knud. 1981. *Topic, Antitopic and Verb Agreement in Non-Standard French* (=*Pragmatics & Beyond: An interdisciplinary series of language studies,* II, 6.). Amsterdam: John Benjamins.

Lapointe, Steven G. 1980. *A Theory of Grammatical Agreement.* Ph.D. Dissertation. New York: Garland 1985.

Larsson, Eva. 1979. *La dislocation en français: Étude de syntaxe générative* (=*Études romanes de Lund,* 28.). Lund: Gleerup.

MacWhinney, Brian. 1976. "Hungarian Research on the Acquisition of Morphology and Syntax." *Journal of Child Language* 3.397–410.

Mahlau, Axel. To appear. "Orden de palabras y estructura oracional en los niños bilingües." To appear in *La adquisición del vasco y del español en niños bilingües,* ed. by Jürgen M. Meisel. Frankfurt am Main: Vervuert.

Meisel, Jürgen M. 1986. "Word Order and Case Marking in Early Child Language: Evidence from simultaneous acquisition of two first languages: French and German." *Linguistics* 24.123–183.

————. 1990. "INFL-ection: Subjects and Subject–Verb Agreement." *Two First Languages: Early grammatical development in bilingual children* (= *Studies on Language Acquisition,* 10.), ed. by. Jürgen M. Meisel, 237–298. Dordrecht: Foris.

————. ed. 1992. *The Acquisition of Verb Placement: Functional categories and V2 phenomena in language development* (= *Studies in Theoretical Psycholinguistics*, 16.). Dordrecht: Kluwer.

————. To appear. "Parameters in Acquisition." To appear in *A Handbook of Child Language* (=*Blackwell Handbooks in Linguistics*), ed. by Paul Fletcher & Brian MacWhinney. Oxford: Blackwell.

Morin, Yves-Charles. 1979. "La morphophonologie des pronoms clitiques en français populaire." *Cahiers de linguistique* 9.1–36.

Müller, Natascha. 1993. *Komplexe Sätze: Der Erwerb von COMP und von Wortstellungsmustern bei bilingualen Kindern (Französisch/Deutsch)* (= *Tübinger Beiträge zur Linguistik, Series A, Language Development*, 16.). Tübingen: Narr.

Müller, Natascha, Berthold Crysmann & Georg A. Kaiser. 1993. "Interactions between the Acquisition of French OBJ-Pro-Drop and the Development of the C-System." Paper presented at the 6th International Congress for the Study of Child Language, Trieste.

Nuckle, Lucie. 1981. *Sur l'acquisition des pronoms clitiques objets chez des enfants francophones: la double et la simple-cliticisation*. Masters Thesis, University of Montréal.

Parodi, Teresa. 1990. "The Acquisition of Word Order Regularities and Case Morphology." *Two First Languages: Early grammatical development in bilingual children* (= *Studies on Language Acquisition*, 10.), ed. by Jürgen M. Meisel, 157–190. Dordrecht: Foris.

Pierce, Amy E. 1989. *On the Emergence of Syntax: A crosslinguistic study*. Ph.D. Dissertation. Cambridge, Mass.: MIT.

Pinker, Steven. 1984. *Language Learnability and Language Development*. Cambridge, Mass.: Harvard University Press.

Pollock, Jean-Yves. 1989. "Verb Movement, UG and the Structure of IP." *Linguistic Inquiry* 20.365–424.

Prinz, Michael. 1991. *Klitisierung im Deutschen und Neugriechischen: Eine lexikalisch-phonologische Studie* (=*Linguistische Arbeiten*, 256.). Tübingen: Niemeyer.

Radford, Andrew. 1986. "Small Children's Small Clauses." *Bangor Research Papers in Linguistics* 1.1–38.

Rizzi, Luigi. 1982. *Issues in Italian Syntax* (=*Studies in Generative Grammar*, 11.). Dordrecht: Foris.

————. 1986a. "Null Objects in Italian and the Theory of *pro*." *Linguistic Inquiry* 17.501–557.

————. 1986b. "On the Status of Subject Clitics in Romance." *Studies in Romance Linguistics* (=*Publication in Language Sciences*, 24.), ed. by Osvaldo Jaeggli & Carmen Silva-Corvalán, 391–419. Dordrecht: Foris.

Roberge, Yves. 1986. "Subject Doubling, Free Inversion, and Null Argument Languages." *Canadian Journal of Linguistics* 31.55–79.

————. 1990. *The Syntactic Recoverability of Null Arguments*. Montréal: McGill-Queen's University Press.

Roberge, Yves & Marie-Thérèse Vinet. 1989. *La variation dialectale en grammaire universelle*. Montréal: Presses de l'Université de Montréal.

Ronat, Mitsou. 1979. "Pronoms topiques et pronoms distinctifs." *Langue française* 44.106–128.

Rothe, Wolfgang. 1966. "Romanische Objektkonjugation." *Romanische Forschungen* 78.530–547.

Safir, Kenneth J. 1985. *Syntactic Chains* (= *Cambridge Studies in Linguistics*, 40.). Cambridge: Cambridge University Press.

Sankoff, Gillian. 1982. "Usage linguistique et grammaticalisation: Les clitiques sujets en français." *Die Soziolinguistik in romanischsprachigen Ländern: La sociolinguistique dans les pays de langue romane*, ed. by Norbert Dittmar & Brigitte Schlieben-Lange, 81–85. Tübingen: Narr.

Strozer, Judith R. 1976. *Clitics in Spanish*. Ph.D. Dissertation (Los Angeles). Ann Arbor: University Microfilms.

Verrips, Maaike & Jürgen Weissenborn. 1992. "Routes to Verb Placement in Early German and French: The independence of finiteness and agreement." Meisel 1992, 283–331.

Weissenborn, Jürgen. 1988. "The Acquisition of Clitic Object Pronouns and Word Order in French: Syntax or morphology?." Manuscript, Max Planck Institute for Psycholinguistics at Nijmegen.

Zwicky, Arnold. 1977. *On Clitics*. Bloomington: Indiana University Linguistics Club.

Zwicky, Arnold & Geoffrey K. Pullum. 1983. "Cliticization vs. Inflection: English *n't*." *Language* 59.502–513.

Case Assignment and Functional Categories in Bilingual Children
Routes of Development and Implications for Linguistic Theory

Achim Stenzel
University of Hamburg

1. Introduction

In this paper, I want to investigate the acquisition of Case marking in two bilingual (German-French) children, as well as aspects of the development of functional categories related to this area. The following topics will be addressed: Is there a universal sequence of case distinctions all children acquire in a fixed order? What is the relation between functional categories and the acquisition of Case marking? What are possible implications for linguistic theory?

2. Theoretical Background

2.1. *Case in a DP Framework*

The framework in which this paper is located is that of Principles and Parameters Theory. Within this approach I adopt recent developments that have become known as "DP analysis". This analysis has been developed to remove apparent idiosyncrasies of various categories and to develop a unified version of X-bar theory that allows a uniform treatment of all categories. In this vein, Abney (1986) proposed that noun phrases be the complement of a functional category DET which would be analogous to the verbal functional category INFL. This results in parallel structures for the projections of both categories. In French, both the verbal and nominal projections are head-initial, whereas in German, the nominal projection is head-initial, but the verbal projection is head-final:

(1)   DP in French and German

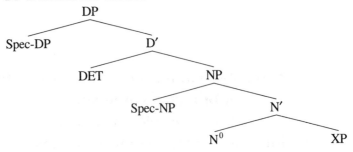

(2)   IP in French

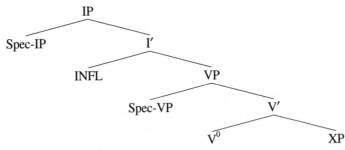

(3)   IP in German

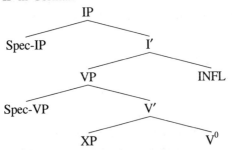

In an analysis of this kind, every lexical projection is "roofed" by a related functional projection. The function of such a structure is to specify the reference of the lexical phrases:

> Determiners and INFL have similar semantic functions. The function of the determiner is to specify the reference of the noun phrase. The noun provides a predicate, and the determiner picks out a particular member of that predicate's extension. The same function is performed in the verbal system by Tense, or Inflection. The VP provides a predicate, that is, a class of events, and Tense locates a particular event in time. (Abney 1986)

For a detailed discussion of the DP in German, see Löbel (1990, 1991), Haider (1988), Olsen (1988, 1989), and also the relevant section in Müller (this volume, chap. 4).[1]

What is the status of abstract Case in a DP framework? In generative theory, Case is seen as a means to structurally license noun phrases at the level of S-structure. This is captured in the formulation of the Case Filter that rules out as deviant any noun phrase with phonetic content that appears in an S-structure position where it cannot be assigned Case. The Case Filter is conceived as a constraint on the distribution of DPs.

This idea of ruling out certain categories in certain positions is common to generative theory, and it is captured in Chomsky's (1986) *Principle of Full Interpretation*. This principle states that every node must have a role in the sentence, and therefore every node must be licensed. In our approach, NPs are licensed as they are complements of a functional head DET. Abney assumes a process called *functional selection (f-selection),* and in phrase structure representations where VP is first sister to INFL and is immediately dominated by I′, VP is f-selected by INFL. Likewise, NPs are f-selected by DET,[2] and f-selection in general is a relation by which the arguments of functional elements are licensed in the same way as the arguments of thematic, i.e. lexical elements are licensed by θ-assignment.[3] The Case Filter may be reinterpreted as the application of the Licensing Condition to DPs:[4]

The Licensing Condition
Every node must be uniquely licensed by entering into a (sufficiently strong) relation with an independently-licensed node. (Abney 1986)

The Case Filter assures that DPs appear in certain positions only, and the relevant criterion is that this position be governed[5] by a potential Case assigner. Abstract Case is the feature that makes categories of a certain type, i.e. DPs, visible for the grammar (cf. Speas 1990). The standard assumption is that Case is assigned to the DP, but Emonds (1985) proposed that Case marking is the projection of some feature of the assigning category onto the assignee. Another approach suggests that the grammar, being a set of well-formedness conditions, checks whether a given DP on S-structure bears a Case feature or not; if not, the sentence is ruled out as ungrammatical.[6] The idea that Case is not assigned, but checked entails that DPs are Case-marked already in the lexicon.

The condition imposed on DPs by the Case Filter is complemented, in Fukui

& Speas (1986), by a requirement that all features a category has to assign *must* be discharged. So a category that *can* assign Case *has* to assign its Case to result in a well-formed structure (cf. Rothstein 1992); Fukui & Speas (1986) call this the "Saturation Principle".

In languages that allow greater variability of word order, such as German or Icelandic, different Case assignment relations are spelt out phonologically as different morphological case categories; in languages that disallow word order variation other than scrambling or dislocation, e.g. French, Swedish or English, morphological variation is greatly reduced.

Case is assigned, under traditional assumptions, to the maximal projection DP and the Case feature percolates to the head D^0; the NP f-selected by D^0 has to agree. Morphological realization of this agreement is language-specific (see the section on case marking in German and French). In German and French (and in English), it is rather more difficult to find evidence for the existence of DET than it is in the case of INFL. Finiteness and V2 effects are clear indicators in favor of the presence of INFL in child grammar (see Meisel 1990, this volume; Meisel & Müller 1992); but neither German nor French display similar cases of head movement in the case of DET. Therefore, it is interesting to look at the findings of Demuth (1992). Demuth studied the acquisition of functional categories in Sesotho, a Bantu language. According to her analysis, Sesotho DPs have the following underlying structure:

(4)

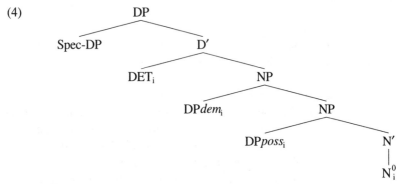

The noun is raised into the DET position where it incorporates the noun class marker assumed to be heading this category. It is not clear from Demuth's presentation whether N^0 is supposed to be head-final or head-initial.[7]

2.2. *Case in German and French*

The morphological realization of structural case varies greatly across languages. German has a system of four morphological case categories, nominative, accusative, dative, and genitive. In general, the pattern described by Chomsky (1981) is followed if we substitute the terms "objective" and "oblique" by "accusative" and "dative", respectively:

(5)   NOM is assigned by AGR
        OBJ is assigned by V
        OBL is assigned by P
        GEN is assigned in a structure of the form [NP__ X′]

and lexical case is assigned as determined by the properties of the assigning category.

German prepositions cannot be easily captured in this schema, since quite a few German prepositions assign the accusative. To a large extent, prepositional Case assignment is semantically predictable. Locative prepositions, e.g., assign dative for stative readings and accusative for directional readings:[8]

(6)   Er ist im-DAT Zimmer
        He is in-the room
(7)   Er geht ins-ACC Zimmer
        He goes into-the room

There is a rich inventory of forms for pronouns, determiners and adjectives. These forms are inflected not only for Case, but also for gender and number. All three categories are marked on one single affix.[9] Nouns are inflected for number and Case, although case marking on nouns in Modern High German is but a residue of a formerly rich system. Adjectives display three different paradigms that are complementarily distributed depending on the determiner: the so-called weak or nominal declension is used after definite articles, the so-called strong or pronominal declension class is used after zero articles, and there is a "mixed" declension made up of endings of both other classes that is used after indefinite articles and possessives (see Table 1). In PPs, under certain conditions, the definite article may (and sometimes must) fuse with the preceding preposition, e.g. *in dem* becomes *im,* or *zu der* becomes *zur.*

*Table 1. Case inflection in German**

(a) personal pronouns

	singular					plural		
nom	*ich*	*du*	*er*	*sie*	*es*	*wir*	*ihr*	*sie*
acc	*mich*	*dich*	*ihn*	*sie*	*es*	*uns*	*euch*	*ihnen*
dat	*mir*	*dir*	*ihm*	*ihr*	*ihm*	*uns*	*euch*	*ihnen*
gen	*meiner*	*deiner*	*seiner*	*ihrer*	*seiner*	*unser*	*euer*	*ihrer*

(b) Definite and indefinite articles

	singular						plural		indefinite
	definite			indefinite			definite		
nom	*der*	*die*	*das*	*ein*	*eine*	*ein*	*die*		(zero)
acc	*den*	*die*	*das*	*einen*	*eine*	*ein*	*die*		
dat	*dem*	*der*	*dem*	*einem*	*einer*	*einem*	*den*		
gen	*des*	*der*	*des*	*eines*	*einer*	*eines*	*der*		

(c) Adjective endings†

	singular									plural		
	masculine			feminine			neuter					
	I	II	III	I	II	III	I	II	III	I	II	III
nom	*-r*	*-e*	*-r*	*-e*	*-e*	*-e*	*-s*	*-e*	*-s*	*-e*	*-n*	*-n*
acc	*-n*	*-n*	*-n*	*-e*	*-e*	*-e*	*-s*	*-e*	*-s*	*-e*	*-n*	*-n*
dat	*-m*	*-n*	*-n*	*-r*	*-n*	*-n*	*-m*	*-n*	*-n*	*-n*	*-n*	*-n*
gen	*-n*	*-n*	*-n*	*-r*	*-n*	*-n*	*-n*	*-n*	*-n*	*-r*	*-n*	*-n*

* Gender distinctions are neutralized in the plural. The use of the genitive for pronouns is obsolete and remains only with a few verbs and prepositions.

† I: strong declension; II: weak declension; III: mixed declension.

According to traditional analysis, French personal pronouns (and interrogative and relative pronouns) are inflected for Case. But, if one accepts the analysis put forth in Kaiser & Meisel (1991), (colloquial) French is adequately described as a pro-drop language.[10] This analysis entails that the tonic pronouns are optional and may be "dropped", and the clitic pronouns are not pronouns in the strict sense, but agreement markers (Kaiser & Meisel 1991; Kaiser 1992). This means that clitics are not in a Case position, but they are coindexed with the relevant argument positions (i.e. the subject or object positions) and have to agree. This is the reason why they appear to be inflected for Case. The tonic pronouns appear in Case positions, but they are invariant. The only forms that appear in Case positions and display morphological variation are the relative and interrogative pronouns *qui* and *que.*

What follows from this analysis as far as the acquisition task is concerned? Obviously, acquisition of clitics depends on a variety of factors: clitics agree for Case, for gender and number. Case assignment, as we have seen, depends on the presence of the functional category DET in the grammar. But does the acquisition of clitics really depend on the presence of DET in the grammar? Kaiser (this volume) shows that the acquisition of subject clitics, being agreement markers, is connected with the acquisition of INFL. Thus we might predict that they appear together with INFL in the grammar. Object clitics on the other hand are the spell-out of a poorly understood agreement phenomenon (see Kaiser 1992, this volume). As very little is known about this kind of agreement, linguistic theory has little to offer for plausible predictions. It rather appears that the acquisition process might shed light on the nature of grammatical structure.

Another area where Case-assignment is relevant for French is Case-assignment by prepositions. Indirect objects (other than clitics) in French receive their Case from a preposition which is very often understood as being semantically empty and being there only for the purpose of assigning Case to indirect object NPs.[11] Consider the following alternation:

(8) *Je donne le livre au   professeur*
     I give   the book to-the teacher[12]
(9) *Je le lui   donne*
     I it to-him give

The preposition is used only with lexical or pronominal indirect objects, but not with the object clitic. The interpretation of this preposition as a semantically "weak" dummy *(prépositions faibles)* is supported by Emonds' (1985) suggestion that indirect objects in German receive their dative case from a preposition that is phonetically null, yet present in phrase structure to satisfy the Licensing Condition:

(10) *Ich gebe* [$_{PP}$ 0 [$_{DP}$ *dem   Mann*]] [$_{DP}$ *das   Buch*]
      I give   the-DAT man   the-ACC book

Clitic doubling is the term for structures where both a clitic and a coindexed tonic pronoun or nominal argument are found:

(11)   *Je ne le$_i$ connais pas ce film$_i$*
         'I not it know not that film'

(12) *Je ne* l_j*'ai pas vu lui*$_j$
'I not him have not seen him'

In these cases, agreement between the clitic and the argument DP is exemplified. The use of the tonic pronoun without the related clitic is restricted to the third person, and ungrammatical in first and second persons:

(13) **Moi vais à Paris en vacances*
'Me go to Paris for holidays'

(14) *Lui vient de Paris*
him comes from Paris
'He comes from Paris.'

With a non-pronominal DP argument, the clitic is not obligatory:

(15) *Mon frère a été à Paris l'année dernière*
my brother has been to Paris last year

Obviously, this grammaticality distribution depends on the person feature of the argument. In the third person, the verb can remain unmarked, as this person seems to be some kind of default, whereas first and second have to be marked to form an agreement chain.[13]

2.3. *Functional Categories in Child Language*

Concerning the development of functional categories in child language, there are a number of possibilities all of which have been advocated in language acquisition research. Two of these positions are at the extreme points of a scale, while others argue for in-between solutions. A more detailed discussion of this matter is found in Müller (1993, this volume).

One position may be called the "No Functional Categories" approach (Radford 1986, 1990a, 1990b; Guilfoyle & Noonan 1988; Parodi 1990b, 1991; Platzack 1992). This hypothesis claims that there is a stage in child language development where the child represents a grammar that is constrained by X-bar-Syntax and other properties of UG, but is characterized by the absence of functional categories. This stage is called "early patterned speech" by Radford (1990a,b), who claims that in this stage children's phrase structures resemble adult small clauses. The opposing view claims that all functional categories are present in child grammar from the beginning (e.g. Poeppel & Wexler 1991, Hyams 1992, Weissenborn 1990) and that these categories contain null elements.

In between these extremes one finds many different proposals (see Müller 1993, this volume) stating that some functional categories may be present in early child grammar, others still lacking, or that there are positions available that are underspecified as far as their feature specification is concerned, and may be specified differently depending on the target language.

What consequences would these hypotheses have for the study of the acquisition of Case marking? If we assume the No Functional Categories Hypothesis to be correct we should be able to find a stage during which there are no functional categories in the children's grammar, although other components of UG are active, especially X-bar syntax since, according to Radford, children's early utterances are characterized as projections of lexical elements. This means that there should be no evidence for COMP, INFL or DET, thus no finite verbs, no Case-marked noun phrases or definiteness effects, no overt complementizers and, in German, no V2 effects. Presence of determiners should be random since they are not placed in an obligatory head position, but adjoined to NP in some way. This suggestion has been made by Roeper (1992).[14] He assumes that some children (but not necessarily all) make use of a so-called "default adjunction capacity" which leads them to adjoin un-analyzed elements to other, already identified categories. A clause containing an early complementizer, at a time when INFL is already accessible, would have the following structure:

(16)

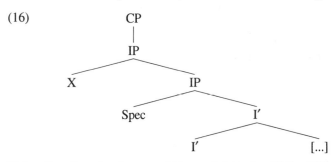

This adjunction structure would be maintained until the "X"-element has been correctly analyzed and identified, and integrated into the grammar.

The crucial claim of this class of hypotheses is that it presupposes (i) X-bar type hierarchical structures in these early utterances and assumes (ii) that the functional categories come in later, and that the Case Filter, being a constraint on the distribution of a functional category, is not operative. The alternative would be to claim that the Case Filter would be reformulated after the acquisition of functional categories, an assumption that is counter-intuitive if we want to see the Case Filter as a principle of UG. If the Case Filter is not yet operative (or rather, applying vacuously since the category it refers to is not yet existent in the grammar), we should expect children's noun phrases to appear in positions where they would be ungrammatical in adult language. For example, we should find prepositionless adverbial phrases because in these phrases the preposition is needed to assign Case to the noun that expresses place, direction or time. As a diagnostic tool, this criterion, on the other hand, loses force because the child might use prepositions not because they are needed for structural reasons, but because of the local or temporal meaning the convey. Another prediction made by this hypothesis is that occurrence of determiners would not be accidental, as the child creates the adjunct position for the purpose to house an element — in this case the determiner — s/he has extracted from the intonation contour of the target; or we should find that children do not systematically distinguish between subjects and non-subjects, although this distinction is required in the target language.

The opposite position, labeled "skeleton theory" by Müller (this volume), assumes that the child, as soon as UG as a module of his cognition has matured or been activated, possesses fully articulated phrase structure representations. The positions for functional categories are present, but morphologically under-specified. This assumption suffers from two drawbacks as far as Case and DPs are concerned: First, the presence of all functional categories in child grammar from early on would mean that the number of functional categories is universally fixed, and second and more important, we would have to explain how children's noun phrases could be interpreted as being DPs and still not be constrained by the Case Filter.

3.   Subjects and Data

The subjects of this study are two of the children of the DUFDE corpus, a boy, Pascal, and a girl, Annika. The children have been studied from 1;8,22 to 4;10,4 (Pascal) and from 2;0,17 to 3;10,26 (Annika). The MLU values and further details are given in chapter 2 in this volume.

3.1. *Previous Studies*

The development of Case marking has been investigated in four other children from the DUFDE project. Here I will summarize the findings by Meisel (1986) and Parodi (1989, 1990a,b).

The child studied in Parodi (1990b), Christophe, is remarkable since he gave up French for a while and started using the language again after some time. In German, this child started to use precursors of personal pronouns at 2;2, as well as uninflected indefinite articles. Around 3;0 accusative and dative markings were present, but there were still unmarked forms. In French, he set out with *ça,* and at 2;2 *moi* and local uses of *à* were added. Between 2;5 and 2;8, he rarely used French at all and returned to the use of *ça* reported for the earliest stages. From 3;3 many tonic subject pronouns were reported, and from 3;4 also subject clitics, with object clitics coming in at 3;6. After 3;8, French deteriorated again.

The other child studied by Parodi (1989, 1990a), Ivar, appears to develop, until 2;11, a two-way system of Case marking in German: Forms governed by INFL are marked as nominative, forms governed by V or P are marked as non-nominative. As this child uses both accusative and dative forms in these contexts, one cannot say which category he uses for these markings. In French, he uses many subject clitics at 2;9, as well as some tonic subject pronouns. As a whole, developments in French happen earlier than in German. After 3;2, there are also many object clitics.

Meisel (1986) studied two children, Caroline and Pierre, from age 1;0 to 4;0 and summarizes their development by postulating three stages. In German, for both children, nominative pronouns come in first, the first determiners being *die* and *der.* Around 2;7 and 2;11, respectively, the children produce the first accusative forms. After that, the two children behave differently: Caroline who develops faster anyway uses the first datives after 2;11, whereas Pierre does not use these forms until the end of the investigation period. In French, Caroline produces determiners and precursors of pronouns at 2;0. Around 2;4, partitive articles and pronouns appear, and from then on the inventory of both subject and object pronouns grows. After 3;3, the use of *moi* and *toi* as subject pronouns is established. Pierre, on the other hand, starts out with a few subject pronouns until 2;11. Then he develops both determiners and object pronouns after 3;1. One must note here that this study was carried out in a different theoretical framework, and that the ages given are rather higher than those of Parodi and — as we will see — myself since Meisel accepted productive use of morphological contrasts as the only decisive evidence for the acquisition of a category.

What is most important is that, although we observe a certain amount of individual variation, the children's development appears to follow a uniform pattern. After a phase during which no morphological distinctions on determiners and pronouns can be made out, the distinction between nominative and non-nominative forms is acquired. The distinction (in German) between accusative and dative is a second step. For French, developmental steps are not equally clear, as Case distinctions do not have as obvious effects on the grammar. Although the development of Christophe displays peculiar features due to his temporary loss of French, he in part follows the same pattern.

3.2. Pascal

In Pascal's case, it has been possible to make out successive stages in the development of both French and German that are identified by characteristic traits.[15]

3.2.1. German

At the first stage, up to 1;8,22, Pascal uses no pronouns at all except two occurrences of *das* (and several of *a,* which seems to be a variant of French *ça* and is used in formulaic expressions):

(17)   *das   ja*   (Pa 1;8,22)
         that-one, yes

As far as determiners are concerned, there is just a sample of forms as *ein,* its variants *a* and *'ne* (=*eine*), or *das.* These forms occur solely in contexts that might be classified as nominative, but they are phonetically underspecified, i.e. undetermined as to their case form:

(18)   a.   *ein/a schiff*   (Pa 1;8,22)
            'one/a ship'
       b.   *ne blum(a/e)*   (Pa 1;8,22)
            'a flower'

The impression one gets from these forms is that the child knows that there is a position to be filled, but that his phonetic representation to go into this position is somehow "underspecified" and so he inserts some kind of filler or "shadow" syllable (Demuth 1992, Peters & Menn 1990) — but see below for discussion.

At the second stage, which spans from approx. 1;9,30 to 2;4,7, the inventory expands rapidly. Pascal acquires the whole range of personal pronouns except for *es, man* and *wir,* and a number of weak and strong demonstratives. Except for one stray form at 2;2,6:

(19)   Adult: *womit fangen wir an?*
                  'what do we begin with?'
        Child: *das*   (Pa 2;2,26)
                  'that'

there are no datives or dative contexts in this stage. At the second stage an
inventory of determiners for nominative and accusative is acquired.

We find that the ratio of correct accusative determiners (tokens) in relation
to all accusative determiners in the recordings grows from 0.5 at 1;9,30 to 0.8
at 2;4,7. What is more interesting is that the relative proportion of "underspecified" forms decreases from 0.55 for pronouns (all cases) and 0.68 for
determiners (all cases) at 1;9,30 to 0.08 for pronouns (all cases) and 0.16 for
determiners (all cases) at 2;4,7. Of the underspecified pronouns at 2;4,7, all six
are accusatives governed by a preposition. The development is clarified in the
graphs in Figures 1 and 2.

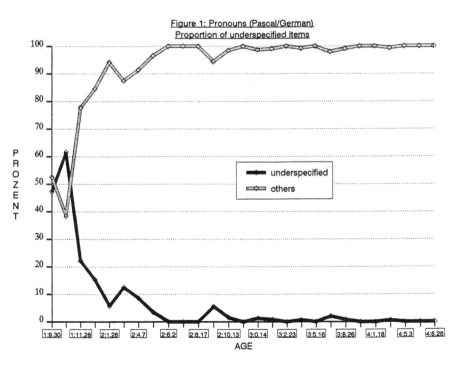

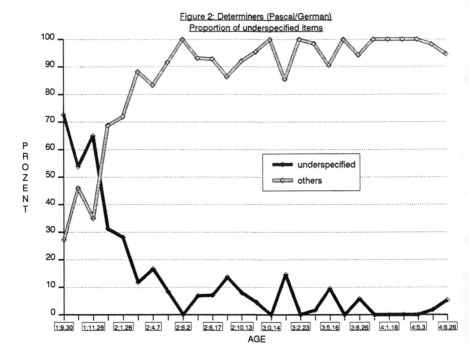

At 2;2,26 we find the first correct dative determiner:

(20)　　*der setz auf dem*　　　　*bett*　　　　　　　　(Pa 2;2,26)
　　　　that one sits on the-DAT bed
　　　　'He is sitting on the bed.'

At the third stage, which I assume to range from 2;4,7 to 2;8,17, many changes occur: this stage is mainly a period of transition. At 2;5,5, a new type of error occurs: dative forms are overgeneralized to accusative contexts. The utterance type in question is:

(21)　　*für dir und (für/von) mir*　　　　　　　　　　(Pa 2;5,5)
　　　　'for you-DAT and for/from me-DAT'

If the second preposition is supposed to be *von,* the dative would be correct, since this is the correct case, but the point I want to make is sufficiently supported by the first part of the utterance.

There is one utterance at this age where an accusative pronoun within a PP is used correctly:

(22) Adult: *wo kommt das hin?*
      'where does this go?'
      Child: *da in diese*   (Pa 2;5,5)
      'there in that-one-ACC'

But there is also evidence from 2;4,7 where the correct dative determiner is used:

(23)   *im eis*   (Pa 2;4,7)
         'in-the-DAT ice'

In some utterances, the determiner is absent although required by the target:

(24)   *in wa[z]er*   (Pa 2;4,7)
         'in water'

More prepositional phrases, but now with the "wrong" dative pronoun, are used two months later:

(25) a. *und- und noch für dir*   (Pa 2;6,2)
          'and still for you-DAT'
      b. *für mir*   (Pa 2;6,2)
          'for me-DAT'

After the transitory period between 2;4,7 and 2;8,17, there follows a longer period (stage IV) where we find a large number of accusative pronouns without and dative pronouns with prepositions. At 2;9,16, we find the first target-like accusative pronoun in the domain of a preposition:

(26)   Pascal
         ein für dich   (2;9,13)
         'one for you-ACC'

One of the most striking features of this stage of development is the quantitative increase of prepositional phrases. The majority of these contexts is dative, so we find an enormous growth of the proportion of datives (target-like or not) among all non-nominative determiners: the ratio grows from 0.2 at 2;7,0 to 0.45 at 3;4,14, and 0.9 at 4;10,4. But this increase in the use of datives is accompanied by a deteriorating rate of performance; Table 2 shows the variability of morphological forms for determiners in dative contexts. For pronouns, similar statements cannot be made since their number is too low to allow significant generalizations of this sort.

Table 2. Surface form employed (proportion) for determiners in dative contexts (Pascal/German)

age	dat	nom	acc	?	tokens
2;4,7	1.0				1
2;5,5			1.0	2	
2;6,2	—	—	—	—	0
2;7,0			1.0	2	
2;8,17	1.0				2
2;9,16		1.0		1	
2;10,13	0.33		0.67		6
2;11,11	0.2	0.2	0.2	0.4	5
3;0,17	1.0				2
3;1,20	0.33	0.16	0.16	0.33	6
3;2,23	0.5		0.5		2
3;4,14	0.46		0.53	0.07	15
3;5,16	—	—	—	—	0
3;6,29	1.0				3
3;8,26	0.54		0.39		13
4;0,12	—	—	—	—	0
4;1,18	0.67		0.33		6
4;4,5	0.37		0.63		19
4;5,3	1.0				2
4;6,13	0.64		0.36		11
4;6,28	0.53		0.41	0.06	17
4;10,4	0.9		0.1		10

As from 2;4,7 onwards, obviously, the dative has been associated with prepositions by Pascal, an interpretation that is supported by overgeneralizations of dative forms to accusative contexts when these are governed by a preposition, and by the near exclusive occurrence of dative contexts in the governing domain of a preposition. This association seems to break up after around 2;10, and the ensuing problems last at least until 4;6.[16]

(27) a. *is- is in mein buch lurchi*   (Pa 2;10,13)
          'is in my book, lurchi'
      b. *ich springe über du*   (Pa 2;10,13)
          'I jump over you-NOM'

c.   *ein ei auf eine schnecke*   (Pa 2;11,11)
     'an egg on a-ACC snail'; pointing to picture of
     snail sitting on an egg
d.   *und auf ein   bein stehen*   (Pa 3;1,20)
     and on one-ACC leg stand
     'and to stand on one leg'
e.   Adult: *auf'm-dat spielplatz? und da   war kein anderes Kind?*
            in the   playground? and there was no   other   child
     Child: *auf de(n) spielplatz*   (Pa 3;1,20)
            'in the-ACC playground'
f.   *denn noch mit den hammer*   (Pa 3;2,23)
     'and then with the-ACC hammer'
g.   *ja, in die toilette ist eine leiter*   (Pa 3;4,14)
     'yes, in the-ACC bathroom is a ladder'
h.   *ja, in die küche ist ein käse*   (Pa 3;4,14)
     'yes, in the-ACC kitchen is some cheese'
i.   *ja, jetzt geht's mit die augen wo die klebt nicht mehr* (Pa 3;4,14)
     'yes, now it's okay with the-ACC eyes, now that they is no
     longer stuck'; talking about his conjunctivitis getting better

What is interesting is that these problems occur with datives only. For accusatives we find that the use of deviant forms is very rare. Considering the fact that almost all determiners in dative contexts as well as the majority of pronouns occur within a PP, one is led to attribute these problems to Case assignment by a preposition, and not to problems with lexical Case.

Verbs that assign lexical Case are rare in Pascal's speech. I have studied the use of both *helfen* and *aider* 'help', as these two verbs should be problematic for children because *aider* assigns objective case in French, but a lexical dative in German. In the whole corpus there were but four uses of *helfen* (all in the same recording), and they all are appropriate:[17]

(28) a.   *und wenn man da ihnen hilft, denn*   (Pa 4;6,13)
           'and if one helps them-DAT there, then...'
      b.   *wenn man da ihnen hilft, denn kriegt man eine maulwurfkarte*
                                                               (Pa 4;6,13)
           'and if one helps them-DAT there, one gets a mole card'; talking
           about board game with picture cards
      c.   *wenn man ihnen hilft*   (Pa 4;6,13)
           'if one helps them-DAT'

d. *wir trinken und helfen ihnen ja?*   (Pa 4;6,13)
    'we drink and help them-DAT, okay?'

In the French data there are only four uses of aider:

(29) a. *tu t'aides (=tu m'aides)*   (Pa 2;4,7)
         'you help me'

     b. *du-du-du aides ça*   (Pa 2;6,2)
         you   help that
         'you help me with that'(?)

     c. *non j'aide pas   maman*   (Pa 4;4,5)
         no, I help Mummy not
         'no, I won't help mummy'

     d. *et ici, si on veut l'aider*   (Pa 4;10,4)
         'and here, if one wants to help them'

All in all, we find the following succession of stages in the development of
Case marking for Pascal:

(30)

I [until 1;8,22]   no inflection; mostly case-neutral forms, no pronouns, very
                   few determiners

II [1;9–2;4]   few determiners, few pronouns, replacement of underspecified
                   by nominative forms, accusative often not target-like

III [2;5–2;9]   improvement of accusative, expansion of lexical inventory,
                   few prepositional phrases (governing dative)

IV [2;10–3;6]   expansion of PP's, Case marking of prepositional comple-
                   ments problematic both for dative and accusative, rapidly
                   increasing inventory

V [3;7–≈4;7]   improvement of accusative, fewer pronouns within PP's,
                   determiners within PP still problematic

The notion of "stage" here shall not mean that one type of linguistic
behavior is replaced by another type, but rather that the set of possible structures
grows: The new structures are added to the older ones, but the older ones are not
given up completely.[18] This will be even more evident for Annika.

3.2.2. *French*

In Pascal's French, there is an initial period where few potentially
Case-marked categories are found. He uses nearly no pronouns, and apart from

the fact that there are also very few noun phrases, also potential Case assigners, i.e. verbs and prepositions, are mostly absent. This stage lasts until 1;8,30, which is, as we shall see, slightly longer than the comparable stage in Pascal's German. The most frequent pronoun is *ça:*

(31) a. Adult: *on prend celui-là?*
          'one takes that one?'
          Child: *celui-là*   (Pa 1;8,22)
          'that one'
      b. *[sese] ça* (=?que c'est ça?)   (Pa 1;8,30)
          'what is this?'

and there are a few clitics:

(32)   *on (r)egarde das*   (Pa 1;8,22)
          'one looks at that'

Also Parodi (1990b) and Meisel (1986) have noted that *on* appears very early.

After that we find increasingly more subject clitics, and the first tonic pronoun appears at 1;11,28:

(33) a. *ça c'est un monsieur*   (Pa 1;11,28)
          'that one is a man'
      b. Adult: *tu connais le jardin d'enfants toi?*
          'you know the kindergarten, you?'
          Child: *moi aussi* (=?*moi aussi je vais au jardin d'enfants*)
          me too   (Pa 1;11,28)
          'I go to the kindergarten, too'

Although the first pronominal objects appear at 1;8,22, they remain rare until 2;4,7 when the frequency of direct object pronouns rises suddenly. A few weeks before that the frequency of noun phrases with a determiner rises considerably, though not drastically at 2;0,30. At 2;4,7, there are more changes: we find that Pascal uses many more subject clitics, tonic subject pronouns, and more prepositional complements:

(34) a. *moi aussi j'aime les maisons*   (Pa 2;4,7)
          'me too, I like the houses'
      b. *moi j'ai (tout) mangé [ə] fromage*   (Pa 2;4,7)
          'me, I have eaten all the cheese'
      c. *il est là le nounours du/de papa*   (Pa 2;4,7)
          'it is there, the teddy of (the) father'

What is especially striking is the late appearance not only of indirect object clitics, but also of pronominal and lexical indirect objects. The first lexical indirect object is used at 2;10,13:

(35)   *au(x) petit(s) giraffe(s)*   (Pa 2;10,13)
         'to the small giraffe(s)'

The first indirect object clitic appears at 3;2,23:

(36)   *mais faut me montrer aussi*   (Pa 3;2,23)
         'but [it] is necessary to show [it] to me, too'

At 3;4,14 we find the first 3rd person indirect object clitics, which differ from the first and second person clitics as they are not homophonous with their direct object counterparts:

(37) a. *va lui   donner*   (Pa 3;4,14)
         go to-him give
         'I'm going to give it to them'
     b. *on va lui donner [salə]*[19]   (Pa 3;4,14)
         'we are going to give [salə] to him'

So I would like to construct a sequence of stages for French that looks like this:

(38) Pascal:

I [until 1;9]   few (deictic) pronouns, few determiners no tonic pronouns
IIa [1;10–1;11]   more pronouns, mostly clitics and "others"
                   incl. *ça*. Transition from IIa to IIb
IIb [2;0–2;2]   might be characterized by increase in noun phrases with
                   determiners
III [2;2–2;9]   productive use of subject clitics and tonic pronouns
(IV [2;10 f.]   development of indirect objects)

It is quite clear that the development of these forms is not, as in the case of German, dependent on the acquisition of a morphological paradigm. As Kaiser (this volume) has shown, one has to distinguish between tonic pronouns on the one hand and clitics on the other, and, more specifically, between subject and object clitics. The interpretation of French as a *pro*-drop-language entails that all pronouns except the clitics have to appear in Case positions, but not all of these positions have to be filled with lexical material. The clitics are coindexed with their respective antecedents and agree in gender, number, and Case.

It is on this level, that of syntactic representation, that the development of French and German is connected: the onset of "grammar" in the sense that the child's utterances are constrained by UG (Bickerton 1990; Meisel 1991a), and the question of the development of functional categories.

3.3. Annika

Annika's development is quite different from Pascal's. In his case, it was possible to distinguish successive developmental steps along a path that was mostly structure-oriented. In Annika's case, on the other hand, we are left with a bewildering picture. As the development of morphological case marking in German does not give conclusive evidence as to Annika's course of acquisition, as we shall see, I want to look for possible evidence for the acquisition of functional categories, especially the verbal functional category INFL.

The motivation for this approach is that the acquisition and integration of INFL has two different consequences for Case marking: on the one hand, INFL (or the two verbal functional categories) allows word order variation in German that makes morphological differentiation of subject and object necessary. On the other hand, it is only with the integration of INFL that the subject may be moved out of its D-structure position and into a Case position, as the specifier of INFL provides a landing-site.[20]

3.3.1. German

I have examined all those utterances that contain a lexically realized Case assigner, i.e. a (finite or nonfinite) verb and/or a preposition. In general, Annika's speech is less conclusive as to the state of grammatical development since she talks less than Pascal.

At 2;0,17, the only utterance containing a lexically realized Case assigner is:

(39) *auch apfel eß*   (An 2;0,17)
       also apple eat
       'he shall eat an apple, too'; feeding a toy monkey

It is impossible to tell whether the finite verb in this utterance is really a finite form or rather a performance "error", since it is still in final position, and both the determiner of the object noun phrase as well as the subject are missing.[21] This word order pattern remains for a long time. At 2;2,22 there are four utterances with the structure "object–nonfinite verb".

(40) a. *[das en glaise] zumache.n (= das gleich zumachen)* (An 2;2,22)
         'close that one right away'
     b. *das auch tasse legen*   (An 2;2,22)
         that too cup put
         'put that in cup, too'

In the last utterance, there is a defective PP that lacks both preposition and determiner. The realization of a Goal without a preposition or a determiner is clearly not targetlike for German, and thus indicates at least the absence of functional categories.

One utterance contains a finite verb in second position with a topicalized object:[22]

(41) *das sagt papi*   (An 2;2,22)
      'daddy says this'

All pronouns in this recording are neuter *das,* the two other nouns are undetermined (*tasse, papi*). At 2;4,18, there are three utterances with the order "object–nonfinite verb", and there are six V2-constructions, two of which are OVS, one is AdvVS, and the remaining are SV:

(42) a. *das hol [is] (=ich)*   (An 2;4,18)
         'that one I get'
     b. *der [vast] (=wäscht)*   (An 2;4,18)
         'that one washes'
     c. *da sitz [is] (=ich)*   (An 2;4,18)
         'there I sit'
     d. *ich mach zu*   (An 2;4,18)
         I make shut
         'I close'; closing a drawer

Of the 61 pronouns in this recording,[23] only 17 appear in potentially Case-assigning contexts; for determiners the ratio is two out of 21. In all these cases, these forms are neuter except for the pronoun *ich* 'I', realized as [is].

At 2;6,18, the majority of utterances fall in two classes: either they are verb-final with a nonfinite verb, or they are verb-second with a finite verb. The verbfinal utterances form the smallest group of these; they belong to an earlier stage of development and their structure is due to the headedness parameter being set to "head-final" for the category V in German.

As the rich sample of V2-constructions shows, it is evident that Annika has acquired verb-second by this time and has integrated some functional category into her grammar to be used as landing-site for moved noun phrases, so we need not bother much about these nonfinite constructions.[24] The following represent about half of Annika's V2-utterances from this date:

(43) a. *es regnet nicht*   (An 2;6,18)
          it rains   not
          'it is not raining'

      b. *und caro nimmt das*   (An 2;6,18)
          'and Caro takes that'

      c. *du behalst (=behältst) das*   (An 2;6,18)
          'you keep that'

      d. *haare hat [s] haare*   (An 2;6,18)
          'hairs has it(?), hairs'; talking about how
          to draw a sun

      e. *das is gut*   (An 2;6,18)
          'that is good'

      f. *das is weg*   (An 2;6,18)
          'that is gone'

      g. *und das is mein*   (An 2;6,18)
          'that is mine'; possessive pronoun unmarked
          for gender, number or case

      h. *das is grünes*   (An 2;6,18)
          'that is green-one'; adjective inflected as
          if indefinite article preceded

      i. *ja ich mal hier*   (An 2;6,18)
          'yes I paint here'

      j. *dann mach ich ein haus*   (An 2;6,18)
          'then I make a house'

      k. *das is ein mund*   (An 2;6,18)
          'that is a mouth'

Note that most of these utterances are SVX, also other structures occur as well.

There are also verb-initial constructions at this age, most of which are questions. Other utterances are cases where the first constituent has been left out. With virtually all of these, it is the direct object that is missing:

(44) a. *darf man*   (An 2;6,18)
          may one
          'one may do that'

b.   *hat er nicht*   (An 2;6,18)
has he not
'he hasn't got/done such a thing'

Of the 116 pronouns in this recording, 46 appear in potential Case assigning contexts. For determiners, the ratio is three out of 42, and they are all indefinites.[25]

Although the recording at 2;7,29 does not contain many verbs, it is interesting to note that these are exclusively in second position, and various constituents are placed in the topic position:

(45) a.   *so   geht das*   (An 2;7,29)
           like-that it   goes
           'that's how it works'
      b.   *das is schöner*   (An 2;7,29)
           'that one is more beautiful'
      c.   *wo's is da löffel*   (An 2;7,29)
           'where is the spoon'

At 2;9,31, there are 23 V2-utterances and five verbfinal utterances. This indicates that Annika has a good command of the requested structures, yet still most pronouns and determiners are neuter or plural so that necessary gender and case differentiations are reduced to a minimum. There are several types of V2 structures:

(46) a.   *ich weiß nicht*   (An 2;9,31)
           I   know not
           'I don't know'
      b.   *ich mach ganz laut*   (An 2;9,31)
           I   make very loud
           'I do it very loudly'
      c.   *ich kann nicht*   (An 2;9,31)
           'I cannot'
      d.   *ich will ni[s] (= ?nicht/nämlich) keinen fisch haben* (An 2;9,31)
           I   want not/namely   no   fish have
           'I don't want to have any fish (you know)'
      e.   *ich koch alles*   (An 2;9,31)
           'I cook everything'
      f.   *ich will alles   zu kochen haben*   (An 2;9,31)
           I   want everything to cook   have
           'I want to have everything I need for cooking'

g. *das ist ein krodil (=krokodil)* (An 2;9,31)
'that is a crocodile'

h. *für die tiere mach ich ein haus* (An 2;9,31)
'for the animals I make a house'

i. *zu   ist jetzt das* (An 2;9,31)
closed is now that
'that is now closed'

j. *was ist denn das* (An 2;9,31)
'what is that'

A first analysis of the sentence structures that Annika uses indicates that in her German, by 2;6,18 at the latest there are two functional categories above VP. One of them is needed as a landing site for the movement of finite verbs that have to incorporate their inflectional affixes, the other obviously attracts the verb similar to the head COMP in adult German, thus allowing the Spec-CP position to be used as a landing site for topicalized elements. Still, it is not at all clear that these categories can be identified with COMP and INFL as they are specified in adult German. They might be specified differently, e.g. as TNS (tense) and AGR (agreement). Müller (this volume) points out that the terms INFL and COMP are completely arbitrary under these assumptions (see also Meisel & Müller 1992). What is important is that there are two functional categories available.

Assuming that the interpretation of the data, namely, that at about 2;6 INFL is implemented in Annika's German, is correct, are we able to make out some step in the acquisition of Case marking similar to that observed in Pascal's data at around 2;4? Let's have a look at the morphological aspects of Case marking.

If one looks at the graphs in Figures 3 and 4 that display the proportion of the various Case contexts for determiners and pronouns, one notes a striking difference: with pronouns, after a phase of considerable variation lasting up to 2;6,18, there are about two thirds nominatives and one third accusatives, with datives coming in at 3;0,29 and never rising above 8%. The huge proportion of nominative contexts can be partly explained by the fact that shifter pronouns also in formulaic utterances like *weiß ich nicht* 'I don't know' have been counted. With determiners, on the other hand, there is a lot of variation. There are 75% nominative contexts at 2;5,18, and 0% at 2;10,27. There are also relatively more dative contexts than with pronouns, between 12% at 3;0,29 and 35% at 3;8,24. I think that this is due to the functions of pronouns and determined nouns in discourse: Pronouns refer to known participants of the situation, whereas

determined nouns are used to introduce new participants. As children prefer
actor–action sequences when reporting an event, they are apt to use an enormous
quantity of subject pronouns.

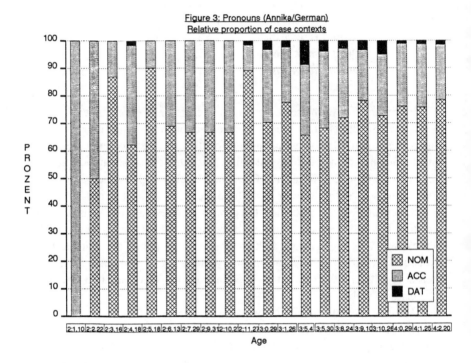

Figure 3: Pronouns (Annika/German)
Relative proportion of case contexts

Annika masters the morphological aspects of Case marking very well, in
fact, she makes very few errors, a fact I want to attribute to an avoidance
strategy. In the earlier recordings, up to about 2;10,27, there are very few forms
other than the pronoun *das* 'that', the shifter pronouns *ich* 'I' und *du* 'you', and
the neuter determiner *das* 'the'. This means that the majority of Case contexts
in her speech require neuter pronouns and determiners, and on neuter forms, as
opposed to masculine and feminine forms, accusative and nominative cannot be
distinguished. It is only as late as 3;1,26 that a larger inventory of pronouns and
determiners is documented.

How should this behavior be explained? One hypothesis might be that
Annika has not mastered gender before 3 years, but this is implausible in the
light of the facts. If Annika had problems with gender, she would be expected
to mark it randomly and make many mistakes, but this is not the case. Rather,

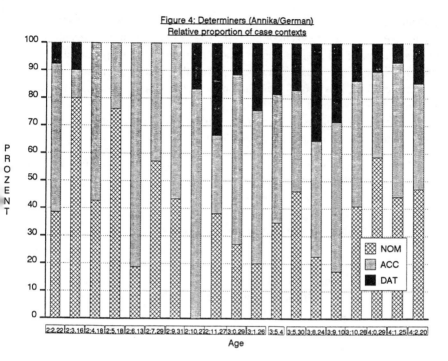

Figure 4: Determiners (Annika/German)
Relative proportion of case contexts

the strictness with which she uses only correctly classified neuter words indicates that she is fully aware of gender distinctions.[26] She makes use of this knowledge and prefers neuter words in order to circumvent the necessity to apply morphological Case marking. She knows that there is something in the morphology of masculine and feminine pronouns and determiners that she does not cope with (or does not want to be bothered with), and goes out of her way to achieve this aim. This behavior lasts as long as about 3;0 or 3;1. Still I do not want to interpret these facts as evidence for late acquisition of abstract Case, in analogy to Pascal where the mastery of the nominative–accusative distinction was understood in this way.

3.3.2. French

What can we expect in the development of the use of pronominal forms in Annika's French, given the discussion in the first section? The task is on the one hand to integrate the functional category DET in the grammar, on the other hand to acquire the inventory of forms and their appropriate distribution in sentence structure. With the development of DET, the Case Filter becomes applicable, and the distribution of all nominal and pronominal elements except the clitics is constrained by it. As these forms, except for the relative pronouns, are not inflected for Case, it is "only" their distribution and person, gender and number agreement that have to be figured out.

Starting with subjects, we find that in the beginning, the vast majority of pronominal forms are *ça* and the subject clitic *il*:

(47) a. *ça aussi dort*   (An 2;0,17)
          'that one also sleeps'

      b. *ça   auch abeille*   (An 2;1,10)
          that-one also bee
          'that is a bee, too'; points to a picture

      c. *[sa e le raiʎ]*   (An 2;2,22)
          'that is the rails'

      d. *ça   petit   [uwi]llage*   (An 2;3,16)
          that small shell; "[uwi]llage"=coquillage
          'that is a small shell'

      e. *ça marron*   (An 2;4,18)
          'that brown'; A. points to color'

(48) a. *il dort*   (An 2;0,17)
          'he sleeps'

      b. *papa [i ε la pa] (=il est là pas)*   (An 2;2,22)
          'Daddy, he is not here'

      c. *elle joue*   (An 2;5,18)
          'she plays'

      d. *non i.l est pas là*   (An 2;5,18)
          'no, it is not here?'

      e. *elle est là*   (An 2;5,18)
          'she is there'

As we can see, the clitic forms are very rare, and do not appear as regularly as *ça*. Apart from a few instances, Annika uses no tonic pronouns. Around 2;6,13, however, the frequency of the clitics rises sharply, and they begin to be used at least as often, if not more, as *ça*:[27]

(49) a. *heum j'sais pas*   (An 2;6,13)
          'oh I don't know'

b. *j'veux pas*   (An 2;6,13)
    'I don't want'
c. *(il) [ə] bien*   (An 2;6,13)
    'he is alright'
d. *c'est [p]omme (=comme) ça*   (An 2;6,13)
    'it is like that'
e. *c'est maman*   (An 2;6,13)
    'that is Mummy'
f. *c'est cassé*   (An 2;7,29)
    'that is broken'
g. *on range*   (An 2;7,29)
    'we tidy up'
h. *j'sais pas (où)*   (An 2;7,29)
    'I don't know where'
i. *il mange*   (An 2;9,31)
    'he eats?'
j. *il mange le pont*   (An 2;9,31)
    'he eats the bridge'; playing with bricks and plush animals
k. *où il est, le l'autre coquillage*   (An 2;9,31)
    'where is it, the other shell'
l. *si c'est la peinture*   (An 2;9,31)
    'yes, that is the paint'
m. *là-dedans il est, le papa*   (An 2;9,31)
    'in there he is, the father'
n. *c'est, c'est moi*   (An 2;9,31)
    'that is, that is me'

Until 2;9,31, there are only five uses of tonic subject pronouns. As from 2;11,27, their frequency rises as well:

(50) a. *non, c'est moi*   (An 2;11,27)
         'no, it is me'
     b. *moi là et puis toi ça*   (An 2;11,27)
         'I there and then you this'; sharing playthings with adult)
     c. *moi aussi*   (An 2;11,27)
         'me too'
     d. *toi avec ça*   (An 2;11,27)
         'you with that one'; giving adult a pencil to draw with

e. *toi aussi*   (An 3;1,26)
    'you too?'
f. *moi aime de chocolat*   (An 3;1,26)
    'I love chocolat'
g. *non toi as pas de téléphone*   (An 3;1,26)
    'no you don't have a telephone'
h. *non moi fais ça*   (An 3;1,26)
    'no I do this'
i. *c'est moi annika [nɛ] sonia [...]*   (An 3;2,24)
    'it is me, Annika, no, Sonia'; looking at photograph
    of children on playground
j. Adult: *qui c'est qui l'a construit comme ça?*
             'who was it who built it like that'
    Child: *moi pas*   (An 3;2,24)
             'me not'
k. *moi a   rien   du tout*   (An 3;2,24)
    me   has nothing at all
    'I have nothing at all'

Annika leaves out the clitic when using the tonic pronoun of the first person, although this usage is restricted to the third person. She continues to do so at 3;7,13:

(51) a. *moi a   cassé*   (An 3;7,13)
          I   has broken
          'I have broken it'
      b. *mais avec qui   a   fait   moi le   œuf?*   (An 3;7,13)
          but with whom has made me the egg
          'but with whom have I made [i.e. colored] the egg?'

Although the forms have been acquired, Annika seems to have problems with subject-verb agreement, as can be seen from the examples in (51). Annika never uses a tonic subject pronoun together with a subject clitic. With clitics, the agreement problems illustrated above do not occur. These structures indicate that subject clitics indeed are to be regarded as spell-out of the AGR component of INFL. Whenever subject clitics of the first or second persons are absent from the utterance, the verb does not agree. In fact, many utterances that have been transcribed as if the verb did agree, may indeed lack subject–verb agreement, but the difference cannot be heard since the differentiation has been lost in the spoken language. Thus not only the utterances in (51), but also some of those in (50) might be characterized by the lack of subject–verb agreement, i.e. (50f,g,h,k)

The first direct object clitics occur at 2;6,13, and the first tonic direct object pronouns occurs at 3;9,19. Nominal and pronominal (including *ça*) direct objects are present from the first recording. In the earlier stages there is only one argument realized in each utterance:

(52) a. *ça aussi*   (An 2;0,17)
          'this too?'
      b. *ça encore*   (An 2;0,17)
          'this too'
      c. Adult: *dans laquelle celle-là ou celle-là?*
                  'into which one, this one or this one?)
          Child: *celle-là*   (An 2;0,17)
                  'this one there'
      d. *personne*   (An 2;2,22)
          'nobody'; playing with a telephone
      e. *celui-là*   (An 2;2,22)
          'that one'; points to object
      f. *ça aussi*   (An 2;2,22)
          'this one too'
      g. *ensuite ça*
          'and then this'; being asked what to play next

Annika uses "transitive" constructions only as late as 2;6,13, but in these the verb may be omitted:

(53) a. *et puis pascale un maison*   (An 2;6,13)
          'and then pascale [makes] a house'
      b. *a annika aussi un sapin*   (An 2;9,13)
          'has Annika also a fir-tree?'
      c. *tout tout annika veut, tout [e]*   (An 2;9,13)
          'all all Annika wants, all eh?'
      d. Adult: *et qu'est-ce qu'il fait cet éléphant?*
                  'and what is he doing, that elephant?'
          Child: *il mange le pont*   (An 2;9,13)
                  'he eats the bridge'
      e. attends annika fait un un autre pont   (An 2;9,13)
          'wait Annika makes another bridge'

What we can note for the time being is that the first direct object clitic coincides
with the frequency rise for subject clitics.

The treatment of *ça* is rather difficult. In some cases, it behaves syntactically like a tonic pronoun, e.g. undergoes clitic doubling:

(54) a. *ça c'est là*   (An 2;4,18)
          'that, it is there'

      b. *eh c'est cassé ça*   (An 2;7,29)
          'it is broken, that one'

      c. *ça c'est le [efa] (=éléphant). maintenant*   (An 2;9,31)
          'that, it is the elephant? now?'

      d. *c'est [tõb] (=tombé?) ça*   (An 3;0,29)
          'it has fallen down, that one'

But in the majority of uses, *ça* functions as a dummy form, being neutral as far
as gender and number are concerned, and has strong deictic value as it supports
and confirms an accompanying gesture.[28] Thus the lack of gender and number
differentiation is compensated by non-linguistic information, i.e. can be gained
from the context. This behavior parallels the overwhelming use of neuter and
plural forms in German.

There are nearly no indirect objects in the French recordings. In the
observation period there is only one indirect object clitic:

(55)   *(rendre)   me   ça*   (An 3;1,26)
          return-INF me-OBJ CL that
          'return that-one to me'

The related tonic forms appear first at 2;11,27:

(56)   *c'est à moi*   (An 2;11,27)
          'it belongs to me?'

and again at 3;1,26:

(57) a. *non ça   rendre   à moi ça*   (An 3;1,26)
          no that-one return-INF to me that-one
          'give that back to me!'

      b. *non à moi ça   là*   (An 3;1,26)
          no to me that one there
          'that doesn't belong to me'

    c.   *c'est à moi*   (An 3;1,26)
        'it belongs to me'
    d.   *c'est à moi*   (An 3;1,26)
        'it belongs to me'
    e.   *parce que ça à moi*   (An 3;1,26)
        because   that to me
        'because that belongs to me'

Then there is a pause with only one use at 3;7,2, and more examples at 3;8,24 and 3;10,26:

(58) a.   *c'est à moi*   (An 3;7,2)
        'it belongs to me'
    b.   *ah non c'est à moi*   (An 3;8,24)
        'oh no, it belongs to me'
    c.   *ça   à toi*   (An 3;8,24)
        that one to you
        'that one belongs to you'
    d.   *dis-moi pas*   (An 3;10,26)
        'tell-me not'; not wanting to be told a word
        she doesn't remember immediately
    e.   *c'est à moi*   (An 3;10,26)
        'it belongs to me'

4. Discussion

So what is it that determines the acquisition of Case marking? There are three questions to be answered:

— What triggers abstract Case in child grammar, and in what way is abstract Case related to functional categories?
— What is the status of the various morphological case categories in the grammar?
— Is there any commonalty behind the apparent variation among the two children?

4.1. Case and Functional Categories

In Pascal's case, it is justified to say that abstract Case has been acquired by the time when the child clearly distinguishes nominative and accusative in German, i.e. no later than 2;4,7. This view is corroborated by a finding by Meisel & Müller (1992). They state that the functional category INFL is fully integrated in Pascal's grammar at around 2;2 or 2;3. This is important because, as we have seen, under the DP approach the Case Filter becomes operative only after functional categories have been acquired.

Soon after the category INFL is present in Pascal's speech, he develops the morphological inventory to express Case relations. There is additional evidence from French: by the time Pascal seems to have acquired two cases in German, he also enters a new stage in the development of French as he acquires productive command of subject clitics. As clitics are elements of an agreement chain, they are governed by the same category that assigns Case to noun phrases. Subject clitics are part of AGR (in INFL), thus they depend on the acquisition of that category for assignment to their proper phrase structure representation. Only after functional categories are present, the agreement relation becomes productive and systematic.

Where Pascal's data suggest that acquisition of INFL and DET are somehow connected, Annika's morphological avoidance strategy obscures the facts. On the one hand, we find that she produces V2 constructions by 2;6,18, and these are true V2 constructions as she obviously is able to topicalize not only subjects, but also objects, adverbials, and wh-words. So there is good evidence for two functional categories above VP in her grammar. Her avoiding overt Case-marking on pronouns and determiners, on the other hand, by preferring neuter or plural forms where the distinction is least clear, in my eyes leads the researcher to the conclusion that the category DET is present in her grammar and the Case Filter is operative. The problem for Annika is that she has not yet built up the full inventory of pronouns and determiners, but is aware of these gaps in her lexicon and tries to circumvent this dilemma (see below for further discussion).

The shadow determiners in my data indicate that prosody might play a role in the triggering of functional categories. The child extracts the approximated intonation contour of determined nouns (cf. Peters 1983; Echols & Newport 1992). At first, these approximations are analyzed and the nominal element is placed into N^0, while the un-analyzed part is assigned to the Roeper-position adjoined to NP. Evidence for this interpretation comes from the fact that these forms are phonologically underspecified. If they were assigned to a projection of their own, they would have to be specified in terms of morphosyntactic features. Thus I would assign to an utterance like (18b) the following structure:

(59)

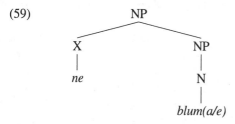

The element under X indicates the position of the underspecified shadow determiner.

What would now serve as a trigger for the nominal functional category DET? The answer might be found in a proposal made by Fukui & Speas (1988). They suggest that every functional category "includes some elements which we may call *Function Features,* or *F-Features,* and other elements which do not assign these features" (Fukui & Speas 1988:138; their italics). Nominative Case, together with [wh] and genitive Case, belongs among these features that form, together with the Case Features assigned by lexical categories, a set, or "grid", of what Fukui & Speas call "Kase" features. They postulate a principle stating that

The Saturation Principle
All positions in a grid must be discharged. (Fukui & Speas 1986:139)

The crucial assumption now is that a category not only has a Theta Grid, but also a Kase Grid.[29]

What kinds of consequences does this explanation have for the theory of language acquisition, and for Case Theory? It follows from Fukui & Speas' approach that Case as far as it is assigned by *lexical categories* does not depend on the implementation of DET in an immediate causality, because the relevant features which are part of the Kase grid of V or P are discharged by the complements of these categories. But with the implementation of INFL in the child's grammar on the other hand, the structural necessity for Case is introduced as the child is pressed to find an element that discharges the nominative feature included in INFL. If we assume that only functional elements can discharge the Kase feature of a functional category, the shadow forms (which may well have developed closer to the phonological target) have to be assigned their status as lexical realizations of a functional category, namely, the category DET. The next step is that DET is introduced into *all* nominal projections. Now the surface distribution of all noun phrases is constrained by the Case Filter, and, in languages where case categories are distinguished, the morphological paradigm has to be learnt.

This approach presupposes that noun phrases are specified with respect to their feature content already in the lexicon and are projected appropriately. As soon as the Case Filter constrains the surface positions of NPs, syntactic distinctions have to be expressed morphologically. The acquisition data, or rather the most plausible explanation of the course of development, thus confirm an account of Case Checking, rather than Case Assignment. This important role of the lexicon and the feature specification of lexical entries clearly has consequences for other components of the theory of grammar.

4.2. *The Role of the Genitive in German*

Radford (1990b) has noted that possessive *'s* is acquired early by English-speaking children. Clahsen et al. (1990) cite evidence from the so-called Simone-corpus collected by Max Miller, as well as evidence from the literature, i.e. Clahsen (1984) and Tracy (1986). These studies indicate that the genitive is acquired rather early, and in any case earlier than the accusative. These findings are incompatible with Pascal's data. Pascal does not use the possessor–possessed construction before 2;8,17, where he omits the inflection:

(60)   *das is mama platz*   (Pa 2;8,17)
         'that is mummy-NOM place'

The first target-like genitive for him is documented at 3;8,26, long after Case is acquired:

(61)   *und mamas ketten sind noch schöner*   (Pa 3;8,26)
         'and mummy's necklaces are still more beautiful'

Pascal instead expresses possession by possessive adjectives:

(62) a. *la-wagen, meins la-wagen (la-wagen=lastwagen)* (Pa 1;10,28)
          'truck, my truck'
      b. Adult: *warte das ist meine!*
                   'wait, that one's mine!)
          Child: *nein*
                   'no!'
          Adult: *doch!*
                   'yes!'
          Child: *nich meine*   (Pa 2;0,30)
                   'not mine!' (=not yours)
      c. *das meins*   (Pa 2;1,28)
          'that one's mine'
      d. *oh! das is mein auto!*   (Pa 2;7,0)
          'oh that is my car'

In Annika's case, the first genitives appear earlier:

(63) a. Adult: *das sind die ohrringe von mama, ne?*
                   'that are the earrings of mummy, right?'
          Child: (picking up the earrings) *mamas*   (An 2;0,17)
                   'mummy's'
      b. Adult: *ist das deine uhr?*
                   'is that your watch?'
          Child: *papa — papas papas papas papas*   (An 2;0,17)
                   'daddy — daddy's daddy's ...'

These prenominal genitives appear earlier than V2 effects or other indicators of
the development of functional categories. Yet they should not be overestimated
since they are uttered without any syntactic context, neither do they occur together
with a possessor noun, nor is any potential Case assigner present. Structures of
the latter kind emerge much later, only after the first datives are attested:

(64) a. *ja von papas schule*   (An 3;1,26)
          'yes from daddy's school'
      b. Adult: *was machst du denn in daniels bett?*
                   'what are you doing in daniel's bed?'
          Child: *das ist daniels*   (An 3;8,24)
                   'that is daniel's?'
      c. *[...] hier in matthias zimmer*   (An 3;8,24)[30]
          '[...] here in Matthias' room'

It appears that early genitives have been extracted from the input and been analyzed not as Case-marked NPs, but as NPs denoting possession. Their function is well understood by Annika, but she uses them as situationally adequate chunks, not being contained in phrase structure.

Tracy (1986) offers an explanation for the early appearance of the genitive suffix: she discusses the possibility that this form is not a case form, but one denoting possession. She has evidence in her data that supports this reading, i.e. child utterances where the genitive suffix is overgeneralized to dative contexts when possession is to be expressed:

(65)   Stephanie
          Father: *wem gehört denn die wiege?*
                   'whose crib is this?'
          Child: Stephanies-GEN   (1;11)
(66)   Malte
          das gehört Maltes   (2;6)
          'that belongs to Malte's-GEN'; pointing to some object)

Tracy's explanation for such early genitive-like expressions of possession would be a problem for Clahsen et al. (1990), who want to employ these early forms as evidence for early acquisition of DET. In their view the child analyzes the prenominal possessor nouns as being Case-marked and hence looks for a possible Case assigner. Finding none, she projects an empty DET element whose AGR feature is the Case assigner.

There are two problems with this analysis. One hinges on the status of the genitive in child language as discussed by Tracy, the other concerns the nature of the bootstrapping operation the child has to perform.

I prefer Tracy's analysis that apparent genitives in early child language rather are possessives, and the POSS feature is essentially a semantic feature that has to be assigned within NP.[31] Under this view we can account for parallel structures for VP/IP and NP/DP once more. The genitive in German and other Germanic languages shares some properties with the nominative. Both cases are assigned by a functional category, INFL for the nominative and DET for the prenominal genitive. Both these cases are assigned to the left and they both are assigned to positions that serve as landing-sites for moved categories:

The positions out of which the nominative and genitive DPs have been moved[32] are the positions where these DPs have been assigned their semantic roles.[33] As the genitive is assigned by DET, it should come in only after DET has been acquired. Before the acquisition of DET, the possessor NP remains *in situ*

(67)

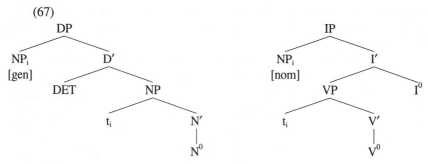

where it receives its semantic role. The *s*-suffix is interpreted by some children as a marker of the semantic role. Possessive adjectives are not marked, since they are appropriately specified as possessor expressions already in the lexicon.

In the analysis by Clahsen et al. (1990), the acquisitional relation between Case and DET is reversed. They assume that the child, noting the morphological difference between nominative and genitive nouns, analyzes the genitive form as Case-marked. Consequently, s/he introduces a new functional category, whose empty head is needed as a Case assigner. This hypothesis suffers from one major drawback: The concept of structural Case can be introduced into the child's grammar only after the grammar contains the functional category DET. Yet in Clahsen et al.'s analysis, the child has to know about Case before s/he acquires the category the Case Filter is meant to constrain.[34]

This hypothesis runs into trouble not only because determiners would be stronger as possible triggers for a functional category, but also because it cannot apply universally. Remember that the Romance languages do not have prenominal genitives, and southern German dialects either. It appears as if in Romance languages, DET cannot house a POSS feature at all, and in the southern German dialects it has to be phonologically realized, and then assigns the dative:

(68) $_{DP}[$ $_{DP}[$ *dem Vater*]-DAT $_{D'}[_D[$*sein*] $_{NP}[$ $_{AP}[$*großes*] *Haus*]]]
       'the father his large house'

4.3. *Morphological Case Categories*

According to Chomsky (1981) and others, there exists a pattern according to which certain morphological cases are associated with certain assigning categories (see above). The genitive would be assigned by the functional category DET, on the one hand, and by [+N]-categories to their complements in languages like German for which the appropriate parameter settings hold. This model accounts for Pascal's developmental sequence, and for his problems with lexical Case assignment.

Pascal's developmental sequence follows the associative pattern in having each case being assigned by only one category, thus exhibiting a bi-uniqueness relation.[35] Also prepositional Case, seen as inherent in German by some authors (e.g. Czepluch 1982) falls under this generalization for Pascal.[36] He overgeneralizes the dative to accusative contexts, although this is explicitly excluded by some researchers (Clahsen 1984; Clahsen et al. 1990; Mills 1985):

(69) a. *für dir und für/von mir* (Pa 2;5,5)
         'for you-DAT and for/from me-DAT'
     b. *und noch für dir*
         'and still for you-DAT'
     c. *für mir* (Pa 2;6,2)
         'for me-DAT'

The decisive property of these contexts is that they are in the domain of a preposition, hence in an environment which is a dative context in the unmarked case. This overgeneralization is remedied only at 2;9,16 when we find the first correct use of an accusative governed by a preposition:

(70)   *ein für dich* (Pa 2;9,16)
         'one for you-ACC'

It is obvious that this pattern is not universal to language acquisition, else it would have appeared in the children studied by Mills (1985), Clahsen (1984), Clahsen, Eisenbeiß & Vainikka (1994) or Tracy (1986), or in others of our children. Still I want to argue that Pascal's developmental sequence reflects a very basic correlation between Case assigner and case category, which in adult German is obscured by other properties of the category P. On the one hand, Schöler, Kratzer, Kürsten & Schäle (1991) report that some of their dysphasic children exhibit the same pattern of overgeneralization, on the other hand, I want to show that there is a non-obvious relation between Pascal's linguistic behavior and that of Annika.

The first dative contexts are much earlier in Annika's data than in Pascal's, but they are not as neatly distributed, since some are governed by a preposition, and some are not, and the most characteristic feature of these earliest datives at 2;0,27 is that in these utterances no forms are found that represent the functional category DET, thus — since Case marking on nouns, and especially proper nouns, is nearly absent — they are not morphologically marked for dative case:

(71) Adult: *wohin machen die eine reise?*
           'where are they traveling?'
     Child: *mit mama*   (An 2;0,27)
            'with mummy'

In one utterance even the preposition is lacking, so there actually is no Case assigner, and the form is analyzed as having a dative context only because from the adults' point of view the missing preposition is inferred as being *von* which governs the dative:

(72)   *foto papa*   (An 2;0,27)
        'picture daddy'

The first prepositions governing the accusative, i.e. some sort of benefactive or directional prepositions, appear at 2;9,31, shortly before the first datives other than unmarked nouns are recorded:

(73)   *für die tiere mach ich ein haus*   (An 2;9,31)
        'for the animals I make a house'

What I want to argue is that Annika, up to a certain point, although she encodes syntactic features, avoids to express them morphologically. At first, she avoids constructions with more than one argument, and later she avoids having to mark Case by using neuter forms nearly exclusively. Then, suddenly, she copes with Case marking, but is this related to the acquisition of functional categories? INFL is implemented in her grammar nearly three months before she uses a growing inventory of Case-marked non-neuter determiners and pronouns. This stage of morpho-lexical expansion coincides with the appearance of the dative and the genitive. Obviously, she develops the need for datives by expansion of her communicative powers, and hence the acquisition of dative forms forces her to expand the inventory of morphosyntactic categories.

So Annika has an "all or nothing" strategy that lets her wait until everything is in place before Case is brought to bear on her grammar, while Pascal is a "structure builder" who adopts a piecemeal (or "building block") approach to structural development by putting together the grammar step by step. After having developed functional categories including DET as well as Case marking as the morphological reflex of a UG component, he begins with the most basic distinction — nominative-accusative — and then proceeds to the next distinction — accusative-dative. I assume that this variation between the children illustrates very general distinctions between learner types.

Acknowledgements

Earlier versions of this paper have been presented at the University of Lund (Sweden) in September 1991, and at the 16th Boston University Conference on Language Development in October 1991. I am grateful to the audiences at these conferences as well as to my colleagues at Hamburg University for the comments they have provided.

Notes

1. Several authors assume that there are in fact, in some languages at least, at least two functional categories above NP. This second nominal functional category is generally assumed to contain some sort of number feature, e.g. Löbel (1990) or Ritter (1991).

2. Felix (1990) assumes a general bi-uniqueness principle to the effect that DET universally selects NP as its complement, and INFL universally selects VP. But cf. Koster (1987) for arguments *against* bi-uniqueness relations in grammatical structure.

3. COMP and P both share properties of lexical and functional categories. COMP is functional, but selects at the same time another functional projection, P on the other hand is lexical, but is selected by another lexical category. Abney (1986) argues that P is in fact a functional category. I will not discuss this issue here, but see Müller (this volume, chap. 9) for the acquisition of COMP by bilingual children.

4. The idea that the Case Filter and θ-theory might be related has already been advanced in Chomsky (1981).

5. Several accounts of the structural conditions for Case assignment have been proposed. The traditional constraint is that it is possible only under government. If we assume nominative case to be assigned by INFL, either the theory of government has to be extended to include INFL (or AGR), as is in fact done by Aoun & Sportiche (1983), or the necessary condition for Case Assignment will have to be c-command (or, cf. Sigurðsson 1989, m-command).

6. Löbel (1992) proposed, similar to Shin (1991), that Case might be a head-level category that heads its own projection. I have not examined the consequences her proposal would have on language acquisition. Maybe Case is a separate functional category in some languages, whereas it is only one of several features of DET in others. Meisel (1991b) has proposed a similar account for NEG(ation) in Basque, French, and Portuguese; definiteness might be another candidate for this kind of language-specific representation, see note 7 below.

7. Some researchers argue that Mainland Scandinavian languages display the same kind of head movement in the DP; the argument runs as follows: The indefinite 'a house' would be rendered as *ett hus* in Swedish, whereas the definite 'the house' would turn out as

huset. In the case of the indefinite article, the noun remains *in situ*, in the definite phrase it has been raised and incorporated into D^0. I would want to question this analysis on the basis of modified noun phrases: If the noun phrase contains an adjective, the respective structures would be *ett stor hus* and *det stora huset*. So, when there is an adjective present, we have an unbound article in both cases, and the adjective is inflected differently. Obviously, at least in Standard Swedish, nouns (and adjectives) agree with their functional governors not only in Case, gender, and number, but also in definiteness. In the case of the unmodified definite noun, the determiner may be left empty as the Φ-features are realized morphologically on the nominal head, Emonds' (1987) Invisible Category Principle being satisfied.

8. Cf. Sigurðsson (1989) for similar relations in Icelandic. Sigurðsson states that Case assignment by prepositions in Icelandic is either fixed, i.e. lexically determined, or semantically predictable.

9. For a study of the acquisition of gender and number in bilingual children, see the papers by Koehn (on morphology) and Müller (chap. 4, on agreement) in this volume.

10. Kaiser & Meisel (1991) argue that colloquial French on the one hand, and standard French on the other hand constitute two distinct systems, and standard French is *not* a *pro*-drop language.

11. This use of a preposition can be compared to the more well-known phenomenon of English *of*-insertion.

12. In French, the prepositions *à* and *de* may fuse with a following masculine or plural definite article. Thus, *à + le* e.g. gives *au*, or *de + les* gives *des*. See Koehn (this volume) for details.

13. See Meisel (this volume) on verbal agreement in child language.

14. A similar proposal by Peter Jordens and Teun Hoekstra, made in a GLOW talk (cf. Hoekstra & Jordens 1994), has come to my attention only after this manuscript had been completed.

15. The acquisition of pronouns in French by Pascal has been studied by Kaiser (this volume).

16. In the majority of the examples in (17), it is, due to the phonological similarity of nominative and accusative endings in colloquial German, not clear whether Pascal uses accusative or nominative forms. What indeed is clear is that the forms he uses are not dative.

17. The difference between dative and accusative is far more salient in the plural than in the singular, since the two forms use different stems: *ihnen* vs. *sie*.

18. This notion of "stage" in language development clearly implies that Universal Grammar is not a production model (and the term "generative" quite misleading), but a model of the constraints that constitute a speaker's linguistic competence. In production, speakers (not only children) may rely on utterances that have been memorized as un-analyzed

wholes and are retrieved from memory whenever they seem to be appropriate. Especially for young children, this may as well concern such structures that belong to earlier developmental stages and mirror the grammatical knowledge of these earlier stages. Peters (1983) explicitly includes with these holistic units sentence frames which can be easily retrieved and have slots to fill with lexical material.

19. The reference of *[salə]* is unclear, it might mean 'fish' for Pascal.

20. See Köppe (this volume) on subject raising in child language.

21. It is also possible that utterances like these might constitute evidence in favor of the existence of two verbal functional categories in child German. Müller (this volume, chap. 9) argues that in such cases, the verb has been raised to a head-final AGR-position, but has failed to be moved on to head-initial INFL.

22. I will argue below that (German) INFL will be acquired by Annika around the age of 2;6. Peter Jordens (p.c.) suggested that the data in (41) might pose a problem for such an analysis, but I think that one single utterance of such a kind does not influence the overall analysis in any way.

23. The basis of these counts were all pronominal forms that occur in the recording, even those that constituted one-word utterances.

24. See note 18.

25. See Müller (this volume, chap. 4) on possible differences between the phrase structure representations of definite and indefinite articles.

26. Koehn (this volume) and Müller (this volume, chap. 4) study the acquisition of gender not by Annika, but by other bilingual children of the DUFDE corpus. Cf. the references cited there, and also Maratsos (1988) on the acquisition of gender in a cross-linguistic perspective.

27. Regina Köppe pointed out that (49a,b,h) could be formulas, i.e. unanalyzed, rote-learned constructions. Yet the remaining number of utterances supports my argument well enough.

28. Note that the child studied by Parodi (1990b), who temporarily gave up most of his French, retained the fairly general use of *ça*, although other pronouns were not used during that period.

29. See Müller (this volume, chap. 9) for a discussion concerning [finiteness] and [wh].

30. As words ending in [s] do not receive the genitive *[-s]* in German, it is not sure whether *Mathias* in this utterance really is [genitive].

31. I would like to point out that the interpretation of POSS as the morphological reflex of a semantic feature is essentially mine, and not intended in Tracy's work.

32. Cf. Fukui & Speas (1986:133): "The specifiers of functional heads are often (in our model, always — see below) moved from within their complement."

33. I do not know whether it is justified to speak of "possessor" as a semantic role, or whether a possessor might even be a θ-role of the NP. I do not want to discuss this issue here and what to make clear that I use the term "semantic role" in an essentially pre-theoretic fashion.

34. Natascha Müller pointed out to me that in the framework of Case Checking I advocated
     above, one could say that genitive NPs might be interpreted by the child as having lexical
     Case. One might then proceed to say that the child recognizes this feature and is forced
     to project a category that in fact bears the feature to be discharged. I still would want to
     argue that at least some children in the beginning do not analyze genitives as being
     Case-marked, but as being marked for possession. This is a semantic feature and can be
     licensed outside of the grammatical feature grid, namely by an NP in the phrase structure
     that has the role or function of Possessor, thus assigns something like a POSS feature —
     data from Hebrew (Ritter 1988, 1991) suggest that the genitive actually is a lexical case.
     I shall explore this hypothesis and its consequences in forthcoming work.

35. But see note 2.

36. Czepluch (1982) argues that in some languages, French among them, the objective-oblique
     distinction has been lost, and that therefore prepositions assign objective case structurally.
     In these languages, indirect objects have to be governed by a preposition, as in his model
     no category can assign the same Case twice. In German, di-transitive verbs assign the
     objective (=accusative) and the oblique (=dative) structurally, and no preposition is
     needed. This contrasts with Emonds (1985) who argues that German indirect objects
     receive their Case universally from a preposition, this preposition being empty.

References

Abney, Stephen. 1986. "Functional Elements and Licensing." Manuscript, Cambridge:
     Mass.: Massachusetts Institute of Technology.

Aoun, Yoseph & Dominique Sportiche. 1983. "On the Formal Theory of Government."
     The Linguistic Review 2.211–236.

Bickerton, Derek. 1990. "Syntactic Development: The brain just does it." Manuscript,
     University of Hawai'i at Manoa.

Chomsky, Noam. 1981. *Lectures on Government and Binding (=Studies in Generative
     Grammar*, 9.). Dordrecht: Foris.

———. 1986. *Knowledge of Language: Its nature, origin, and use.* New York: Praeger.

Clahsen, Harald. 1984. "Der Erwerb von Kasusmarkierungen in der deutschen Kinder
     sprache." *Linguistische Berichte* 89.1–31.

Clahsen, Harald, Sonja Eisenbeiß & Anne Vainikka. 1994. "The Seeds of Structure: A
     syntactic analysis of the acquisition of Case marking." *Language Acquisition
     Studies in Generative Grammar (=Language Acquisition and Language Disorders,*
     8), ed. by Teun Hoekstra & Bonnie D. Schwartz, 85–118. Amsterdam: John
     Benjamins.

Czepluch, Hartmut. 1982. "Case Theory and the Dative Construction." *The Linguistic
     Review* 2.1–38.

Demuth, Katherine. 1992. "Accessing Functional Categories in Sesotho: Interactions at the morpho–syntax interface." Meisel 1992, 83–107.

Echols, Catherine & Elissa Newport. 1992. "The Role of Stress and Position in Determining First Words." *Language Acquisition* 2.189–220.

Emonds, Joseph. 1985. *A Unified Theory of Syntactic Categories* (=*Studies in Generative Grammar*, 13.). Dordrecht: Foris.

———. 1987. "The Invisible Category Principle." *Linguistic Inquiry* 18.613–632.

Felix, Sascha W. 1990. "The Structure of Functional Categories." *Linguistische Berichte* 125.46–71.

Fukui, Naoki & Margaret Speas. 1986. "Specifiers and Projection." *MIT Working Papers in Theoretical Linguistics* 8.128–172.

Guilfoyle, Eithne & Máire Noonan. 1988. "Functional Categories and Language Acquisition." Paper presented at the 13th Boston University Conference on Language Development.

Haider, Hubert. 1988. "Die Struktur der deutschen Nominalphrase." *Zeitschrift für Sprachwissenschaft* 7.32–59.

Hoekstra, Teun & Peter Jordens. 1994. "From Adjuncts to Head." *Language Acquisition Studies in Generative Grammar* (=*Language Acquisition and Language Disorders*, 8), ed. by Teun Hoekstra & Bonnie D. Schwartz, 119–149. Amsterdam: John Benjamins.

Hyams, Nina. 1992. "The Genesis of Clausal Structure." Meisel 1992, 371–400.

Kaiser, Georg A. 1992. *Zur Grammatik der klitischen Personalpronomina im Französischen und Portugiesischen: Eine synchronische und diachronische Analyse.* (=*Editionen der Iberoamericana*, Reihe III, 44.) Frankfurt am Main: Vervuert.

Kaiser, Georg A. & Jürgen M. Meisel. 1991. "Subjekte und Null-Subjekte im Französischen." *'DET, COMP und INFL': Zur Syntax funktionaler Kategorien und grammatischer Funktionen* (=*Linguistische Arbeiten,* 263), ed. by Gisbert Fanselow & Susan Olsen, 110–136. Tübingen: Niemeyer.

Koster, Jan. 1987. *Domains and Dynasties. The Radical Autonomy of Syntax* (=*Studies in Generative Grammar*, 17). Dordrecht: Foris.

Löbel, Elisabeth. 1990. "D und Q als funktionale Kategorien in der Nominalphrase." *Linguistische Berichte* 127.232–264.

———. 1991. "Typologische Aspekte funktionaler Kategorien in der Nominalphrase." *Zeitschrift für Sprachwissenschaft* 9.135–169.

———. 1992. "KP/DP-Syntax. Interaction of Case Marking with Referential and Nominal Features." *Theorie des Lexikons. Arbeiten des SFB 282*, 33.

Maratsos, Michael. 1988. "The Acquisition of Formal Word Classes." *Categories and Processes in Language Acquisition*, ed. by Yonata Levy, I. Schlesinger, Martin Braine, 31–44. Hillsdale, N.J.: Erlbaum.

Meisel, Jürgen M. 1986. "Word Order and Case Marking in Early Child Language: Evidence from simultaneous acquisition of two first languages: French and German." *Linguistics* 24.123–183.

———. 1990. "INFL-ection: Subjects and subject–verb agreement." Meisel 1990, 237–298.

———. 1991a. "Verbal Functional Categories in Early Grammatical Development." Unpublished Working Paper, University of Hamburg.

———. 1991b. "The Development of Sentence Negation." Manuscript, University of Hamburg.

———. (ed.). 1990. *Two First Languages.* (=*Studies in Language Acquisition,* 10.) Dordrecht: Foris.

———. (ed.). 1992. *The Acquisition of Verb Placement: Functional categories and V2 phenomena in language development* (=*Studies in Theoretical Psycholinguistics,* 16.). Dordrecht: Kluwer.

Meisel, Jürgen M. & Natascha Müller. 1992. "On the Position of Finiteness in Early Child Grammar: Evidence from simultaneous acquisition of two first languages: French and German." Meisel 1992, 109–138.

Mills, Anne E. 1985. "The Acquisition of German." *The Cross-Linguistic Study of Language Acquisition,* ed. by Dan I. Slobin, 141–254. Hillsdale, N.J.: Erlbaum.

Müller, Natascha. 1993. *Komplexe Sätze. Der Erwerb von COMP und Wortstellungs-mustern bei bilingualen Kindern (Französisch/Deutsch)* (=*Tübinger Beiträge zur Linguistik,* Series A: *Language Development,* 16.). Tübingen: Narr.

Olsen, Susan. 1988. "Die deutsche Nominalphrase als 'Determinansphrase'." Manuscript, University of Stuttgart.

———. 1989. "Das Possessivum: Pronomen, Determinans oder Adjektiv?" *Linguistische Berichte* 120.133–153.

Parodi, Teresa. 1989. "Kasus bei Ivar." Unpublished Working Paper, University of Hamburg.

———. 1990a. "Kasus bei Ivar im Alter zwischen 3 und 5 Jahren." Unpublished Working Paper, University of Hamburg.

———. 1990b. "The Acquisition of Word Order Regularities and Case Morphology. Meisel 1990, 157–190.

———. 1991. "Funktionale Kategorien im bilingualen Erstspracherwerb und im Zweitspracherwerb." Spracherwerb und Grammatik. *Linguistische Untersuchungen zum Erwerb von Syntax und Morphologie.* (=*Linguistische Berichte,* Sonderheft 3.), ed. by Monika Rothweiler, 152–165.

Peters, Ann M. 1983. *The Units of Language Acquisition* (=*Cambridge Monographs and Texts in Applied Psycholinguistics.*). Cambridge: Cambridge University Press.

Peters, Ann M. & Lise Menn. 1990. "The Microstructure of Morphological Development: Variation Across Children and Across Languages." Manuscript, University of Hawai'i/ University of Colorado.

Platzack, Christer. 1992. "A Grammar Without Functional Categories: A syntactic study of early Swedish child language." Meisel 1992, 63–82.

Poeppel, David & Kenneth Wexler. 1991. "Finiteness and V2 Effects Implicate the Existence of Functional Categories and Headmovement in Early German Grammar." Paper presented at the 16th Boston University Conference on Language Development, 18.10.1991.

Radford, Andrew. 1986. "Small Children's Small Clauses." *Bangor Research Papers in Linguistics* 1.1–38.

———. 1990a. "The Syntax of Nominal Arguments in Early Child English." *Language Acquisition* 1.195–223.

———. 1990b. *Syntactic Theory and the Acquisition of English Syntax.* Oxford: Blackwell.

Ritter, Elisabeth. 1988. "A Head-Movement Approach to Construct-State Noun Phrases." *Linguistics* 26.909–929.

———. 1991. "Two Functional Categories in Noun Phrases: Evidence from Modern Hebrew." *Perspectives on Phrase Structure: Heads and Licensing (=Syntax & Semantics* 25.), 37–62, ed. by Susan D. Rothstein. San Diego, Ca.: Academic Press.

Roeper, Thomas. 1992. "From the Initial State to V2: Acquisition principles in action." Meisel 1992, 333–370.

Rothstein, Susan. 1992. "Case and NP Licensing." *Natural Language and Linguistic Theory* 10.119–139.

Schöler, Hermann, Petra Kratzer, Frank Kürsten & Heike Schäle. 1991. "Inflection: A comparison of dysphasic and 'normal' children." Paper presented at the Conference "Crossing Boundaries: Formal and Functional Determinants of Language Acquisition," Tübingen, October 1991.

Shin, Hyo-Shik. 1991. "Die KP-Analyse der Nominalphrase." Paper presented at the 13th Annual Meeting of the Deutsche Gesellschaft für Sprachwissenschaft, Aachen, 27.2.–1.3.1991.

Sigurðsson, Halldór A. 1989. "Verbal Syntax and Case in Icelandic: A comparative GB approach." Dissertation, University of Lund.

Speas, Margaret J. 1990. *Phrase Structure in Natural Language (=Studies in Natural Language and Linguistic Theory*, 21). Dordrecht: Kluwer.

Tracy, Rosemary. 1986. "The Acquisition of Case Morphology in German." *Linguistics* 24.47–78.

Weissenborn, Jürgen. 1990. "Functional Categories and Verb Movement: The acquisition of German syntax reconsidered." *Spracherwerb und Grammatik. Linguistische Untersuchungen zum Erwerb von Syntax und Morphologie (=Linguistische Berichte Sonderheft 3),* ed. by Monika Rothweiler, 190–224.

NP-Movement and Subject Raising

Regina Köppe
University of Hamburg

1. Introduction

Recent research in language acquisition has addressed the issue of NP-movement from different perspectives, relating it to the debate on the continuity hypothesis (e.g. Guilfoyle & Noonan 1988) in contrast to maturational views (e.g. Borer & Wexler 1987). The questions that will be dealt with in this paper are the following: When do children have access to NP-movement? Is the availability of NP-movement subject to maturation or is it, as UG principle, available from early on, even though its application is linked to the emergence of a functional category providing a landing site for movement? To address these questions, I focus on early word order in both German and French, as well as on the differentiation of various classes of verbs according to the base position of their subjects.

2. Theoretical Background

Within the framework of generative theory, NP-movement constitutes one possible option of the movement process *Move α*. Traditionally, NP-movement is assumed to apply in specific constructions where two conditions are met:

(1)   The subject position (Spec-IP) is not assigned a theta-role.

(2)   An NP generated in a VP-internal position is not assigned Case in this position.

Typically, NP-movement applies in passive constructions. According to Jaeggli (1986), the external theta-role is absorbed in passive sentences, and the verb does not assign structural Case to the object NP. This NP then has to be moved to Spec-IP in order to receive Nominative Case. In other words, the D-structural object becomes the superficial subject, as shown in (3a–b).

(3) a. $[_{IP}$ $[_{NP}$ e] *was* $[_{VP}$ *caught* $[_{NP}$ *a frog*]]]
     b. $[_{IP}$ $[_{NP}$ *a frog_i*] *was* $[_{VP}$ *caught* $[_{NP}t_i$]]]

In the case of raising verbs like *seem* (German *scheinen*, French *sembler*, *paraître*, etc.), there is also no theta-role assignment to the subject position. Further, the moved NP is not an object (since raising verbs are intransitive), but the subject of an embedded nonfinite clause, from which it raises to Spec-IP of the matrix clause. This is shown in (4a–c).

(4) a. *Peter_i seems* [t_i *to be tired*]
     b. *Pierre_i (me) semble* [t_i *être fatigué*]
     c. *weil Peter_i (mir)* [t_i *müde zu sein*] *scheint*

Burzio (1986) has proposed that the same movement process also concerns the subjects of some intransitive verbs which he calls ergative verbs.[1] Burzio shows that the subjects of ergative verbs are generated in the object position and have to be moved to the subject position:

(5) a. *Peter_i [arrives t_i]*
     b. *Pierre_i [arrive t_i]*
     c. *weil Peter_i [t_i ankommt]*
         'because Peter arrives'

The passive-like behavior of ergative verbs follows from the same conditions (1) and (2) which also account for passive and raising constructions. In fact, Burzio points out that condition (1) — as a lexical property of ergative verbs — is sufficient. The fact that the object position does not receive Case from the verb is automatically accounted for by Burzio's finding that "all and only the verbs that can assign θ-role to the subject can assign (accusative) Case to an object" (Burzio 1986:178). In other words, as Grewendorf (1989:3) reformulates it, "the subject position has no theta-role iff the object position has no Case".

Originally, Burzio's analysis of ergative verbs was proposed for Italian, where *ne*-cliticization and auxiliary selection can be used to distinguish ergative verbs from other intransitive verbs. Since then, various ergativity tests for other languages have been proposed (e.g. Grewendorf 1989; Legendre 1989; Sorace

1991). A central property of ergative verbs in French and in German seems to be auxiliary selection, just as in Italian. All French verbs that choose *être* 'to be' as perfect auxiliary are ergative verbs. Note, however, that there are other properties by which French ergative verbs can be identified; see Legendre (1989), who proposes a number of ergativity tests for French. German ergative verbs choose the auxiliary *sein* 'to be'. Grewendorf (1989) further distinguishes "one-place" ergative verbs like *ankommen* 'to arrive', *wachsen* 'to grow', *sterben* 'to die', etc. and "two-place" ergative verbs, which can occur with an indirect Dative object: *gelingen* 'to succeed', *passieren* 'to happen', *unterlaufen* 'to occur to', etc.

Recently, it has been proposed that all subjects are generated in a VP-internal position where they receive their external theta-role and that all subjects have to be raised to Spec-IP in order to be assigned Nominative Case (Kuroda 1988; Sportiche 1988; Koopman & Sportiche 1991). Concerning the underlying position of the subject, Sportiche (1988) and Koopman & Sportiche (1991) assume that the subject NP is generated as a sister to VP, both constituents forming a small clause (V″), whereas most other researchers assume that subjects are generated in Spec-VP. I will follow the latter proposal, since for the present analysis, this issue is not a crucial one.

Turning now to the obligatoriness of NP-movement, note that this movement process is not universally motivated by the Case Filter. Languages like Spanish or Italian allow for Nominative assignment to a VP-internal position (see Jaeggli 1986; Contreras 1987). With respect to German, the obligatoriness of NP-movement also has been questioned. Consider the examples in (6) and (7) below, taken from von Stechow & Sternefeld (1988:463) for passive and from Grewendorf (1988:156) for ergative verbs:

Passive
(6)   a.   *weil e^i [dem Kind das Buch^i geschenkt wurde]*   (VP-internal)
      b.   *weil das Buch$_i$ [dem Kind t$_i$ geschenkt wurde]* (NP-movement)[2]
           'because the book has been given to the child'

Ergative verbs
(7)   *weil dem Linguisten <u>ein Fehler</u> unterlaufen ist*   (VP-internal)
      'because a mistake has occurred to the linguist'

Grewendorf (1988, 1989) plausibly argues that VP-internal NPs such as those in (6a) and (7) are coindexed with an empty expletive pronoun in Spec-IP. Nominative Case is thus assigned to the expletive pronoun and can be inherited by the NP. In Grewendorf's view, the fact that number agreement between INFL and the subject position is determined by the VP-internal NP provides evidence for his analysis. Note however that this point is far from being settled since NP-movement in German is closely related to the analysis of German in terms of scrambling (see von Stechow & Sternefeld 1988; Fanselow 1990).

3. NP-movement in Early Child Language

In the literature on language acquisition, the issue of NP-movement has been taken up by only a small number of researchers. Several authors claim that NP-movement is not available in early child language. Borer & Wexler (1987), for instance, explain acquisition data concerning passive and ergative verbs with the maturation of the ability to form A-chains. By contrast, Guilfoyle & Noonan (1988) suggest that the functional projection IP is not yet present in early child grammar and, consequently, that no landing site is available for NP-movement. This "no functional categories" hypothesis (see Radford 1986, 1990) continues to be discussed in current research on grammatical development.

3.1. Passive, Raising, and Ergative Verbs

As noted above, Borer & Wexler (1987) argue that the ability to form A-chains matures in the course of syntactic development. This hypothesis is based on two observations concerning English child language. First, it appears that young children have the capacity to produce and to understand lexical passives, but not syntactic passives. Syntactic or verbal passives (e.g. *the doll was seen*) are a result of NP-movement, whereas lexical or adjectival passives (e.g. *the doll was combed*) do not involve movement. The second observation is that children seem to overgeneralize causative constructions to intransitive verbs, as shown in (8) below, even though causativization in English is only possible with some ergative verbs, as shown in (9).

(8) *the doll giggled*   →   [*]*Peter giggled the doll*
(9) *the doll moved*   →   *Peter moved the doll*

According to Borer & Wexler, the causative rule is a syntactic rule which, in the presence of a thematic role, adds an external thematic role. With respect to the observation that children causativize intransitive verbs, Borer & Wexler assume that thematic relations between verb and subject have to be changed: The external theta-role (the intransitive subject) has to be internalized when a (second) external argument is added. In adult English, however, where causativization is only possible with ergative verbs, thematic relations can remain unchanged when adding an external argument, given that ergative verbs do not assign an external theta-role. Borer and Wexler thus hypothesize that children analyze ergative verbs like other intransitive verbs, i.e. their subject is generated in the subject position and not in the object position. According to this view, it is only the maturation of the ability to form A-chains that allows children to adjust their representation of ergative verbs and, consequently, to choose the second option of the causative rule.

Borer & Wexler's maturation hypothesis has been subject to criticism on theoretical as well as on empirical grounds. As Guilfoyle & Noonan (1988) point out, the crucial disadvantage of any maturation theory lies in its low explanatory power. It is hard to see which data could present evidence to falsify a maturational account. Moreover, the ability to form A-chains is not an independent principle, but consists of the interaction of several principles: *Move* α, theta theory, and the projection principle. Guilfoyle & Noonan emphasize that it is not clear how this interaction could mature, given that all three principles are assumed to be already present in the child's grammar.

Guilfoyle & Noonan's account of Borer & Wexler's findings on passive is as follows: all principles of UG are present from the beginning of language development, but maturation only concerns the domain where these principles operate, i.e. the domain of phrase structure. More precisely, Guilfoyle & Noonan assume that lexical categories are present in the grammar of young children, while functional categories emerge later in development. They thus argue that NPs cannot be moved simply because there is no landing site available before the emergence of INFL and its projection. The "no functional categories" hypothesis has the advantage to be easier to verify, since the presence of a given functional category in a developing grammar can be shown independently on the basis of e.g. word order, agreement phenomena, the presence of clitic elements, etc. (see Meisel; Kaiser; Stenzel; Müller, this volume, chap. 9). In consequence, this hypothesis, making stronger claims with respect to the power of UG during early linguistic development and at the same time leading to clearer predictions for this development, should be preferred as point of departure.

With respect to empirical objections to Borer & Wexler's (1987) findings, Eisenbeiß (1990) notes that young children acquiring German (aged 2;3 to 3;5) produce and understand syntactic passives, which are marked in German by the auxiliary *werden* 'to become'. Moreover, she points out that children even appear to interpret lexical passives, which select the auxiliary *sein* 'to be', as syntactic passives. Jakubowicz (1989) comes to similar conclusions in analyzing French children's acquisition of passive and raising constructions (ages 3;0–7;5). Finally, Pierce (1989), testing the comprehension of passive in Spanish children, is also not able to corroborate Borer & Wexler's findings.

Concerning the lexical representation of ergative verbs, Pierce (1989) and Deprez & Pierce (1991) argue that the fact that VS order is only used frequently with ergative verbs in data from the acquisition of English constitutes evidence for the assumption that ergative verbs are analyzed correctly as such from the beginning. Clark (1985), on the other hand, reports that overgeneralizations of the causative construction to intransitive verbs — apparently including those ergative verbs which do not allow causativization — have been frequently observed in English as well as in French child language, e.g. [*]*She comed it*, [*]*Je travaille les cailloux* 'I am working the stones' (Clark 1985:734–735).

3.2. Early Subjects

In this section, I will briefly present current hypotheses on early sentence structure in order to formulate predictions concerning early word order and the position of the subject in French and in German.

Whereas a number of researchers argue that functional categories are still lacking in early child grammar (Radford 1986; Guilfoyle & Noonan 1988; Meisel 1990, this volume; Müller 1993, this volume, chap. 9; etc.), others assume a more developed sentence structure containing IP (e.g. Clahsen et al. 1992; Pierce 1989) or even CP (Verrips & Weissenborn 1992; Weissenborn 1990), even for the earliest stages of grammatical development. Note that the debate has focused mainly on verb raising (movement of the finite verb) and subject–verb agreement. Less attention has been paid to NP-movement, and, more specifically, subject raising. Most authors assume — more or less implicitly — that if verb raising to INFL is possible, subject raising to Spec-IP follows automatically.

A different view is favored by Pierce (1989) and Deprez & Pierce (1991). Although they claim that the functional category IP is present from the beginning, they nevertheless argue that in French child language verb raising developmentally precedes subject raising. This view is based on the observation that in their data, during a first phase, 77% of lexical subjects occur in a postverbal position. These VS constructions are assumed to result from verb raising to INFL, whereas subjects still remain in Spec-VP. According to Pierce, these postverbal subjects are licensed on the assumption that in early French, Nominative Case can be assigned to the VP-internal subject. During a second phase, then, Pierce observes that the rate of postverbal subjects decreases simultaneously with an increase of pronominal subjects. According to Pierce, the declining number of postverbal subjects indicates that subject raising has begun to operate.

In addition, I want to point out that Borer & Wexler's (1987) maturation theory, as well, when applied to the question of subject raising from VP, should predict the occurrence of VS structures where the verb, but not the subject, has been raised.

3.3. *Theoretical and Empirical Considerations as a Background for the Analysis of the Availability of NP-Movement*

We now turn to more detailed evidence on the availability of NP-movement in early child language. From the preceding sections, it becomes apparent that the presence or non-presence of functional categories plays a crucial role for the possibility of movement rules to apply. More precisely, a) given that NP-movement requires a landing site (Spec-IP) located in the INFL projection, and b) given that there is good evidence to assume a stage where the child's grammar does not yet contain the category INFL and its projection (cf. also Meisel; Kaiser; Stenzel; this volume), it follows that the analysis should focus on the period before and after the emergence of INFL, and that one should investigate whether Spec-IP is available as a landing site from early on.

Considering when and how the ability to move NPs develops, the next question to address is the kind of evidence one can obtain. Here the analysis should mainly concern constructions that implicate NP-movement and that can be observed at the same developmental stage where INFL supposedly emerges. Such constructions are primarily subject raising from VP to Spec-IP as well as subject raising for ergative verbs. Of course, passive and raising verbs like *scheinen* 'to seem' also involve NP-movement, but constructions like (4b,c) or (6), for instance, which are quite complex and/or involve subordinate clauses, are produced relatively late and thus cannot present evidence on the availability of NP-movement during the crucial phase of development.

A closer look at the DUFDE data confirms these considerations on passive and raising. We find very few passive constructions. For instance, in Ivar's data from age 1;5 up to age 6;3, there are no more than 24 passives (German: 16;

French: 8), the first examples appearing at the age of 3;4. Most of these are lexical passives (Iv 3;04,23 *und dann war das abgerißt* 'and then this was torn off'), and the few verbal passives are all target-like with respect to the position of the subject (e.g. Iv 4;07,24 *und dann wirst du gekocht* 'and then you will be cooked'). In addition, in neither language do we find any instances of constructions involving raising verbs like *scheinen* 'to seem' or *paraître* 'to appear'. This situation is perhaps not unexpected, as we are dealing with naturalistic, spontaneous data where one does not find sufficient instances of those rather specific constructions throughout the period of observation; the results of Borer & Wexler (1987), Eisenbeiß (1990) and Jakubowicz (1989) are all based on experimentally elicited data.

The analysis of early speech and especially of subject raising to Spec-IP might provide additional insights concerning the status of NP-movement. For instance, if subject raising occurs regularly as soon as a landing site for NP-movement is available in the child's grammar, then one might reasonably assume that — in terms of UG — the option making NP-movement obligatory is chosen first, and that possible exceptions to this rule have to be learned later.

As a first hypothesis, we might assume that the structure of VPs in early child language is the same as in the standard analysis of German and French, with the subject being generated in Spec-VP. With respect to the base position of subjects within VP in early child language, it is difficult to find evidence for a fixed subject position. This might be the reason why Pierce (1989) and Deprez & Pierce (1991), for instance, consider the ordering of subject and verb within VP to be optional in French child language. Müller (1993) and Meisel (this volume) propose similar analyses for early German as well.[3] These are shown in (10) below.

(10) French   German

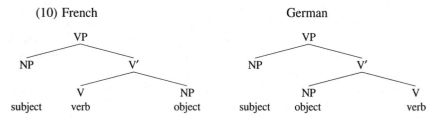

It is often assumed that the structure of IP in early German differs from the adult structure in the sense that IP is analyzed as head-initial rather than as head-final (e.g. Clahsen 1991; Clahsen et al. 1992; Weissenborn 1990; Müller 1993, this volume, chap. 9)[4], as shown in (11).

(11) French   German

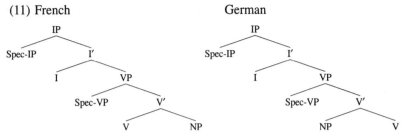

In order to determine the role of the emerging IP with respect to the availability of NP-movement, and also in order to determine how the child analyzes structures containing verb and subject, we have to ask which linear order of sentential elements should be expected in early child language before and after the emergence of INFL.

A closer look at the underlying configuration of VP and IP in both languages reveals only one major difference between French and German: in French VPs, the object position follows the verb, whereas in German, it precedes the verb. This structural difference accounts for the following distribution: In German, linear order of elements is the same (SV) in VP and in IP, with the exception of transitive verbs. In early German, a preference for the order SOV (or, more precisely, OV since early utterances mostly contain only one argument) may indicate that the child still produces VPs, whereas SVO order would indicate that subject and verb have been raised. Note that, contrary to French or English, subjects of ergative verbs, being generated in the object position, are nevertheless preverbal in German, so that it is virtually impossible to decide whether they are correctly analyzed by the child.

In French, the linear order of base generated elements in IP and VP only differs for ergative verbs, their subject originating in the postverbal object position (VS in contrast to SV(O) for intransitive and transitive verbs). In French, the main question will thus be whether children are able to differentiate between the structural representation of ergative and intransitive verbs.

It is also important to note that subjects do not have the same status in the two languages. In German, subjects are (in general) obligatory and have to be raised to Spec-IP[5] in order to receive Nominative Case, whereas in French, lexical subjects do not necessarily have to be present if the sentence contains a subject clitic. According to Roberge (1986) and Kaiser & Meisel (1991; see also Kaiser, this volume), who analyze subject clitics as INFL elements capable of identifying *pro*, colloquial French can be regarded as a null subject language. In other words, lexical subjects can be missing if a subject clitic is present, as shown by the example in (12). Alternatively, they can also appear together with the clitic in a preverbal position (Spec-IP) as in (13) or in a postverbal position as in (14).[6]

(12) $[_I$ *il mange*$_j$ $[_{VP}$ t$_j$ *une pomme*]]
        'he eats an apple'

(13) $[_{IP}$ *Pierre*$_i$ $[_I$ *il mange*$_j$ $[_{VP}$ t$_i$ t$_j$ *une pomme*]]]
        'Peter he eats an apple'

(14) $[_I$*il mange*$_j$ $[_{VP}$ t$_i$ t$_j$ *une pomme*] *Pierre*$_i$]
        'he eats an apple Peter'

If French can be considered to be a null subject language, it is possible to analyze (14) analoguous to the "free inversion" of the subject in languages like Italian or Spanish. According to Burzio (1986), these postverbal subjects are adjoined to the VP (cf. also Rizzi 1982) in the case of transitive and intransitive verbs. Postverbal subjects of ergative verbs, however, remain in the object position within VP as in (15).

(15) $[_I$il arrive$_j$ $[_{VP}$ t$_j$ Pierre]]
        'he arrives Peter'

In this perspective, it is important to observe that, on the one hand, subject raising occurs in only some of the structures possible in French, and, even more important, postverbal subjects in early child language cannot automatically be classified as resulting from verb raising without subject raising (cf. Pierce's 1989 analysis). Instead, we must consider the possibility that postverbal subjects have been moved to the right (with the clitic element missing), or in the case of ergative verbs, that VS structures are simple VPs with both verb and subject remaining in their base positions.

Another problem for the analysis of subject raising in French and German child language is the large number of utterances with simple SV structure. Here it is virtually impossible to decide whether the two elements have undergone raising to IP or whether they are in their base positions within VP. Consequently, in order to find clear evidence for movement of the subject and/or the verb, it is necessary to take into account the linear position of subject, object, and verb in relation to sentence-internal negation (which I assume to be located between IP and VP, cf. Dieck 1989) and to non-finite parts of the verbal complex. Furthermore, agreement phenomena may help to classify verb form as finite (= i.e. raised to INFL) (cf. Meisel, this volume), so that subjects preceding such finite verbs can be assumed to be raised to Spec-IP.

4.   The Data

The subjects of this study are Pascal and Ivar. The period of observation is defined in terms of MLU, beginning with an MLU value of around 1.7 (corresponding roughly to the first combinations of verbs with noun phrases) up to the time when MLU exceeds 3.0 in both languages. For Pascal, this period covers the subjects' ages ranging from 1;10,0 to 2;5,5, for Ivar, from 2;2,7 to 2;6,6.

4.1. *French*

During a first stage, which lasts from 1;8,22 to 1;11,28 (Pascal) and from 2;2,7 to 2;4,9 (Ivar), verbs mainly occur with only one argument, either subject or object, or with adverbials. Examples are shown in (16) and (17).

(16)	a.	*ouvrir chaussures*	(Pa 1;10,28)
		'open-INF shoes'	
	b.	*là mett(re)*	(Pa 1;10,28)
		'there put-INF'	
(17)	a.	*mouton sauter*	(Iv 2;2,7)
		'sheep jump-INF'	
	b.	*tombé da*	(Iv 2;2,7)
		'fallen there'	

With transitive verbs, it is mostly the subject that is omitted, whereas with intransitive and ergative verbs, the subject is in general present. During this first stage, there is no evidence — such as clitic subjects, negation following finite and preceding non-finite verbs, etc. — for the existence of the functional projection IP (see also Meisel, this volume). Then, at the ages of 2;1,0 (Pa) and 2;4,23 (Iv), respectively, major changes take place, indicating the availability of INFL and its projection IP.[7] Both children use clitic subjects, as shown in (18) and (19).

(18)	a.	*elle fait dodo la poupée*	(Pa 2;1,0)
		' she sleeps the doll'	
	b.	*maman elle est là*	(Pa 2;1,0)
		'mummy she is there'	

(19) a. *il dort*   (Iv 2;4,23)
         'he sleeps'
     b. *tu vois*   (Iv 2;4,23)
         'you see'
     c. *je mange*   (Iv 2;4,23)
         'I eat'

In addition, the position of subject and verb preceding sentence-internal negation indicates that both verb raising and subject raising are available. This configuration is illustrated in (20) and (21).

(20) a. *est pas les enfants*   (Pa 2;1,0)
         'is not (at) the kindergarten'
     b. *margarine tombe pas*   (Pa 2;1,0)
         'margarine falls not'
(21) a. *je veux pas*   (Iv 2;4,23)
         'I want not'
     b. *teddy tombe pas*   (Iv 2;4,23)
         'teddy bear falls not'

Finally, Ivar combines modal *veux* with infinitives, as in (22).

(22)   *je veux manger*   (Iv 2;4,23)
         'I want (to) eat'

Interestingly enough, in exactly the same recording we can observe for both children that verbs are combined for the first time with more than one argument, i.e. with subjects and objects.[8] Examples are shown in (23) and (24) below.

(23)   *papa réparé de roller de pacal*   (Pa 2;1,0)
         'daddy repaired Pascal's scooter'
(24)   *natasa man[z]er brot*   (Iv 2;4,23)
         'Natascha eat-INF bread'

These developmental facts make it clear that verb raising does not precede subject raising in grammatical development, as examples of subject and verb raising occur simultaneously in the French data. This, in turn, presents good evidence for the claim that in French NP-movement to Spec-IP is possible as soon as the projection IP is present in the children's grammar. Moreover, since we do not observe utterances exhibiting subject raising without verb raising, it appears that movement of both categories is possible at the same point of development. As is evidenced in Tables 1 and 2, there do not seem to be any restrictions on raising of different types of subjects, e.g. raising of pronominal subjects (stressed pronouns) vs. raising of lexical subjects (nouns or NPs). Pierce's (1989) assumption as well as the predictions one can derive from Borer & Wexler's (1987) maturation theory, namely that verb raising developmentally precedes subject raising, are thus disconfirmed by our data.

Table 1. Pascal — subject–verb order, French

age	preverbal subjects							postverbal subjects						
	+SR		?SR		TOTAL			+CL		−CL		TOTAL		
	NP	PR	NP	PR	NP	PR	TOT	NP	PR	NP	PR	NP	PR	TOT
1;08,22				5	5		**5**							
1;10,00										1		1		**1**
1;10,28			1		1		**1**	2		1		3		**3**
1;11,28		1		2		3	**3**			1		1		**1**
2;01,00	2		1	1	3	1	**4**	2		1		3		**3**
2;01,28				3		3	**3**			2		2		**2**
2;02,26	6	2		3	6	5	**11**	1	1			1	1	**2**
2;04,07	4	12		11	4	23	**27**	10	11		1	10	12	**22**
2;05,05		8	1	3	1	11	**12**	3	2	2	1	5	3	**8**

+SR = subject raising clearly evidenced by placement of negation and/or placement of finite and non-finite verb

?SR = no clear evidence for subject raising, but the order of constituents is the same as in +SR structures

+CL = VS order with preverbal subject clitic

−CL = VS order without subject clitic

NP = nouns or noun phrases

PR = all kinds of pronouns (with the exception of French subject clitics)

Tables 1 and 2 also disconfirm Pierce's (1989) observations concerning lexical subjects. In the data of Ivar and Pascal, there is no stage characterized by a high rate of postverbal subjects, nor does the rate of postverbal subjects decrease at any specific point in development. With respect to the use of preverbal vs. postverbal subjects — recall that the adult model provides both structures, as in (13) and (14) above — it appears that even though there is no special preference for postverbal subjects, interindividual differences nevertheless seem to play a certain role.

REGINA KÖPPE

Table 2. Ivar — subject–verb order, French

age	preverbal subjects							postverbal subjects						
	+SR		?SR		TOTAL			+CL		−CL		TOTAL		
	NP	PR	NP	PR	NP	PR	TOT	NP	PR	NP	PR	NP	PR	TOT
2;02,07			2	1	2	1	3			1	1	1	1	2
2;03,05			8	1	8	1	9			1	1	1	1	2
2;04,09			4	5	4	5	9	2				2		2
2;04,23	2	1		2	2	3	5			2		2		2
2;05,07	2	3	9	1	11	4	15	2		4		6		6
2;06,06	1	2	2	2	3	4	7	1		3		4		4

Ivar, for instance, initially appears to prefer preverbal subjects (see also Parodi 1990). The number of postverbal subjects only increases at a time when Ivar already uses clitics and right dislocations (2;5,7). In consequence, it is plausible to explain earlier postverbal subjects as right-dislocated structures where the clitic is simply missing. Note also that some of these subjects follow the VP (2;3,5 *c'est kaputt nounours* 'it is broken the teddy bear', 2;5,7 *(veut) un noeud ivar* '(wants) a knot Ivar'). In simple VS sentences like *tire pas ivar* 'pulls not Ivar' (2;6,6), however, the position of the subject cannot be determined. Burzio's (1986) assumption that subjects of ergative verbs remain in the object position cannot be verified on the basis of these few examples.

Pascal does not seem to prefer preverbal subjects as clearly as Ivar. However, early instances of postverbal subjects are difficult to explain: most of the utterances containing postverbal subjects seem to be rote-learned forms like *où il est* 'where is he' followed by a noun phrase. Nevertheless, there are also many postverbal subjects following the complete VP (1;10,28 *c'est mal encore la plante*, 'it is still bad the plant', 1;11,28 *est partie l'enfant nadia* 'is gone (to the) kindergarten Nadia', 2;1,0 *souffler les bougies nadia* 'blow-INF the candles Nadia').

These observations clearly indicate that postverbal subjects do not remain in Spec-VP, their base position, as was argued by Pierce (1989), but that they have been adjoined to the right of the VP. This structure is also frequent in adult French (with the difference that the clitic is omitted in the children's speech). Considering Pierce's analysis in a little more detail, it also becomes apparent that constructions containing subject clitics are excluded from her count of pre- vs. postverbal subjects. Rather, these constructions are counted in a different column as instances of right dislocations. In other words, utterances are classified differently, depending on whether or not a clitic subject pronoun precedes the verb when a non-clitic subject follows it. It is very likely that the decrease of postverbal subjects she observes in her data simply reflects the fact that, at a given age, right-dislocated subjects appear more often with a clitic and that, in consequence, they are not counted as postverbal any more.

The percentages of pre- and postverbal subjects in the data studied here are given in Tables 3 and 4. In both tables, columns show whether or not they have undergone subject raising (preverbal subjects) and whether or not a subject clitic is present (postverbal subjects).

Table 3. Ivar — preverbal and postverbal subjects, French

	preverbal %		postverbal %	
age	+SR	?SR	+CL	−CL
2;02,07		60		40
2;03,05		82		18
2;04,09		82	18	
2;04,23	72	29		29
2;05,07	72		9	19
2;06,06	64		9	27

Table 4. Pascal — preverbal and postverbal subjects, French

	preverbal %		postverbal %	
age	+SR	?SR	+CL	−CL
1;08,22		100		
1;10,00				100
1;10,28		25	50	25
1;11,28	25	50		25
2;01,00	17	33	33	17
2;01,28	60			40
2;02,26	84		16	
2;04,07	55		43	2
2;05,05	60		25	15

A further observation that should be mentioned is that postverbal subjects in constructions with simple VS order, at least in Pascal's data, occur almost exclusively with ergative verbs, whereas SV order is preferred with intransitive verbs. Examples are shown in (25) and (26) below.

(25)   *tombé le monsieur*   (Pa 2;1,28)
         'fallen the man'

(26)   *ça pique*   (Pa 1;11,28)
         'this pricks'

These structures may tentatively be interpreted as ergative constructions, with the subject being generated in the object position. Nevertheless, this analysis will have to be tested empirically on more material. One could also consider the possibility that such postverbal subjects occupy a position adjoined to VP, modeled on the right dislocation construction. Nevertheless, one would then have to explain why this model is not used (or used to a lesser extent) with subjects of intransitive and transitive verbs. Recall that Burzio's (1986) analysis has postverbal subjects of ergative verbs not "right-dislocated", but remaining in the object position. A third possibility is suggested by Pierce (1989), who assumes that the position of the subject, Spec-VP, may be optional within VP, i.e. the specifier can be generated to the left or to the right of the verb. It is obvious that in this view nearly every possible order of subject and verb could be accounted for, thus weakening its explanatory power considerably. Unless the empirical evidence does not permit any other account than to assume free variation of subject–verb order — which, I think, is not the case — one should prefer a more constrained hypothesis.

Under these considerations, the fact that Pierce (1989) and Deprez & Pierce (1991) make similar observations like those presented in (25) and (26) for English, but not for French, may have been brought about because structures containing clitic subjects have been omitted from their French data.[9]

Tables 5 and 6 show the first occurences of verb and subject raising for each verb class. Note that these tables contain only counts for those utterances in which verb and subject raising are clearly evidenced by the position of the elements with respect to negation and/or with respect to the occurrence of subject clitics. Taking a closer look at subject raising with different verb classes, it is interesting to note that ergative verbs are among the first verbs exhibiting verb and subject raising. For Pascal, they remain, for several months, the only verb class in which raised subjects can be observed. Examples are shown in (27) and (28).

(27)   *maman elle est là*   (Pa 2;1,0)
         'mummy she is there'

Table 5. Pascal — Raising, French		
age	verb raising	subject raising
1;10,28		
1;11,28		E?
2;01,00	E	E
	T?	
2;01,28		
2;02,26		
2;04,07		T

Table 6. Ivar — Raising, French		
age	verb raising	subject raising
2;02,07		
2;03,05		
2;04,09		
2;04,23	T	T
		E
2;05,07	E	
	I?	
2;06,06	I	I

T = transitive, I = intransitive, E = ergative, ? = unclear example

(28)   *teddy tombe pas*   (Iv 2;4,23)
        'teddy bear does not fall'

Intransitive verbs, on the other hand, do not show clear instances of subject raising during the period of observation; rather, they are mostly combined with clitic subjects, as shown in (29) and (30).

(29)   *il pleure*   (Pa 2;4,7)
        'he cries'

(30)   *et puis elle tourne pas*   (Iv 2;6,6)
        'and then she does not turn around'

Given the relatively low number of utterances in the data on which this analysis is based, it is difficult to find conclusive evidence for the claim that the difference between ergative and intransitive verbs does not reflect the scarcity of examples in the data, i.e. that, accidentally, there were no combinations of intransitive verbs with lexical subjects. On the other hand, remember that with French ergative verbs, the base-generated order of subject and verb (VS) within VP differs from normal order (SV(O) for transitive and intransitive verbs). Contrary to Borer & Wexler's (1987) claim, we do not find any empirical evidence which prevents us from assuming that children are indeed able to analyze ergative verbs correctly. This assumption is confirmed by the observation that subjects of ergative verbs occur more often in a postverbal position than subjects of other verb classes. Note also that overgeneralizations of the causative construction, as observed by Borer & Wexler, cannot be found in our data.

Assuming then that young children rely on formal and structural properties of the input language in constructing their grammar, they indeed seem to be able to detect that subjects of ergative verbs are generated in a postverbal position. This means that the underlying order of the VP is correctly analyzed. Moreover, the observation that ergative verbs show verb and subject raising earlier than intransitive verbs possibly indicates that it is exactly this irregularity of ergative verbs that facilitates or even triggers subject raising as soon as Spec-IP is available.

4.2. German

In German, the word order of early utterances presents certain problems for the analysis proposed above. From the ages of 1;10,28 (Pa) and 2;3,5 (Iv) onwards, we observe a number of utterances exhibiting SVO order, thus suggesting verb and subject raising only by their order of elements. Consider, for example, (31) and (32).

(31) a.   *so i mach [kua kua]*   (Pa 1;10,28)
          'like this she makes [kua kua]'
     b.   *papa mach diese*   (Pa 2;1,0)
          'daddy make these'
(32) a.   *i will nounours*   (Iv 2;3,5)
          'I want teddy bear'
     b.   *das nimm en deddi*   (Iv 2;3,5)
          'this one takes a teddy bear'

Several other early utterances exhibiting either postverbal subjects or postverbal negation might also be interpreted as first instances of verb raising. Examples are shown in (33–34) and (35–36), respectively.

(33)   *[ə] schokolade diese*   (Pa 2;1,0)
          'is chocolate this one'
(34) a.   *such deddi das*   (Iv 2;3,5)
          'seeks teddy bear this'
     b.   *war das ivar*   (Iv 2;3,5)
          'was this Ivar'
(35)   *ich will nich*   (Pa 2;1,0)
          'I want not'
(36)   *kommt das (nich)*   (Iv 2;3,5)
          'comes this (not)'

Clear evidence for verb and subject raising, however, where both subject and verb precede sentence-internal negation, is available only from the ages of 2;1,28 (Pa) and 2;4,9 (Iv) onwards.

Table 7. Pascal — subject–verb order, German

	preverbal subjects									postverbal subjects								
	+SR		?SR		−SR		TOTAL			+SR		?SR		−SR		TOTAL		
age	NP	PR	NP	PR	NP	PR	NP	PR	TOT	NP	PR	NP	PR	NP	PR	NP	PR	TOT
1;10,28			1	3			1	3	4									
1;11,28			1				1		1									
2;01,00			2	6			4	6	10			7			1	7	1	8
2;01,14												7				7		7
2;01,28		13	2	7		2	2	22	24				1			1		1
2;02,26		1		2				3	3	1		1				2		2
2;04,07	1	36		2			1	38	39				1	1		1	1	2
2;05,05	1	15		6	1		2	21	23	1		6	3			8	3	11

Table 8. Ivar — subject–verb order, German

	preverbal subjects									postverbal subjects								
	+SR		?SR		−SR		TOTAL			+SR		?SR		−SR		TOTAL		
age	NP	PR	NP	PR	NP	PR	NP	PR	TOT	NP	PR	NP	PR	NP	PR	NP	PR	TOT
2;02,07				1				1	1									
2;03,05			7	31	2		9	31	39		1	1	2	3		4	3	7
2;04,09	1	3	9	31	1	1	11	15	26				1	3	2	3	3	6
2;04,23	1	3	2	5			3	8	11		3	3	2			3	5	8
2;05,07	6	5	1	11		3	7	19	26		4	3	1	1		4	5	9
2;06,06	4	5	4			1	7	7	14	1	2	1			1	3	3	6

As in French, no difference between raising of pronominal subjects and raising of lexical subjects can be observed, as is evidenced in tables (7) and (8). Note also that in some cases it is possible in adult German to omit the subject, a possibility which is also reflected in the children's speech (*geht nich* 'does not work', *is nich da* 'is not there', etc.). Nevertheless, such target-like omissions are not counted in the present analysis.

Table 9. Pascal — subject raising, German

| | preverbal % | | postverbal % | |
age	+SR	?SR	+SR	−SR
1;10,28		50	50	
1;11,28			100	
2;01,00		72	22	6
2;01,14		100		
2;01,28	68		20	12
2;02,26	60		40	
2;04,07	92.5		5	2.5
2;05,05	79		18	3

Table 10. Ivar — subject raising, German

| | preverbal % | | postverbal % | |
age	+SR	?SR	+SR	−SR
2;02,07		100		
2;03,05	2	59	28	11
2;04,09	12.5	31	44	12.5
2;04,23	84		16	
2;05,07	69		20	11
2;06,06	75		15	10

Tables (9) and (10) show the percentages of subject raising in relation to the linear position of the subjects. Concerning postverbal subjects, the situation in German differs from that of French. In the adult language, German V2 effects allow for XVS(O) structures in which the subject occupies a postverbal position. In these structures, the verb has been raised to COMP (with a maximal projection preceding it), and the subject has been raised to Spec-IP in order to receive Nominative Case. In early child language, however, there is considerable debate as to whether COMP is already available at the same time when INFL is present. Müller (1993, this volume, chap. 9; see also Meisel & Müller 1992) argues that during the time-span discussed in this paper, the category COMP is not yet available in the grammar of Pascal and Ivar. Because Müller assumes that both children's German sentence structure contains IP as well as AGRP, she argues that in verb-second structures like *hier kommt pascal* 'here comes Pascal'

(Pa 2;1,14) or *da kann man sitzen* 'there can one sit' (Iv 2;5,7), the adverb has been raised to Spec-IP, whereas the subject has been raised to Spec-AGRP in order to receive Nominative Case.

If, on the other hand, one would argue that only *one* functional category is necessary (see also Meisel, this volume), subjects of such verb-second sentences should be regarded as remaining in preverbal Spec-VP. Taking Case assignment and case marking into consideration does not lead us any further here, given that a) moved NPs receive Nominative Case, and b) Nominative is the first case to be acquired (probably by default, see Stenzel, this volume). In other words, during the early phases of grammatical development, Nominative marking of a given NP does not present any evidence concerning its position, i.e. whether it is in its base position or whether it has been raised to Spec-IP. Moreover, Stenzel (this volume) notes that during this phase, very few NPs are case-marked at all.

Finally, what is interesting in comparison to the French data is that in German again, the verbs exhibiting two different orders of base generated constituents within VP and in IP are among the first verbs to be raised (see tables 11 and 12). In German, this differing verb class is the class of transitive verbs, exhibiting SOV order at D-structure within VP, whereas it is SVO (or XVSO) at the level of S-structure. Another observation which deserves further research is that in German as well, verb and subject raising of intransitive verbs occurs late.

(37) a. *tippen papa*   (Pa 2;1,24)
          'type daddy'
      b. *nein der paßt nicht*   (Pa 2;5,5)
          'no this one does not fit'

These observations are in conflict with Clahsen's (1988) analysis of German child language. Clahsen states that verb raising initially is limited to modals and intransitive verbs ending in *-t*. According to Clahsen, *-t* is not yet analyzed as an agreement feature, but seems to mark "low transitivity". Clahsen's analysis has also been questioned by Weissenborn (1990) and Verrips & Weissenborn (1992), who, analyzing the same data, do not come to the conclusion that verb raising is limited to intransitive verbs. The fact that verb and subject raising with intransitive verbs has been observed to occur later than with other verbs exhibiting different orders of subject and verb within VP and within IP thus might again lead us to conclude that children use their knowledge of the structural relations between verbs and their arguments within VP in developing the INFL projection.

Table 11. Pascal — Raising, German

age	verb raising	subject raising
1;10,28		T?
		E?
1;11,28		
2;01,00	E	T?
	I?	
2;01,14	E	
2;01,28		E
		T?
2;02,26	T	
2;04,07	I	
2;05,05		I

Table 12. Ivar — Raising, German

age	verb raising	subject raising
2;02,07	T?	
	E?	
2;03,05	E	E?
		T?
2;04,09	T	T
	E	E
	I	I

T = transitive, I = intransitive, E = ergative, ? = unclear example

5. Conclusion

In sum, the availability of NP-movement is closely related to the emergence of the functional category INFL in the child's grammar. Further, there is no empirical evidence for the maturational constraint proposed in Borer & Wexler (1987). The analysis also shows that NP-movement is possible in both languages as soon as the landing site Spec-IP is present in the child's grammar. The data thus provide evidence in favor of Guilfoyle & Noonan's (1988) claim that UG principles are present from early onwards, and that they can apply as soon as the necessary structures, i.e. functional projections, have emerged.

In addition, the occurrence of postverbal subjects in French is not due to verb raising to INFL with the subject remaining in its base position, as has been proposed by Pierce (1989). Instead, the analysis of French subject clitics as INFL-elements leads to a different account for structures containing postverbal subjects in early French, which can be analyzed as right dislocations where the subject clitic is missing.

Concerning the status of NP-movement in German, conclusive evidence in favor of its optionality has not been found. This may be due to the fact that complex structures which are assumed to have VP-internal subjects in German are not produced by the children during the observation period. Note, however, that subject raising to Spec-IP, the earliest case of NP-movement occuring, is effected in most of the cases and thus might constitute some evidence for the obligatoriness of this process in German.

Finally, the data suggest that both children are able to analyze correctly lexical properties of verbs and to develop a VP structure from very early on. It also has been proposed that the recognition of structural differences in the ordering of verbs and their complements at the level of VP might serve as a trigger for the development of the functional projection IP.

Acknowledgements

I would like to express my thanks to all members of the DUFDE project for their helpful and encouraging discussion. I am also grateful to Lynn Eubank for his most valuable comments and suggestions.

Notes

1. The term "unaccusative" for this verb class is also used frequently in the literature. I will nevertheless follow the terminology from Burzio (1986), who points out that the terms "unergative" vs. "unaccusative" originally stem from Relational Grammar (Perlmutter 1978). In Burzio's GB analysis, the traditional term "intransitive" is opposed to "ergative".

2. Von Stechow & Sternefeld (1988) state that the meaning of the two sentences is not exactly equivalent and that the sentence involving movement seems to be pragmatically marked.

3. Note that Radford's (1986) small-clause analysis of early child language (see also Parodi 1990) offered the possibility to generate the "subject" NP either to the left or to the right of the "XP predicate".

4. There are various hypotheses concerning the further development of this structure. What is important for the present analysis, however, is not whether early utterances are IPs or CPs or whether there is an intermediate AGRP (cf. Müller 1993; this volume, chap. 9), but whether there is some kind of functional category above VP that has a left specifier serving as landing site for NP-movement.

5. Further *wh*-movement of the subject to Spec-CP (as a result of the German verb-second effect) will not be considered here.

6. According to this analysis of colloquial French, the "standard" SVO order belongs to a different variety of French. Interestingly enough, the subjects of such SVO sentences are often restricted to proper names in colloquial French:
   $[_{IP}$Pierre$_i$ $[_I$ mange$_j$ $[_{VP}$t$_i$ t$_j$ une pomme]]]

7.   For a detailed analysis of the emergence of IP and the use of subject clitics, see Meisel (this volume) and Kaiser (this volume).

8.   Bickerton's (1990) theory of acquisition, explaining the "onset of syntax" as a consequence of biological maturation of the child's brain at a given time, could account for this observation quite well. As Bickerton's view of the "onset of syntax" mainly concerns the development of hierarchical relations, i.e. phrase structure, one could plausibly relate this "onset of syntax" to the emergence of INFL. Note, however, that our data might present some problems for Bickerton's assumption that the earliest multiword utterances are not syntactically structured and simply reflect the word order of the input language. Concerning the combination of objects and verbs, Pascal sticks to the target-like VO order in French, whereas he prefers OV structures in German. In adult German, however, OV structures (subordinate clause) as well as VO orders (main clause) can be observed. Ivar, on the other hand, uses OV and VO orders in both languages up to the age of 2;5. What is interesting here, and still deserves further research is the frequent occurrence of OV structures in French, since the French input does not provide such an order. In both cases, then, the order of objects and verbs does not exclusively reflect the input, but could instead be interpreted as resulting from the presence of some kind of VP-structure.

9.   With respect to Clark's (1985:711) observation that in various studies on the acquisition of French, subject-verb order in French is reported to be highly variable with intransitive verbs, one might ask whether these results are possibly caused by counts in which intransitive and ergative verbs are not differentiated.

References

Bickerton, Derek. 1990. "Syntactic Development: The brain just does it." Manuscript, University of Hawai'i at Manoa.

Borer, Hagit & Kenneth Wexler. 1987. "The Maturation of Syntax." *Parameter Setting (= Studies in Theoretical Psycholinguistics)*, ed. by Thomas Roeper & Edwin Williams, 123–172. Dordrecht: Reidel.

Burzio, Luigi. 1986. *Italian Syntax. A Government-Binding Approach (= Studies in Natural Language and Linguistic Theory)*. Dordrecht: Reidel.

Clahsen, Harald. 1988. *Normale und gestörte Kindersprache: Linguistische Untersuchungen zum Erwerb von Syntax und Morphologie*. Amsterdam: John Benjamins.

———. 1991. "Constraints on Parameter Setting: A grammatical analysis of some acquisition stages in German child language." *Language Acquisition* 1.361–391.

Clahsen, Harald, Teresa Parodi & Martina Penke. 1992. "Frühe IPs: Stufe I beim Erwerb des Deutschen." Paper presented at the 14th Annual Meeting of the German Society for Linguistics (DGfS), University of Bremen, February 1992.

Clark, Eve. 1985. "The Acquisition of Romance, with Special Reference to French." *The Crosslinguistic Study of Language Acquisition*. Vol. 1, ed. by Dan I. Slobin, 687–782. Hillsdale, N.J.: Erlbaum.

Contreras, Heles. 1987. "Small Clauses in Spanish and English." *Natural Language and Linguistic Theory* 5.225–243.

Deprez, Viviane & Amy Pierce. 1991. "Negation and Functional Categories in Early Grammar." Paper presented at the GLOW Workshop on Language Acquisition, University of Leiden, April 1991.

Dieck, Marianne. 1989. *Der Erwerb der Negation bei bilingualen Kindern (Französisch–Deutsch): Eine Fallstudie*. Masters thesis, University of Hamburg.

Eisenbeiß, Sonja. 1990. "Zum Passiverwerb in der deutschen Kindersprache." Manuscript, University of Düsseldorf.

Fanselow, Gisbert. 1990. "Scrambling as NP-movement." *Scrambling and Barriers* (= *Linguistik aktuell/Linguistics Today*, 5.), ed. by Günther Grewendorf & Wolfgang Sternefeld, 113–140. Amsterdam: John Benjamins.

Grewendorf, Günther. 1988. *Aspekte der deutschen Syntax: Eine Rektions-Bindungs-Analyse (Studien zur deutschen Grammatik*, 33.). Tübingen: Narr.

———. 1989. *Ergativity in German* (= *Studies in Generative Grammar*, 35.). Dordrecht: Foris.

Guilfoyle, Eithne & Máire Noonan. 1988. "Functional Categories and Language Acquisition." Manuscript, Montreal: McGill University.

Jaeggli, Osvaldo. 1986. "Passive." *Linguistic Inquiry* 17.587–622.

Jakubowicz, Celia. 1989. "Maturation or Invariance of Universal Grammar: Principles in language acquisition." *Probus* 1.283–340.

Kaiser, Georg A. & Jürgen M. Meisel. 1991. "Subjekte und Null-Subjekte im Französischen." *'DET, COMP und INFL': Zur Syntax funktionaler Kategorien und grammatischer Funktionen* (= *Linguistische Arbeiten*, 263.), ed. by Susan Olsen & Gisbert Fanselow, 110–136. Tübingen: Niemeyer.

Koopman, Hilda & Dominique Sportiche. 1991. "The Position of Subjects." *Lingua* 85.211–258.

Kuroda, Sige-Yuki. 1988. "Whether We Agree or Not: A comparative syntax of English and Japanese." *Lingvisticae Investigationes* 12.1–47.

Legendre, Géraldine. 1989. "Unaccusativity in French." *Lingua* 79.95–164.

Meisel, Jürgen M. 1990. "INFL-ection: Subjects and Subject-Verb Agreement." *Two First Languages: Early grammatical development in bilingual children* (= *Studies on Language Acquisition*, 10.), ed. by Jürgen M. Meisel, 237–298. Dordrecht: Foris.

Meisel, Jürgen M. & Natascha Müller. 1992. "On the Position of Finiteness in Early Child Grammar: Evidence from the simultaneous acquisition of two first languages: French and German." *The Acquisition of Verb Placement* (= *Studies in Theoretical Psycholinguistics*, 16.), ed. by Jürgen M. Meisel, 109–138. Dordrecht: Kluwer.

Müller, Natascha. 1993. *Komplexe Sätze: Der Erwerb von COMP und von Wortstellungsmustern bei bilingualen Kindern (Französisch/Deutsch)* (= *Tübinger Beiträge zur Linguistik, Series A: Language Development, 16.*). Tübingen: Narr.

Parodi, Teresa. 1990. "The Acquisition of Word Order Regularities and Case Morphology." *Two First Languages: Early grammatical development in bilingual children* (= *Studies on Language Acquisition*, 10.), ed. by J.M. Meisel, 157–190. Dordrecht: Foris.

Perlmutter, David. 1978. "Impersonal Passives and the Unaccusative Hypothesis." *Berkeley Linguistic Society IV*, 157–189. Berkeley: University of California.

Pierce, Amy. 1989. *On the Emergence of Syntax: A crosslinguistic study*. Dissertation, Cambridge, Mass.: Massachusetts Institute of Technology.

Radford, Andrew. 1986. "Small Children's Small Clauses." *Bangor Research Papers in Linguistics* 1.1–38.

———. 1990. *Syntactic Theory and the Acquisition of Syntax*. Oxford: Blackwell.

Rizzi, Luigi. 1982. *Issues in Italian Syntax* (= *Studies in Generative Grammar,* 11.). Dordrecht: Foris.

Roberge, Yves. 1986. "Subject Doubling, Free Inversion, and Null Argument Languages." *Canadian Journal of Linguistics* 31.55–79.

Sorace, Antonella. 1991. "Unaccusativity and Auxiliary Choice in Non-Native Grammars of Italian and French: Asymmetries and predictable indeterminacy." Paper presented at the 16th Boston University Conference on Language Development, October 1991.

Sportiche, Dominique. 1988. "A Theory of Floated Quantifiers and its Corollaries for Constituent Structure." *Linguistic Inquiry* 19.425–449.

von Stechow, Armin & Wolfgang Sternefeld. 1988. *Bausteine syntaktischen Wissens: Ein Lehrbuch der generativen Grammatik*. Opladen: Westdeutscher Verlag.

Verrips, Maaike & Jürgen Weissenborn. 1992. "Routes to Verb Placement in Early German and French: The independence of finiteness and agreement." *The Acquisition of Verb Placement* (= *Studies in Theoretical Psycholinguistics*, 16.), ed. by Jürgen M. Meisel, 283–337. Dordrecht: Kluwer.

Weissenborn, Jürgen. 1990. "Functional Categories and Verb Movement: The acquisition of German syntax reconsidered." *Spracherwerb und Grammatik: linguistische Untersuchungen zum Erwerb von Syntax und Morphologie (Linguistische Berichte, Sonderheft 3/1990)*, ed. by Monika Rothweiler, 190–224. Opladen: Westdeutscher Verlag.

Parameters Cannot Be Reset
Evidence from the Development of COMP

Natascha Müller
University of Hamburg

1. Introduction

Recent work in generative grammar has been guided by the idea of developing a theory of grammar in which structural variation across languages results from the interaction of parameterized universal principles rather than from a language-particular rule system. This research has been motivated by what is generally called the logical problem of language acquisition (cf. Hornstein & Lightfoot 1981), i.e. the problem of how children acquire a language on the basis of limited and degenerate data. If the parameter-setting approach to language variation turns out to be successful, then the task of language acquisition may reduce to the learning of lexical items and their idiosyncratic properties (cf. Felix 1990).

Early child language differs in crucial ways from the respective adult grammar, e.g. the lack of agreement and tense markings, the use of target-deviant word order patterns, the lack of modal auxiliaries. This observation might lead to the hypothesis that child grammars violate the principles of UG. However, if certain options are parameterized and thus need to be specified in the acquisition process, it is conceivable that the child explores the range of variation defined by the parameterized options. This variation should be observed essentially with functional categories, if Chomsky's (1989) suggestion turns out to be correct, namely that parametrization mainly relates to functional as opposed to lexical categories.

Functional categories are assumed to be bundles of abstract grammatical features (cf. Felix 1990). These grammatical features are drawn from a universal inventory. The claim that language variation relates to the system of functional categories may be interpreted at least in the following two ways:

—   languages may differ with respect to which grammatical features they select, although Felix (1990) and Rizzi (1991b) point out that some features are selected universally. The feature "gender" is not selected by every natural language, for instance.

—   languages may differ with respect to the distribution of grammatical features across the different syntactic positions (cf. Felix 1990). One example is the distribution of the finiteness operator [+F] (cf. Platzack & Holmberg 1989 and further below).

If these suggestions turn out to be correct, then it is quite reasonable to assume that functional categories may be unavailable at early points of language development and that the abstract grammatical features in the children's grammars may be distributed in a way deviating from the adult counterpart, where these options are permitted by UG.

Recently, some researchers have proposed a more constrained version of parameter theory. Among others, Valian (1988, 1990) has pointed out that the current version of the parameter model cannot accurately describe the way the child arrives at the target grammar. Given the fact that the data the child is exposed to are sometimes contradictory, s/he could switch parameter values an infinite number of times and as a consequence never settle on the correct value. This clearly raises a fundamental theoretical problem. Apart from theoretical shortcomings, there is also empirical evidence in favor of the assumption that children do not constantly switch the value of parameters during the acquisition process. Obviously, the theory of UG must be buttressed by a theory of acquisition which constrains how parameters are set. What is needed then is a constraint which requires that parameters cannot be reset during language development. The parameter-setting constraint (Clahsen 1990; cf. also Penner 1992, Roeper & Weissenborn 1990, and Weissenborn 1990b) has been formulated in order to meet these requirements. It states that fixed parameters cannot be reset.

In what follows, I will present within this framework a syntactic analysis of the word-order patterns used by bilingual children in French and German embedded clauses. I will attempt to present empirical evidence in support of the following two claims:

(i)   The development of functional categories is characterized by the children's exploration of the options offered by UG. More specifically, some abstract grammatical features may be missing during the earliest stages and they may be distributed in a target-deviant way even when the child has discovered their relevance for the respective input language. In other words, it is possible that children choose the wrong value of a parameter.

(ii) Parameters cannot be reset during the course of development.

2. Functional Categories in Child Grammar

2.1. *On the Availability of Functional Categories in Early Child Grammar*

Recently, many logical possibilities for the acquisition of functional categories in child language have been explored. Some researchers (Guilfoyle & Noonan 1988; Parodi 1990; Penner 1990; Platzack 1992; Radford 1986, 1987) argue that the very early stages are characterized by the absence of functional categories in the children's syntactic representation of sentences. Radford (1986, 1987) assumes that the clauses children produce resemble small clauses in the adult system. Clahsen (1990), Guilfoyle & Noonan (1988), Meisel (1991) and Pierce (1992) suggest that young children's "clauses" are really VPs. These approaches may be referred to as the short-clause-hypothesis. Other researchers, like Hyams (1992), Poeppel & Wexler (1991), Verrips & Weissenborn (1991, 1992), and Weissenborn (1990b) argue for the existence of fully articulated, but morphologically underspecified structures. I will refer to this hypothesis as the skeleton-hypothesis (for a more detailed discussion of both approaches cf. Müller 1991).[1] The analyses have empirically relevant implications. Whereas both predict language variation with respect to the distribution of grammatical features, only the short-clause analysis predicts that languages may vary with respect to the number and hierarchy of syntactically relevant functional projections. Additionally, the task of the language learner differs considerably under the short-clause and the skeleton analysis. If we assume the skeleton hypothesis to be correct, then the child's task is reduced largely to determining the distribution of grammatical features.[2] Following the short-clause analysis, the child has to find out (1) which grammatical features are relevant in the respective language,[3] (2) how the relevant grammatical features are distributed across different syntactic positions, and related to this last point (3) how many functional projections, i.e. syntactic positions are needed.[4] One desirable consequence of the short-clause hypothesis is that the universal inventory is not mixed up with the actual representation in the syntax of the particular language.

Currently, the study of the similarities and the differences among natural languages has led to contradictory results (cf. e.g. Fukui & Speas 1986; Iatridou

1990; Platzack & Holmberg 1989; Pollock 1989) and thus cannot serve as a basis for a decision in favor of one hypothesis. Examining language development can therefore play an important role in theory development. If we can show that children's syntactic representations differ from the target grammar not only with respect to the distribution of the relevant grammatical features but also with respect to the number of functional projections "activated", this would lead us to the assumption that the short-clause hypothesis is more plausible than the skeleton hypothesis.

In between these limiting proposals a number of other analyses have been presented which assume that the children's grammars contain some under-specified functional projections. This view has been advanced among others by Clahsen (1990), Clahsen & Penke (1992), Gawlitzek-Maiwald, Tracy & Fritzen-schaft (1992), Meisel (1990), Meisel & Müller (1992) and Roeper (1992). Note that this approach is compatible with both the short-clause and the skeleton hypothesis. The idea of incompletely specified functional projections has been explored with respect to feature specification and the architecture of functional projections. As far as the architecture is concerned, Lebeaux (1988), Hoekstra & Jordens (1991), and Roeper (1992) argue that adjunction structures are the precursors of fully articulated adult-like structures. They assume that categorial analysis is a later step in the acquisition process and that it triggers X-bar-structures.

In what follows I will confine myself to the problem of how the functional category COMP is discovered by children. Before I turn to a brief overview of the findings of other researchers concerning the development of the functional category COMP in child grammar, I will summarize some of the basic facts in the corresponding adult grammars.

2.2. The Adult Systems

It is generally agreed that French is an S-INFL-V-O language (cf. Pollock 1989), whereas German is a verb-second language with underlying O-V-INFL order (cf. Platzack 1983). Non-finite verbal elements appear in the position preceding complements in French and in the position following complements in German. This holds for main as well as subordinate clauses. Both are assumed to be verb-raising languages, i.e. the finite verb moves from its base-position V into INFL. The V2-phenomenon in German main clauses is derived by movement of the finite verb into COMP and by movement of any maximal projection into Spec-CP. Interestingly enough — though much weaker — French has a verb-second effect as well (residual V2-phenomenon, cf. Rizzi 1991b). Verb-second patterns show up in root interrogative sentences (subject-clitic inversion). It has been proposed that the differences between the two languages are related essentially to two parameters. The headedness parameter is specified differently for INFL in French, where IP is head-initial, and in German, where it is head-final. This is the surface position of the finite verb in French main clauses and in German subordinate clauses, which are verb-final. The other difference concerns the value of the finiteness (or verb-second) parameter suggested by Platzack & Holmberg (1989) which specifies the position of the operator [+F] in syntax. According to these authors, [+F] is located in COMP in German, i.e. in the position of the [WH]-operator, and in INFL in French. Under these assumptions we would thus have the structures in (1) and (2) for German and French respectively:[5]

(1)　a.　GERMAN

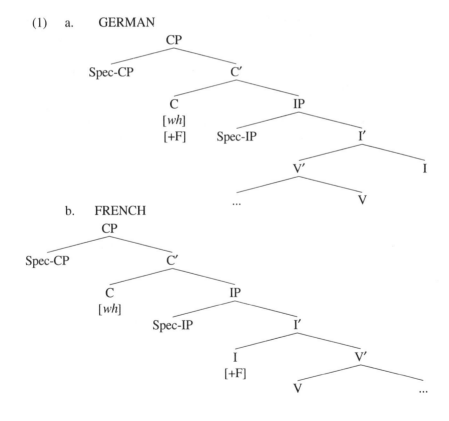

b.　FRENCH

2.3. *CP in Early Child Grammar*

Two hypotheses are discussed in the recent literature with respect to the availability of CP as compared to IP in early child grammar. Some researchers argue in favor of the assumption that CP is available only after IP has already been established (cf. Clahsen 1990; Gawlitzek-Maiwald et al. 1992; Guilfoyle & Noonan 1988; Haverkort & Weissenborn 1991 for French; Meisel & Müller 1992; Penner 1992; Roeper 1992; Rothweiler 1989; de Villiers 1992). Evidence in support of this hypothesis is the lack of complementizers and V2-effects (in V2 and residual V2-languages) at a point of development where there is no doubt that INFL is available in child grammar. Others hypothesize that IP and CP are available simultaneously (Hyams 1992; Poeppel & Wexler 1991; Verrips & Weissenborn 1991; Weissenborn 1990a,b). The evidence for this view are V2-effects (in V2 languages) and root wh-questions which show up at the same time the acquisition data indicate the presence of IP.

Both approaches make the implicit claim that V2-effects are necessarily related to the C-system in adult grammar and thus, the presence or absence of V2-effects is taken to be an indicator for the presence or absence of CP in child grammar. The plausibility of this assumption for V2-languages in general is weak given the fact that there are V2-languages such as Yiddish (cf. Diesing 1990) and Icelandic (cf. Platzack 1983, 1986) where V2-effects are not restricted to main clauses, but show up as well in embedded clauses where COMP is filled already. The following examples are taken from Diesing (1990:50).

(2) a.   *Vuhin   geyt ir?*
          where-to go   you
          'where are you going?'

     b.   *Zi iz gekumen zen ver frier   vet   kontshen*
          she is come   see who earlier would finish
          'she has come to see who would finish ealier'

     c.   *Vemen hot er nit gevolt az ot di bikher zoln   mir geben?*
          who   has he not wanted that the books should we give
          'to whom did he not want us to give the books'

In what follows, I will argue that V2-constructions in developing V2-languages and root interrogatives in developing V2- and residual V2-languages are most plausibly represented as IP-structures.

3. The Analysis

The analysis starts at a point of development where INFL is already available in the children's grammars. Nothing will be said on the question of whether there is an earlier phase during which INFL is not available and on the structure of the children's utterances (cf. Meisel 1990, this volume).

As a point of departure I will first give a brief survey of the relevant observations concerning the shape of very early child grammars, based on Meisel & Müller (1992) and Müller (1991). It is argued there that INFL/AGR is present in child grammars from early on, but that COMP, on the other hand, is initially missing. I will expand one particular point of my analysis (Müller 1991), i.e. the problem of how to integrate COMP into the children's grammar. The major purpose of the discussion will be to show (i) that the integration of COMP into German child grammar differs among the children studied here and (ii) that — due to the constraint that parameters cannot be reset — differences with respect to the acquisition of word order in German embedded clauses can be observed.

3.1. The Data

The subjects of this study are two boys — Ivar and Pascal — and one girl — Caroline. The age period studied covers about four years of the children's language development. Ivar has been studied from the age of 1;5 to 5;10, Pascal from 1;5 to 4;7, and Caroline from 1;6 to 5;0 (for a detailed description of the research project see Köppe, this volume, chap. 2).

4. Early Child Grammar without COMP

In the data from all three children there is evidence to suggest that properties of INFL are present from very early on (cf. Meisel 1986, 1990, this volume). The children make productive use of verb inflection to mark person and number agreement between subjects and verbs and begin to produce subjects systematically in both languages (Ivar at approx. 2;4, Caroline at approx. 2;1, and Pascal at approx. 2;2).

At this point of development, where both INFL and AGR and V2-patterns in German are clearly established, the children do not yet use complementizers. Meisel & Müller (1992) and Müller (1990, 1991) argue that the lack of complementizers can be explained neither by the supposedly too complex semantics of complementizers nor by the supposedly too complex character of embedded constructions. They conclude that the complementizer system is still not available in the children's grammars. Their arguments are based on the following observations.

Although the children do not use complementizers during this period, they already have full command of adverbs and prepositions which serve to express semantic relations similar to those of complementizers in the target language. Furthermore, two of the children (Caroline, Ivar) produce complex constructions expressing logical subordination (for examples, cf. Meisel & Müller 1992). Interestingly enough, all three children make productive use of the clause connectors *und* and *et* ('and') not only as utterance introducers (or initiators), but also as true co-ordinating conjunctions. This shows that the children are able to construct syntactically conjoined clauses. It seems clear that an approach which accounts for the lack of complementizers in terms of the formal and cognitive complexity of embedded constructions runs into severe problems.

Another observation concerns the interpretation of pronouns (pronominal subordination) in complex clauses which lack complementizers (cf. Roeper 1991). In adult German, verbs like *glauben* 'think' and *sagen* 'say' allow embedded V2-clauses without complementizers, in addition to V-final *daß*-'that'-clauses. The embedded V2-clause may be interpreted as a quotation or as a subordination, depending among other things on the reference of the pronoun in the embedded clause. Pronouns in the children's complex clauses which are not introduced by a complementizer do not have a subordinated interpretation, but instead a quotation reading.

(3) a. *ich sagst du — du wi[n] brot   oder würstchen*   (Iv;3;2,14)
         me tell you you want bread or   sausages
         'you ask me whether I want bread or sausages'
     b. *mir sagst du ob ich brot oder würstchen will*
(4) a. *...kannst du ihn k-trag k-hast du auch k-eh äh*
         can   you him ask   have   you also a
         hast du auch so   ein haus ne?   (Iv;3;4,9)
         have you also such a   house
         'can you ask him whether he has a house like this too'
     b. *kannst du ihn fragen ob er auch so ein haus hat*

In order to interpret the second clause in examples (3) and (4) as a subordination, the child should have used the pronouns indicated in (3b) and (4b).

Note also that the children use imperatives and interjections in their complex clauses which are not introduced by a complementizer. This suggests that these clauses are analyzed as quotations:

(5)   *dit — eh tirez   [n]a langue*   (Iv;2;9,5)
             says   stick out the tongue
             'he says stick out your tongue'

(6)   *ja   und i-ich hab gesagt — oh is gut   mein aua*   (Iv;3;0,19)
             yes and I   have said   oh is okay my   booboo
             'and I've said it's okay my booboo'

(7)   *n[ə]   sage — mach das hier*   (Pa;2;1,28)
             Nadia sagt   mach das hier
             'Nadia says do this here'

It again appears that we are dealing with syntactically non-subordinated constructions whose appearance we would predict under the view that the C-system initially is not available.

The assumption that the complementizer system is still missing in the children's grammar is lent further support by the fact that the French data from all three children lack examples of constructions which depend on the existence of the C-system, namely inversion in root interrogatives. The lack of inversion constructions in early French has also been reported by Weissenborn (1990b) for monolingual children.

Under the view that the functional category COMP is the one that bears the WH specification in adult grammar, one consequence of the claim that the children's grammars still lack the complementizer system would be that the WH specification is not present. Interestingly enough, it can be observed that the children leave out the *wh*-element in embedded questions. However, they already make productive use of root interrogative constructions introduced by a *wh*-word in both languages during the period discussed. A priori this seems to require the existence of the WH specification.

(8)   *demander maman — là   il est*   (Iv;2;6,6)
             ask   Mommy there it is
             'I will ask Mummy where it is'

(9)   *où   il est (le) nounours*   (Iv;2;6,6)
             where it is   the teddy?
             'where is the teddy?'

(10)   *i muß i muß fragen mama — ha-hat hat die k[j]ebe* (Iv;2;10,11)
         I have   to ask Mummy has   the glue
         'I have to ask Mummy where she's put the glue'
(11)   *wo is der auto*   (Iv;2;8,15)
         'where is the car?'
(12)   *guck mal — ich hab,hab   ich*   (Ca;2;6,22)
         look   I   have,have I
         'look what I have'
(13)   *was is das denn darein*   (Ca;2;10)
         'what is that in there'

In order to solve this conflict, a refinement of the *wh*-feature system is needed. Following Rizzi (1991b), the non-selected *wh*-specification of main clauses has to be distinguished from the lexically selected *wh*-specification of embedded clauses. He assumes that, among the other autonomously licensed specifications (like e.g. the tense specification of the whole sentence), the *wh*-specification of main clauses occurs in INFL. The position of the *wh*-specification in embedded clauses is COMP.

> The first question to ask is how the *wh*-specification can occur in main clauses. I will assume that this, as well as any other substantive feature specification cannot occur "for free" in a structure, and must be licensed somehow. The occurrence of *wh* in an embedded Comp is determined by a standard licensing device, lexical selection. What about main questions? Of course, the theory of licensing cannot be too demanding: there must be at least a position in a structure whose properties and specifications are independently licensed, i.e. a point which the chain of licensings can be anchored to, and start from. It is natural to assume that such a position can be the main inflection (or one of the main inflectional heads, if some version of the Split-INFL-hypothesis is adopted, as in Pollock 1989), the head that also contains the independent tense specification of the whole sentence. I would like to propose that among the other autonomously licensed specifications, the main inflection can also be specified as *wh*. (Rizzi 1991b:4)

That the main inflection can also be specified as *wh* is suggested by the fact that in some natural languages the verb manifests a special morphology in interrogatives. Assuming that the distinction between the selected and the non-selected *wh*-specification and the arguments against the existence of the C-system in early child grammar are correct, the children's developing grammars can be said to include only non-selected *wh*. Furthermore, under the view that the main inflection can be specified as *wh*, the use of root interrogatives is consistent with the assumption that the children's grammars still lack the complementizer system.

Another important observation is that root *wh*-question formation always displays the target-like V2-pattern in the children's German data. If we analyze root *wh*-interrogatives as IP- and not as CP-structures, this could be accounted for by the assumption that the *wh*-element is positioned in Spec-IP and the finite verb in INFL (for further details of the analysis see below).

In German, verb-second patterns start to appear with temporals (*jetzt* 'now'), locatives (*da* 'there') and objects.[6] The appearance of topicalization would also be expected under the analysis presented by now since it is quite conceivable that the child, having recognized the relevance of non-selected +*wh* (defining the interrogative sentence type), has discovered the importance of non-selected -*wh* (defining the declarative sentence type) as well. Note that both *wh*-question formation and topicalization are generally taken to be instances of one movement process, namely $\overline{\text{A}}$-movement.[7]

Meisel & Müller (1992) present a syntactic analysis of V2-constructions which is based on the "split-INFL-hypothesis" according to which some INFL-features are held to be independent heads (cf. Chomsky 1989; Pollock 1989). They suggest that the children's grammars contain two verbal functional categories (above VP) which they call AGR and INFL[8] respectively. Furthermore, they argue in favor of Pollock's analysis, namely that INFL dominates AGR (cf. structures (25) and (26) for German and French respectively).[9] In other words, finite verbs in the children's grammar of German and French first have to move to AGR before they can be raised to INFL. As far as the position of the finiteness operator is concerned, the authors assume that it is assigned to the highest functional head, INFL, in both languages, i.e. that INFL is analyzed as a possible landing site for finite verbs in both languages. The use of V2-constructions in German and SVX-patterns in French indicates that IP is head-initial in both languages. Directionality is interpreted in Meisel & Müller (1992) as the result of the lack of COMP and the decision to place [+F] in INFL as one option (presumably the default-value) of the finiteness-parameter.

One consequence of deriving the V2 effect in German by movement of the finite verb into INFL and by movement of any maximal phrase into Spec-IP is that $\overline{\text{A}}$-movement can also be accounted for in the absence of COMP. More specifically, I want to argue that Spec-IP may function both as an A-position and as an $\overline{\text{A}}$-bar position in the children's grammar of German (cf. Müller 1991). Thus, Spec-IP can host subjects[10], *wh*-elements and topicalized non-subjects. This possibility has been suggested by Diesing (1990) for adult Yiddish (cf. also

Horvath 1981 for Hungarian and Rizzi 1991a) which shows V2-effects in embedded clauses. One consequence of this analysis is that being an A-position depends on whether or not a theta-role or nominative Case can be assigned. In view of the absence of verb second patterns in the children's grammar of French it seems reasonable to assume that, here, adjunction to IP is the only option in the case of $\overline{\text{A}}$-movement. Note that topicalization always results in V3-patterns in French.

(14)	*ici on peut dormir*	(Iv;2;5,7)
	'here you can sleep'	
(15)	*ça on met*	(Iv;2;5,7)
	this we put	
	'we put this there'	
(16)	*un petit peu ça pique*	(Pa;2;4,7)
	a little bit it pricks	
	'it pricks a little bit'	
(17)	*là il pleure*	(Pa;2;4,7)
	'there he cries'	
(18)	*là elle est cassée*	(Ca;2;2,9)
	'there it is broken'	
(19)	*la chaussure on va jouer*	(Ca;2;4,8)
	the shoe we will play	
	'we will play with the shoe'	

The analysis presented so far has consequences for the assignment (or checking) of nominative Case in the children's grammar of German and French. One characteristic of V2-languages such as German is that the subject of a main clause may precede or immediately follow the finite verb. In non-V2- or residual V2-languages such as French, V2 effects are restricted to clitic subjects, hence the ungrammaticality of *a Jean lu le livre? 'has John read the book'. On the basis of these observations, Rizzi & Roberts (1989) develop the idea of directionality of nominative Case assignment. The authors suppose that in French, nominative Case can only be assigned leftward (here: Spec-IP), while in Germanic languages such as German either direction (leftward or rightward; here: Spec-IP or Spec-AGRP) of assignment is chosen.[11] Under these assumptions, raising of *a* into a position above the subject *Jean* (Spec-IP) represents a Case Filter violation in French, since nominative Case can only be assigned leftward here.

Furthermore, Meisel & Müller (1992) report that all three children sometimes use verb-final patterns in German main clauses which they interpret as evidence in favor of a head-final AGRP in German.[12] The observation that these patterns are completely absent in the French data suggests that AGRP is analyzed as a head-initial projection here.[13]

(20)   *(p)apa lenkrad   sitz*   (Iv;2;4,7)
        Daddy steering wheel sit
        'Daddy sits at the steering wheel'

(21)   *(var) ein [s]iff macht*   (Iv;2;5,21)
        Ivar a   boat builds
        'Ivar builds a boat'

(22)   *da so   macht* (da=der)   (Pa;2;2,12)
        it like this goes
        'it goes like this'

(23)   *das,das wo   is*   (Pa;2;5,5)
        it   where is
        'where is it'

(24)   *diese   da   drauf is*   (Ca;2;10)
        this one there on top is
        'this one is there on top'

Following Meisel & Müller (1992), the finite verb has not moved far enough in examples (20)–(24). Since examples of verb-final patterns in German main clauses are very infrequent, nothing forces us to assume that V-movement in the children's grammars derives from principles which are different from those in the respective adult grammar. Nevertheless, it seems to be the case that performance factors may sometimes interfere with grammatical principles (cf. Meisel 1990).[14]

The analysis so far would involve structures like the ones in (25) and (26) for German and French respectively (see next page).[15]

Meisel & Müller (1992) present further empirical evidence in favor of two positions for finite verbs in the children's grammars. They observe that the children use constructions of the type *jetzt sagt der das sagt* 'now says he it says' in which the same verb appears twice, initially and finally.

Furthermore, all three children use constructions which contain a finite modal auxiliary verb and a finite main verb (cf. Müller 1991).

(25)   German

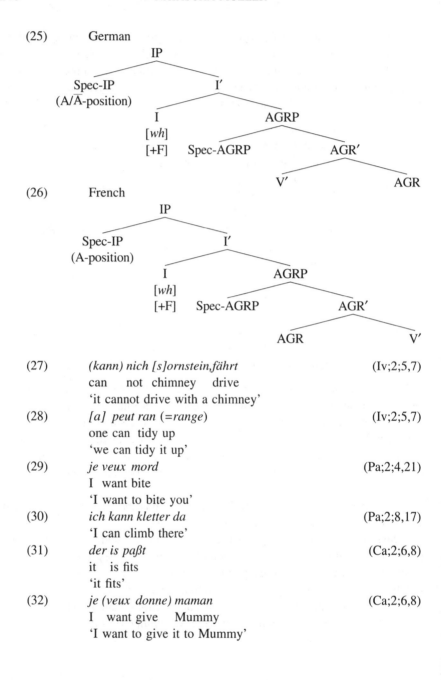

(26)   French

(27)   *(kann) nich [s]ornstein,fährt*   (Iv;2;5,7)
     can   not chimney   drive
     'it cannot drive with a chimney'

(28)   *[a] peut ran (=range)*   (Iv;2;5,7)
     one can tidy up
     'we can tidy it up'

(29)   *je veux mord*   (Pa;2;4,21)
     I want bite
     'I want to bite you'

(30)   *ich kann kletter da*   (Pa;2;8,17)
     'I can climb there'

(31)   *der is paßt*   (Ca;2;6,8)
     it   is fits
     'it fits'

(32)   *je (veux donne) maman*   (Ca;2;6,8)
     I   want give   Mummy
     'I want to give it to Mummy'

Note that copying constructions of the type *jetzt sagt der das sagt* and the verb final pattern in German (cf. examples (20)–(24)) are excluded with modal auxiliaries. These distributional facts can be accounted for if we assume that INFL is specified as modality and that modal auxiliaries are base-generated in INFL.[16]

So far, the distribution of finite verbs was taken as empirical evidence for the existence of the second functional projection AGRP, namely that all finite verbs which show up in AGR also appear in INFL (V2-position), but not vice versa (modal auxiliaries are excluded from AGR). Although I think that we need two functional categories, neither of which corresponds to adult COMP, in order to account for the children's utterances during this developmental phase (but see Meisel this volume for a different view), exactly which features are generated under the syntactic position labelled AGR remains a matter for further empirical investigation. Since the children, according to Schlyter's (1990) analysis, mark lexical aspect (change-of-state vs. non-change-of-state) during the period discussed, aspect might be a possible candidate. Interestingly enough, most of the verbs which show up in the syntactic position labelled AGR have the 3rd person inflection. However, not only 3rd person singular forms, e.g. *ist* 'is', but also 3rd person plural forms, e.g. *sind* 'are', *ham* 'have', are used in this position.[17] Meisel (1986, 1990) reports that the children already make productive use of 1st and 2nd person singular verb forms during this developmental phase. Since AGR seems to be restricted to verb forms with 3rd person singular and plural inflectional affixes, I hypothesize that number is another possible candidate for the feature specification of AGR (cf. the discussion in Müller 1991). I think these observations clearly demonstrate that it is worth reflecting upon the category labelled AGR here once more in detail. For the development of subject-verb agreement see Meisel (this volume).

To summarize, then, there is evidence for the existence of two functional, verbal categories and for the claim that AGRP is head-final in German and head-initial in French, whereas IP is head-initial in both languages, where INFL minimally contains [+F], non-selected *wh*, and modality. Note that INFL contains those specifications which according to Rizzi (1991b) are autonomously licensed.

I want to come back to the hypothesis that [+F] is associated with INFL in French and German child grammar during the period discussed. I assume that "[+F] in INFL" represents the default-setting of the finiteness parameter. This follows from markedness theory since it describes the smaller language. If the arguments against the existence of the C-system are valid, the actual grammar

does not provide the child with all the necessary information s/he needs in order
to choose some marked option of the finiteness parameter. Since the child seems
to have recognized the importance of finiteness in the respective grammars on
the one hand, and since COMP (or the importance of selected *wh*) has not yet
been discovered at this point of development on the other hand, the default-value
"[+F] in INFL" is used.

5. The Integration of COMP

In the course of further development, all children start producing subordinated embedded clauses which are introduced by complementizers. This happens in
Ivar at 2;11 in both languages, in Caroline at 2;6 in French and at 3;1 in
German, and in Pascal at 2;5 in French and at 2;9 in German. According to the
present analysis this indicates that lexically selected *wh* is available in the
children's syntactic representation of sentences. Main clauses now show standard
word order in both languages. This is also the case in French subordinate clauses.
From the very beginning, all three children have full command of the position
of the finite verb in French embedded clauses. In view of these observations it
seems plausible to assume that lexically selected *wh* is associated with a new
syntactic position (namely COMP) in the French grammars of all three children
and that this category does not contain the finiteness operator as required by the
target system. Note that now there are examples of inversion in root interrogatives in the French corpora which we would expect to show up in the
presence of COMP; cf. e.g. *comment s'appelle ma copine?* 'how is my girlfriend
called?', *où où où est le grand garçon (de l'école)?* 'where is the tall boy from
school?'.

In German, Pascal's and Caroline's embedded clauses show the required
verb-final pattern. These children acquire the word order for German subordinate
clauses without error. I suggest that Caroline and Pascal correctly associate the
syntactic position of lexically selected *wh* with the already existing verbal
functional category which contains the finiteness operator (INFL), i.e. both [+F]
and lexically selected *wh* are assigned to the same syntactic position. This
amounts to saying that they have set the verb-second parameter to the value
required by adult German. Following Clahsen (1990), the children restructure the
former INFL node, i.e. no independent COMP node is projected, and their
grammar can be said to contain a "rich COMP node". That this analysis is
indeed plausible becomes evident if we have a closer look at Ivar's development.

In Ivar's German, there is a striking similarity between the word order patterns of main clauses and embedded clauses. In both main clauses and embedded clauses the finite verb immediately follows the subject or a non-subject constituent, i.e. it appears in third position, if a complementizer is present.

(33)   *[vis] du <u>war</u> bibi*   (Iv;3;1,24)
           'when you were a baby'

(34)   *ich will   wenn du   <u>hast</u> ruhe, ich hab   ruhe oder*   (Iv;3;3,12)
           I   want if   you have calm I   have calm right
           'if you are quiet then I will be calm'

(35)   *erst wenn wir <u>sind</u> fertig   mit   das*   (Iv;3;4,9)
           just when we   have finished with it
           'just when we have finished it'

(36)   *wenn da   <u>komm</u> andere schiffe dann gehn die   dagegen*
           when there come other   boats   then   go   they against it
                                             (Iv;3;4,23)
           'when other boats come there then they go against it'

(37)   *...daß   dann <u>sagt</u> er...*   (Iv;3;5,7)
             that then   says he
           'that he says then...'

(38)   *du wi[n] daß mama <u>nimm</u> das weg ne*   (Iv;3;7,17)
           'you want that Mummy takes it away right?'

(39)   *guck mal wie   des   <u>is</u> groß*   (Iv;3;8,1)
           look   how this is big
           'look how big this is'

(40)   *was ich <u>hab</u> gemacht*   (Iv;3;10,25)
           '(look) what I have done'

(41)   *sagen wir mal daß das <u>is</u> ein baum*   (Iv;3;10,25)
           'let's say that this is a tree'

Up to the age of 4;4, of all the 167 embedded clauses, only 7 (4%) have the finite verb in clause-final position. The primary goal of the following discussion will be to demonstrate that COMP is integrated differently into Ivar's grammar of German. I want to suggest that [+F] and lexically selected *wh* are distributed across different categories, namely INFL and COMP, as in French. Thus, it seems that Ivar has set the finiteness parameter to the wrong value for German, which means that [+F] and lexically selected *wh* are not assigned to the same syntactic category. This explains why the presence of a complementizer does not prevent the finite verb from moving to the V2-position (=INFL) in his grammar. The analysis for German embedded clauses would thus involve a structure like the one in (42):

(42)   Ivar (German)

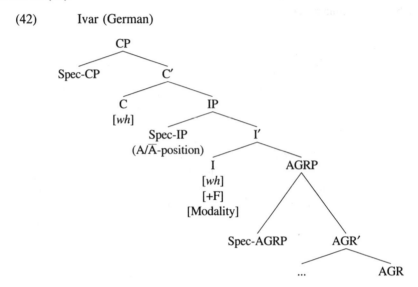

The question is how we can account for Ivar's wrong choice concerning the value of the finiteness parameter for German. I want to argue that Ivar does not analyze first complementizers as functional categories and that he, therefore, projects a new category in syntax which is superfluous.

It can be observed that the category COMP in Ivar's grammar of German develops out of a lexical category, namely the preposition *für* 'for'.[18] Such a development is not observed in Caroline's or in Pascal's German. The lexical nature of the forerunner *für* might lead Ivar to the hypothesis that a new category which is lexical is needed in syntax in order to generate complementizers. If "complementizers" are first analyzed as lexical categories, they cannot be associated with functional [+F], i.e. they are not generated in INFL which contains [+F] in Ivar's grammar. This amounts to saying that the choice of a syntactic position for complementizers is made before Ivar has discovered that they constitute functional categories. As a consequence, the finiteness parameter is set to the wrong value for German.

What evidence is there to suggest that complementizers develop out of the preposition *für*?

At the age of 2;7, i.e. 4 months before adult-like complementizers begin to appear, Ivar starts to use the preposition *für* which introduces not only NPs, but also whole sentences. It is interesting to note that these sentences may contain a finite or a non-finite verb form.

für+NP

(43)	*der [got] f[um] f[um] jeans*	(Iv;2;8,1)
	'this belongs to jeans'	
(44)	*für [ga]-fü tie[j]e*	(Iv;2;8,15)
	'for animals'	
(45)	*für de-den [n]öwe*	(Iv;2;8,15)
	'for the lion'	
(46)	*fu du der geschenk*	(Iv;2;11,7)
	'for you the gift'	

für+S

(47)   *f[um] tiere   weg nich [n]aufen*   (Iv;2;7,17)
         for   animals away not run
         'in order for the animals not to run away'

(48)   *muß da   sei   rein guck pour pour tie[j]e   nich*
         has there to go in   look for   animals not
          nich weg[n]aufen   (Iv;2;8,1)
         not away-run
         'this has to go in there in order for the animals not to run away'

(49)   *f[o] de f[o] de reiten komm du*   (Iv;2;9,18)
         for   it ride   come you
         'you come in order to ride it'

(50)   *emm das das für k[j]em[d]en*   (Iv;2;10,11)
               this   for to comb
         'this is for to put in your hair'

(51)   *das für k[j]emmen deine haare*   (Iv;2;10,11)
         this for to comb   your hair
         'this is for to put in your hair'

(52)   *fü,für nich der [n]öwe beißt* (=Löwe)   (Iv;2;11,21)
         for   not the lion   bites
         'in order for the lion not to bite'

Cf. also later in the developmental process:

(53)   *das is für der rauch geht hoch, in das hau*   (Iv;3;4,9)
           this is for the smoke goes up,   in the house
           'in order for the smoke to go up...'

(54)   *f[um] björn hat das abgerißt*   (Iv;3;4,23)
           for   Björn has it off-torn
           'because Björn has torn it off'

(55)   *so föm föm für die kinder, kann das abrissen*   (Iv;3;4,23)
           for   the children can it   off-tear
           'in order for the children to tear it off'

There is more evidence to suggest that *für* is categorized as a preposition: Besides the form *für*, Ivar uses the variants *fo, fum, föm* which do not correspond to the target language. In adult German, some prepositions may fuse with case-marked articles, cf. *am, zum*. In contrast to prepositions, complementizers are invariant in German. This is also true for Ivar's language use. Furthermore, Ivar never uses complementizers in combination with NPs at later points in his development.

Another observation supporting the claim that complementizers first constitute lexical categories is that early elements introducing clauses are base-generated *weil* 'because', *wenn* 'if', *als* 'when', specified as [-wh]. During the age period from 2;11 to 3;1 no moved *wh*-words introduce embedded clauses. If we assume that functional categories differ from lexical categories with respect to the specifier-system (cf. Fukui & Speas 1986; Raposo & Uriagereka 1990; Speas 1990), i.e. functional heads assign certain inflectional (Kase-) features (e.g. [+F], [+wh], [+AGR]) under agreement and these features are licensed by a particular (adjacent) specifier (cf. Speas 1990), then the absence of embedded *wh*-words in Ivar's grammar is a natural consequence of the assumption that COMP, the syntactic position of complementizers, is specified as (non-Kase assigning) [-wh]. In other words, since COMP does not contain selected [+wh], for instance, it does not license a specifier as a landing site for embedded *wh*-movement. Note that subordinating conjunctions and moved *wh*-words appear simultaneously in Caroline's and Pascal's German embedded clauses.

The next step comprises the integration of functional COMP into Ivar's grammar of German which is evidenced by the use of *wh*-words introducing embedded clauses. From the age of 3;2 onwards, Ivar starts making productive use of *wh*-words in embedded clauses. Thus, lexically selected [+wh] is part of the child's category system. It seems reasonable to suppose that Ivar has discovered the functional category COMP. However, the integration of functional

COMP into the grammar does not entail the correct word order in German embedded clauses. Up to the age of 4;4, Ivar's embedded clauses mainly show main-clause word order with the finite verb in third position. Interestingly enough, there are examples of the V2-effect in embedded clauses, such as *weiß du warum da sind so böse tiere* 'know you why there are that vicious animals' (cf. also (36) and (37)). This observation seems to confirm the analysis given above for German V2-constructions in non-embedded contexts (Spec-IP=Ā-position).

Note that the occurrence of the V2-effect in German embedded clauses does not depend on the type of element which introduces the clause (subordinating conjunction *wenn* 'when', complementizer *daß* 'that', *wh*-word *warum* 'why'). Another interesting aspect is that V2-effects are restricted to German embedded clauses. Crucially, the subject surfaces in the position immediately following the element introducing the embedded clause in French. Again, we have reason to believe that the analysis presented above is plausible, where I argued that in French, Spec-IP functions exclusively as an A-position.

We can account for these observations if we claim that selected [+*wh*] is associated with the earlier developed syntactic position of base-generated *für* and *weil*, *wenn*, *als*, but not with INFL containing [+F] as a consequence of the assumption that fixed parameters (the verb-second parameter) cannot be reset. Thus, Ivar ends up with a structure like the one in (42) for German.

The question is how Ivar arrives at the target-like V-final pattern in German embedded clauses. The data from Ivar clearly show that the acquisition of the V-final pattern in German embedded clauses is a step-by-step (or item-by-item) learning process. Note that under the assumption that fixed parameters cannot be reset, we would also expect a long drawn-out learning process.

From the age of 4;4 onwards, V-final patterns appear quite frequently in embedded clauses. The relative proportion of V-final patterns amounts to 50% in one third of all recordings during the age period from 4;4 to 4;11. An obvious assumption would be that the occurrence of V-final patterns is random. However, this conclusion is premature. It seems to be the case that their usage is subject to severe restrictions. It can be observed that the patterns appear with particular verbs only, namely with main verbs in the present tense. The pattern is excluded with modal and temporal auxiliaries (in the present and past) and with main/copula verbs in the past tense like *war* 'was'. During the period discussed, the data do not contain a single example of the use of a modal or temporal auxiliary or a main/copula verb in the past tense like *war* in clause-final position.

(56)   ...*weil   einmal wenn der <u>war</u> hier...*   (Iv;4;4,14)
            because once   when he was here
            'because when he stayed here once...'

(57)   *wenn ich <u>hab</u> ein dach <u>gebaut</u>*   (Iv;4;6,20)
            when I   have a   roof built
            'when I have built a roof'

(58)   *wenn Mama   <u>hat</u> hühner <u>gebraten</u>*   (Iv;4;4,14)
            when Mommy has chicken fried
            'when Mommy has fried chicken'

(59)   *wenn Gundula <u>is</u>   <u>weggegangen</u>*   (Iv;4;4,14)
            when Gundula has away-gone
            'when Gundula has gone'

(60)   *und wenn der <u>will</u> <u>arbeiten</u>*   (Iv;4;5)
            'and if he will work'

(61)   ...*wenn ich dich <u>verhexe</u>...*   (Iv;4;4,14)
              if   I   you bewitch
            'if I bewitch you'

(62)   ...*wenn man kein bibi <u>hat</u>...*   (Iv;4;8,19)
              if   you no   baby have
            'if you don't have a baby...'

(63)   *und weißt du   was was ich <u>hab</u> <u>gesehn</u>*   (Iv;4;4,21)
            and know you what what I   have seen?
            'and do you know what I have seen?'

(64)   *ich (will) was   grünes was du   nicht <u>siehst</u>*   (Iv;4;4,14)
            I   want something green that you not   see
            'I want something green that you don't see'

(65)   *ich sehe was alles   [s]warz <u>is</u>*   (Iv;4;4,14)
            I   see that everything black   is
            'I see those things that are black'

(66)   *ich sehe was gelb   <u>is</u>*   (Iv;4;4,14)
            I   see what yellow is
            'I see something that is yellow'

(67)   *weißt du wie wir mußt die tür   <u>machen</u>*   (Iv;4;5,14)
            know you how we must the door make?
            'do you know how we have to make the door?'

(68)   *ich weiß gar   nich wie wir's <u>machen</u>*   (Iv;4;6,13)
            I   know really not how we it do
            'I really don't know how we do it'

(69) *...daß du sollst geld <u>haben</u>*   (Iv;4;9,15)
    that you shall money have
    'that you shall have money'

(70) *...daß du <u>bist</u> im mama- im im   haus*
    that you have in Mummy-in the in the house
    <u>geblieben</u>   (Iv;4;9,15)
    stayed
    'that you have stayed in the house'

(71) *ich möchte auch daß der bibi bei mir <u>bleibt</u>* (Iv;4;6,13)
    I   want also that the baby with me stays
    'I also want that the baby stays with me'

(72) *...daß ich <u>wiederkomme</u>*   (Iv;4;9,15)
    that I   back-come
    'that I come back'

A further observation is that embedded clauses which contain a main verb in the present tense do not seem to be treated in a uniform way, that is some show the target-like V-final pattern and some show main clause word order. It looks as if the V-final pattern is optional in these cases.

(73) *...daß dann <u>sagt</u> er...*   (Iv;4;4,14)
    that then says he
    'that he says then'

(74) *...daß sie <u>haben</u> keinen geld   mehr* (Iv;4;8,4)
    that they have no   money anymore
    'that they don't have money anymore'

(75) *wir tun nur so daß hier <u>gibt's</u>   zwei* (Iv;4;9,29)
    we do only so that here are there two
    'we only do as if there are two here'

(76) *ich möchte auch daß der bei mir <u>bleibt</u>* (Iv;4;6 13)
    I   want also that he with me stays
    'I also want that he stays with me'

(77) *...daß ich es <u>weiß</u>*   (Iv;4;7,24)
    that I it know
    'that I know it'

(78) *ich möchte daß der mund ausgeschnitten <u>is</u>...* (Iv;4;10,29)
    I   want   that the mouth out-cut   is
    'I want that the mouth is cut out'

(79)   ...wenn du _trinkst_ den...   (Iv;4;4,21)
          'if you drink it'
(80)   ...wenn-wenn du _tust_ dein finger _rein_   (Iv;4;5,28)
          'if you put your finger in'
(81)   aber wenn da _sind_ ganz viele...   (Iv;4;6,20)
          'but if there are very many...'
(82)   ...wenn der immer _aufpustet_   (Iv;4;4,14)
          'when he always inflates'
(83)   wenn ich dir die brille   _gebe_   (Iv;4;9,1)
          if   I   you the glasses give
          'if I give you the glasses'
(84)   wenn ich emm f[um] drei bis zwei   _zauber..._
          if   I   for   three into two (by magic) turn
                                                                        (Iv;4;9,1)
          'if I turn three into two by magic'

Cf. also the following examples:

(85)   wenn das _is_ unten   (Iv;4;10,29)
          'if this is below'
(86)   wenn das unten _is_   (Iv;4;10,29)
          'if this below is'

This finding might constitute an empirical challenge to the claim about the constraints imposed on the occurrence of V-final patterns. However, we again can observe restrictions with respect to the occurrence of these patterns. V-final patterns start being obligatory with main verbs in the present tense, depending on the type of the lexical item which introduces the embedded clause. The following sequence can be observed. At first, V-final patterns appear categorically in embedded clauses (containing a main verb in the present tense) introduced by _was_ 'what'. Then follow _damit_ 'in order to', _wer_ 'who', _wo_ 'where', _daß_ 'that', _wenn_ 'if', and _wie_ 'how'. The crucial observation is that the difference between _wh_-elements, subordinating conjunctions and complementizers like _daß_ does not seem to be of any importance here. It thus appears to be the case that the V-final pattern with main verbs in the present tense is learned separately for each lexical C-element introducing embedded clauses. Note that even in cases where the V-final pattern is already obligatory with a particular C-element, it is not generalized to embedded clauses which are introduced by the same

C-element and which contain a modal or temporal auxiliary or a main/copula verb in the past tense like *war* 'was'.

The question arises, of course, how we can account for the observed restrictions. Assuming that my analysis of Caroline's and Pascal's acquisition data is correct, Ivar has to learn that complementizers are placed in the syntactic position which contains [+F], i.e. in INFL in his grammar. Furthermore, he has to learn this separately for each complementizer, if we assume that the verb-second parameter cannot be reset during the course of development. Note that IP has everything Ivar needs in order to generate complementizers. Spec-IP can function as an $\overline{A}$-position and thus it can host *wh*-elements. INFL is specified as *wh*, which can either be autonomously licensed or lexically selected. In cases where a particular complementizer is positioned in INFL, his grammar generates the V-final pattern, since the finite verb has to remain in head-final AGR (cf. structure (42)). In summary, then, it appears to be the case that what seems to be instantaneous in Caroline's and Pascal's acquisition of the word order in German embedded clauses corresponds to a long drawn-out learning process in Ivar. Restructuring of his German IP is a step-by-step process.

I do not discuss at length here the question of why the V-final pattern is excluded with modal and temporal auxiliaries and main/copula verbs in the past tense like *war* in Ivar's grammar of German (cf. Müller 1991). Meisel's (1985) and Schlyter's (1990) studies of the acquisition of tense and aspect show that the children begin to mark tense (present vs. past) at the point of development where COMP is integrated into their grammar. Having recognized the importance of tense, the child has to determine the distribution of the [PAST]-specification in her/his grammar. I argued in Müller (1991) that Ivar assigns [PAST] to INFL, i.e. to the syntactic position which is specified as autonomously licensed [+F], [Modality], and [*wh*]. We thus obtain a structure for German as in (87) (see next page).

Modal and temporal auxiliaries and main verbs in the past tense thus have to be positioned in INFL in order to be specified as [Modality] and/or [+PAST]. If we base our arguments on distributional properties of finite verbs (cf. above), the observation that modal and temporal auxiliaries and main verbs in the past tense are excluded from the position of head-final AGR in Ivar's grammar of German may indicate that these verbs are base-generated in INFL (cf. Müller 1991).

As is clear from the feature specification of INFL in structure (87), an apparent conflict arises in embedded clauses which contain a modal or temporal auxiliary or a main verb in the past tense. These elements have to be positioned in INFL in order to be specified for [Modality] and/or [+PAST]. As far as the

(87)   Ivar (German)

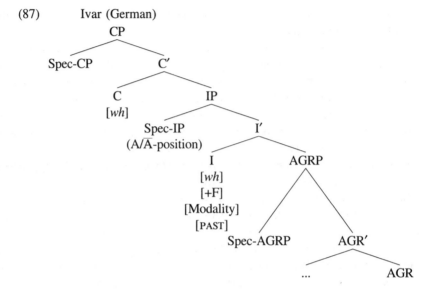

position of complementizers is concerned, the only option is to place them within a projection of COMP in these cases. As a result, the finite verb surfaces in the position immediately following the subject or a non-subject constituent, i.e. in third position.

Developmentally, there is quite some change to be observed from the age of 4;11 onwards in Ivar. The relative proportion of verb-final patterns among all embedded clauses never drops below 90%. Furthermore, embedded clauses with main clause word order appear at 5;2 at the latest. This developmental phase sees the sudden use of modal and temporal auxiliaries and main verbs in the past tense in clause-final position in embedded clauses. These elements appear in clause-final position "out of the blue", i.e. no gradual developmental pattern that obtains for main verbs in the present tense can be observed.

According to the analysis presented in this paper, the observation that most of Ivar's embedded clauses show target-like verb-final patterns from the age of 4;11 onwards suggests that Ivar has discovered for the majority of C-elements that they are positioned within a projection of INFL and not of COMP in structure (87). Thus, the first learning task, namely the restructuring of INFL as rich COMP, has been achieved by that time. Due to the described conflict, Ivar has to reconsider the distribution of the grammatical features [Modality] and [PAST]. Two interpretations are possible here. First, it may be suggested that the modality and the tense specification are assigned to head-final AGR in Ivar's grammar of German, i.e. AGR is restructured as shown in (88). If this were the case, however, we would expect an item-by-item learning process as in the case of restructuring INFL as rich COMP. As we are dealing with a sudden step in development, it may also be very tentatively suggested that Ivar projects a new verbal (head-final) functional category in syntax which is specified as [Modality] and [PAST]. This would be a plausible analysis, if we had enough empirical evidence for two (head-final) verbal functional categories in adult German as well. This last point, however, is far from being settled (cf. e.g. Iatridou 1990). The proposed analyses would involve structures like the ones in (88) and (89) respectively:

(88)   Ivar (German)

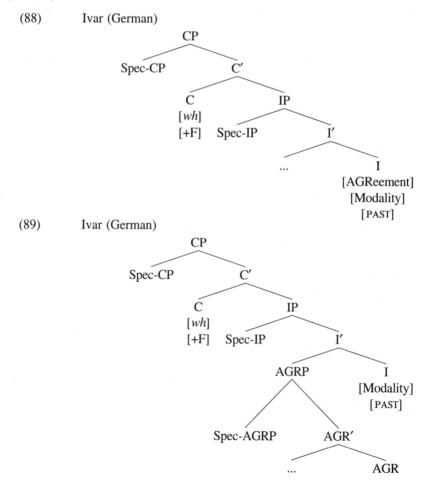

(89)   Ivar (German)

I want to leave open the question of whether structure (88) or structure (89) is to be preferred (cf. Müller 1991 for a discussion of this issue).

If the analysis presented for Ivar's development in German is correct, then we should obtain the same conflict in Caroline's and Pascal's grammar of German. I argued in favor of an analysis according to which modal auxiliaries are base-generated in INFL in the German grammar of all children during the phase where COMP has not been developed yet.[19] Note that this is the wrong analysis for adult German. Caroline and Pascal have to reconsider the distribution of these verbs by the time they restructure their INFL node as a rich COMP node (the rich COMP node cannot contain two types of base-generated elements at the same time, a complementizer and a modal auxiliary). As soon as INFL is restructured as a rich COMP node, modal auxiliaries can no longer be base-generated in this node. The conflict mentioned is not visible in Caroline's and Pascal's case since the restructuring of the INFL node results from the setting of the finiteness parameter to the correct value in the grammar of these children and therefore is not a step-by-step process as in Ivar's case.

6.   Discussion

I have suggested that the reason for Ivar's development is that he does not analyze first complementizers as functional categories but instead as lexical categories and that consequently, lexically selected [wh] and [+F] are distributed across different categories. We have to ask further the reasons for the wrong classification of complementizers.

There is no doubt that subordinating conjunctions in adult German share many properties with lexical categories such as prepositions.[20] For instance, they encode similar semantic relations (temporal, causal) and they appear in front of sentences and noun phrases respectively (cf. Müller 1991 for a discussion of this issue). Thus, there may be confusion with respect to the categorial status of these elements in the child's grammatical system. If we consider the fact that subordinating conjunctions are used by the children only at a later point in development where they already make productive use of prepositions, the hypothesis about the wrong classification of subordinating conjunctions becomes even more plausible. Note that authors like Bickerton (1981), Koopman & Lefèbvre (1981), Washabaugh (1975), Woolford (1979) argue for some English- and French-based creoles that prepositions (for, pour) are possible precursors for complementizers.

The approach presented so far claims that the development of the two languages of the bilingual children proceeds along two separate, language-specific paths (cf. Meisel 1986, 1990). There are several observations which suggest that transfer from French into German is probably not the reason for Ivar's development. First, I have tried to show that Ivar's German embedded clauses display V2-effects. There are no examples of the occurrence of inversion in his French embedded clauses. Secondly, some monolingual German children also have problems with this domain of the grammar and they produce the same word order patterns which have been observed in Ivar (cf. Gawlitzek-Maiwald et al. 1992).[21] Thirdly, usage of a preposition as a precursor for complementizers can also be found in monolingual children. The English children studied by Brown (1973), Adam and Eve, use *for* to introduce finite clauses (the data are taken from the CHILDES database at the Max-Planck Institute for Psycho-linguistics at Nijmegen). Some examples of this usage are:

Adam

    (90)   *for Mummy help me reach*
    (91)   *look out for children shout*
    (92)   *for the sun get in my eyes*
    (93)   *for all ladybugs get in it*

Eve

    (94)   *for for a horse had a have a drink of water*
    (95)   *for for bus stops*
    (96)   *it's a bathtub for a boy get in*
    (97)   *that for we cook our meat for*

A fourth point is that Ivar makes the correct choices in cases where other parameters (e.g. the headedness-parameter) are concerned.

Under the approach proposed in this paper recognition of the relevance of grammatical features is determined by the categorial analysis of lexical material. However, this does not answer the question of why certain grammatical features, lexically selected [wh] for instance, are integrated only at a later point in development. Why does the child not pay attention to the relevant lexical material during earlier phases? I want to very tentatively suggest that recognition of relevant grammatical features is determined, among other things, by an invariant chronology which is independent of the input. This amounts to saying that children will start testing whether selected [wh] is relevant in the respective input language only after they have tested the relevance of other grammatical features, taken from a universal inventory. A chronology for parameter-setting is a desirable consequence of this hypothesis (for further discussion cf. Müller 1991).

Acknowledgements

I want to thank Susanne E. Carroll, Peter Jordens, Georg Kaiser, Caroline Koehn, Regina Köppe, Jürgen M. Meisel, Zvi Penner, Tom Roeper, Achim Stenzel, and Jürgen Weissenborn for comments on earlier versions of this paper.

Notes

1. Weissenborn (1990b) suggests that there is an initial stage in the acquisition of German where the children use residual, but not generalized V-to-C-movement. The important assumption is that the CP is available for syntactic processes from very early on.

2. Note that according to the skeleton-analysis the child should be said to determine which grammatical features are *not* relevant in the input language.

3. If we assume the short-clause analysis to be correct, then the child has to decide which features are relevant in the respective language. This decision, however, has to be made only for those features which are not selected universally. Finiteness, for example, is seen as a universal feature and thus is excluded from the set of possible choices (cf. Felix 1990; Rizzi 1991b).

4. Platzack & Holmberg (1989) suggest a parameter which specifies the occurrence of AGR a) in syntax or b) not in syntax. Whether a language chooses option a) or b) depends on the kind of subject–verb agreement.

5. For the assumption that lexical categories differ from functional categories in their specifier-system, cf. below.

6. Fronting of temporals and locatives is much more frequent than fronting of objects.

7. For a detailed discussion of $\overline{A}$-movement in adult and child language see Müller (1991).

8. Meisel & Müller (1992) use the category label TENSE for the syntactic position which minimally contains [+F]. Since the children do not seem to have discovered the PAST-feature yet (cf. Meisel 1985; Schlyter 1990), this terminology is misleading.

9. This hierarchy of functional projections is incompatible with Haverkort & Weissenborn's (1991) analysis of clitic placement in positive imperatives. I do not want to discuss this problem here. Note, however, that there is a selectional interdependency between complementizers and tense (*that* selects [+tense], *for* selects [-tense]) in the adult grammar which suggests that INFL (or TENSE) dominates AGR and not vice versa (cf. Zubizarretta 1992).

10. I take Kuroda's (1988) and Sportiche's (1988) analysis of subjects to be uncontroversial, namely that they originate in a position within VP and are A-moved into their s-structure position.

11. The existence of copying constructions such as *(du) nimmst du 'ne blaue* 'you take you a blue (one)', *i bin i ein hirsch* 'I am I a deer', *wir wolln wir eine (kutsche) machen* 'we want we a cab make', where the subject appears pre- and postverbally, in the German data from all children and the absence of such examples in French suggests that this may indeed be the correct generalization (cf. Müller 1991 for further discussion).

12. Caroline uses this pattern only once. In the data from Ivar and Pascal, the finite verb shows up in clause-final position in 4% of all finite multi-word sentences.

13. Peter Jordens, Monika Rothweiler, and Jürgen Weissenborn have pointed out to me that verbs like *macht* 'makes' and *sitz* 'sit' may also be interpreted as non-finite verb forms in child grammar. Note however that this interpretation is not very plausible for *is* 'is'.

14. We know that this is valid for adults as well.

15. I argued in Müller (1991) that adjunction to IP is base-generated (cf. also de Villiers 1991). Thus, the d-structure for those constructions derived by adjunction would look as follows:

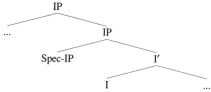

16. If we take modal auxiliaries to be the lexical spell-out of INFL, INFL is the highest functional category in the children's syntactic representation of sentences, as suggested in Meisel & Müller (1992). For a different view cf. Haverkort & Weissenborn (1991), Verrips & Weissenborn (1992), and Weissenborn (1990b) among others.

17. Again, these verb forms also show up in the V2-position, cf. the example of a copying construction at a later point of development (3;04,23) *...wenn da sind eh da sind [n]öwen sind in meine ca[s]* 'when there are eh there are lions are in my cages'.

18. The hypothesis that prepositions are precursors for complementizers has also been explored for monolingual English children. Nishigauchi & Roeper (1987) find that *for* is the first lexical item which the children use in order to introduce clauses.

19. Note that in contrast to modality, the [PAST]-specification is not available in Caroline's and Pascal's grammar during this first developmental phase.

20. This is also valid for subordinating conjunctions in relation to adverbs.

21. There seems to be a quantitative difference between monolingual and bilingual acquisition of word order in embedded clauses which still has to be accounted for. To my knowledge the literature on monolingual language acquisition has not yet reported on a case like Ivar where the acquisition process takes approximately two years.

References

Bickerton, Derek. 1981. *Roots of Language*. Ann Arbor: Karoma.

Brown, Roger. 1973. *A First Language: The early stages*. Cambridge, Mass.: Harvard University Press.

Chomsky, Noam. 1989. "Some Notes on Economy of Derivation and Representation." *MIT Working Papers in Linguistics* 10.43–74.

Clahsen, Harald. 1990. "Constraints on Parameter Setting: A grammatical analysis of some acquisition stages in German child language." *Language Acquisition* 1.361–391.

Clahsen, Harald & Martina Penke. 1992. "The Acquisition of Agreement Morphology and its Syntactic Consequences." Meisel 1992, 181–223.

de Villiers, Jill. 1991. "Why Questions?." *Papers in the Acquisition of WH: Proceedings of the UMass Roundtable, May 1990*, ed. by Thomas L. Maxfield & Bernadette Plunkett, 155–173. Amherst, Mass.: GLSA Publications.

————. 1992. "On the Acquisition of Functional Categories: A general commentary." Meisel 1992, 423–443.

Diesing, Molly. 1990. "Verb Movement and the Subject Position in Yiddish." *Natural Language and Linguistic Theory* 8.41–79.

Felix, Sascha. 1990. "The Structure of Functional Categories." *Linguistische Berichte* 125.46–71.

Frazier, Lynn & Jill de Villiers, eds. 1990. *Language Processing and Language Acquisition* (=*Studies in Theoretical Psycholinguistics*, 10.). Dordrecht: Kluwer.

Fukui, Naoki & Margaret Speas. 1986. "Specifiers and Projections." *MIT Working Papers in Theoretical Linguistics* 8.128–172.

Gawlitzek-Maiwald, Ira, Rosemary Tracy & Agnes Fritzenschaft. 1992. "Language Acquisition and Competing Linguistic Representations: The child as arbiter." Meisel 1992, 139–179.

Guilfoyle, Eithne & Máire Noonan. 1988. "Functional Categories and Language Acquisition." Paper presented at the 13th Annual Boston University Conference on Language Development, Boston, October 1988.

Haverkort, Marco & Jürgen Weissenborn. 1991. "Clitic and Affix Interaction in Early Child Romance." Paper presented at the 16th Annual Boston University Conference on Language Development, Boston, October 1991.

Hoekstra, Teun & Peter Jordens. 1994. "From Adjuncts to Head." *Language Acquisition Studies in Generative Grammar* (=*Language Acquisition and Language Disorders*, 8.), ed. by Teun Hoekstra & Bonnie D. Schwartz, 119–149.

Hornstein, Norbert & David Lightfoot, eds. 1981. *Explanations in Linguistics*. London: Longman.

Horvath, Julia. 1981. "Aspects of Hungarian Syntax and the Theory of Grammar." Diss., Los Angeles: University of California.

Hyams, Nina. 1992. "The Genesis of Clausal Structure." Meisel 1992, 371–400.

Iatridou, Sabine. 1990. "About Agr(P)." *Linguistic Inquiry* 21.551–577.

Koopman, Hilda & Claire Lefèbvre. 1981. "Haitian Creole pu." Muysken 1981, 201–221.

Kuroda, S.-Y. 1988. "Whether We Agree or Not: A comparative syntax of English and Japanese." *Lingvisticae Investigationes* 12.1–47.

Lebeaux, David. 1988. *Language Acquisition and the Form of the Grammar.* Diss., University of Massachusetts at Amherst.

Meisel, Jürgen M. 1985. "Les phases initiales du développement de notions temporelles, aspectuelles et de modes d'action." *Lingua* 66.321–374.

————. 1986. "Word Order and Case Marking in Early Child Language: Evidence from simultaneous acquisition of two first languages: French and German." *Linguistics* 24.123–183.

————. 1990. "INFL-ection: Subjects and subject-verb agreement." Meisel 1990, 237–298.

————, ed. 1990. *Two First Languages: Early grammatical development in bilingual children* (=*Studies on Language Acquisition*, 10.). Dordrecht: Foris.

————. 1991. "Early Grammatical Development: Verbal functional categories." Manuscript, University of Hamburg.

————, ed. 1992. *The Acquisition of Verb Placement: Functional categories and V2 phenomena in language development* (=*Studies in Theoretical Psycholinguistics,* 16.). Dordrecht: Kluwer.

Meisel, Jürgen M. & Natascha Müller. 1992. "Finiteness and Verb Placement in Early Child Grammars: Evidence from the simultaneous acquisition of two first languages: French and German." Meisel 1992, 109–138.

Müller, Natascha. 1990. "Erwerb der Wortstellung im Französischen und Deutschen: Zur Distribution von Finitheitsmerkmalen in der Grammatik bilingualer Kinder." Rothweiler 1990, 127–151.

————. 1991. *Komplexe Sätze: Der Erwerb von COMP und von Wortstellungsmustern bei bilingualen Kindern (Französisch/Deutsch).* Diss., University of Hamburg. To appear in Tübinger Beiträge zur Linguistik (*Language Development*, 16.). Tübingen: Narr.

Muysken, Pieter, ed. 1991. *Generative Studies on Creole Languages.* Dordrecht: Foris.

Nishigauchi, Taisuke & Thomas Roeper. 1987. "Deductive Parameters and the Growth of Empty Categories." *Parameter Setting* (=*Studies in Theoretical Psycholinguistics*, 4.), ed. by Thomas Roeper & Edwin Williams, 91–121. Dordrecht: Reidel.

Parodi, Teresa. 1990. "The Acquisition of Word Order Regularities and Case Morphology." Meisel 1990, 158–190.

Penner, Zvi. 1990. "On the Acquisition of Verb Placement and Verb Projection Raising in Bernese Swiss German." Rothweiler 1990, 166–189.

———. 1992. "The Ban on Parameter Resetting, Default Mechanisms, and the Acquisition of V2 in Bernese Swiss German." Meisel 1992, 245–281.

Pierce, Amy. 1992. *Language Acquisition and Syntactic Theory: A comparative analysis of French and English child grammars.* Dordrecht: Kluwer.

Platzack, Christer. 1983. "Germanic Word Order and the COMP/INFL Parameter." *Working Papers in Scandinavian Syntax* 2.1–45.

———. 1986. "The Position of the Finite Verb in Swedish." *Verb Second Phenomena in Germanic Languages (=Publications in Language Sciences,* 21.), ed. by Hubert Haider & Martin Prinzhorn, 27–47. Dordrecht: Foris.

———. 1992. "A Grammar without Functional Categories: A syntactic study of early Swedish child language." Meisel 1992, 63–82.

Platzack, Christer & Anders Holmberg. 1989. "The Role of AGR and Finiteness in Germanic VO Languages." *Scandinavian Working Papers in Linguistics* 43.51–76.

Poeppel, David & Kenneth Wexler. 1991. "Finiteness and V2 Effects Implicate the Existence of Functional Categories and Head Movement in Early German Grammar." Paper presented at the 16th Annual Boston University Conference on Language Development, Boston, October 1991.

Pollock, Jean-Yves. 1989. "Verb Movement, Universal Grammar, and the Structure of IP." *Linguistic Inquiry* 20.365–424.

Radford, Andrew. 1986. "Small Children's Small Clauses." *Bangor Research Papers in Linguistics* 1.1–38.

———. 1987. "The Acquisition of the Complementizer System." *Bangor Research Papers in Linguistics* 2.55–76.

Raposo, Eduardo & Juan Uriagereka. 1990. "Long-Distance Case Assignment." *Linguistic Inquiry* 21.505–537.

Rizzi, Luigi. 1991a. "Proper Head Government and the Definition of A-Positions." Paper presented at the GLOW meeting, Leiden, March 1991.

———. 1991b. "Residual Verb Second and the Wh-Criterion." *Technical Reports on Formal and Computational Linguistics* 2.1–28.

Rizzi, Luigi & Ian Roberts. 1989. "Complex Inversion in French." *Probus* 1.1–30.

Roeper, Thomas. 1991. "The Meaning of *that:* A (partially) parametric treatment of subordination and quotation." Paper presented at the Conference 'Crossing Boundaries: Formal and Functional Determinants of Language Acquisition', Tübingen, October 1991.

———. 1992. "From the Initial State to V2: Acquisition principles in action." Meisel 1992, 333–370.

Roeper, Thomas & Jürgen Weissenborn. 1990. "How to Make Parameters Work: Comments on Valian." Frazier & de Villiers 1990, 147–162.

Rothweiler, Monika. 1989. *Nebensatzerwerb im Deutschen: Eine empirische Untersuchung zum Primärspracherwerb*. Ph.D. Dissertation, University of Tübingen.

———, ed. 1990. *Spracherwerb und Grammatik: Linguistische Untersuchungen zum Erwerb von Syntax und Morphologie (=Linguistische Berichte Sonderheft*, 3.). Opladen: Westdeutscher Verlag.

Schlyter, Suzanne. 1990. "The Acquisition of Tense and Aspect." Meisel 1990, 87–154.

Speas, Margaret. 1990. *Phrase Structure in Natural Language (=Studies in Natural Language and Linguistic Theory*, 21.) Dordrecht: Kluwer.

Sportiche, Dominique. 1988. "A Theory of Floating Quantifiers and its Corollaries for Constituent Structure." *Linguistic Inquiry* 19.425–449.

Valian, Virginia. 1988. "Positive Evidence, Indirect Negative Evidence, Parameter Setting, and Language Learning." Manuscript, Hunter College New York.

———. 1990. "Logical and Psychological Constraints on the Acquisition of Syntax." Frazier & de Villiers 1990, 119–145.

Verrips, Maaike & Jürgen Weissenborn. 1991. "The Acquisition of Functional Categories Reconsidered." Paper presented at the Conference 'Crossing Boundaries: Formal and functional determinants of language acquisition', Tübingen, October 1991.

———. 1992. "Routes to Verb Placement in Early German and French: The independence of finiteness and agreement." Meisel 1992, 283–331.

Washabaugh, William. 1975. "On the Development of Complementizers in Creolization." *Working Papers in Language Universals* 17.109–140.

Weissenborn, Jürgen. 1990a. "Functional Categories and Verb Movement in Early French and German." Paper presented at the DFG-colloquium, Nijmegen, May 1990.

———. 1990b. "Functional Categories and Verb Movement: The acquisition of German syntax reconsidered." Rothweiler 1990, 190–224.

Woolford, Ellen. 1979. "The Developing Complementizer System of Tok Pisin: Syntactic change in process." *The Genesis of Language*, ed. by Kenneth C. Hill, 108–124, Ann Arbor: Karoma.

Zubizarreta, Maria-Luísa. 1992. "Word Order in Spanish and the Nature of Nominative Case." Manuscript, University of Southern California.

Index of Names

Index of Subjects

In the series LANGUAGE ACQUISITION AND LANGUAGE DISORDERS (LALD) the following titles have been published thus far:

1. WHITE, Lydia: *Universal Grammar Second Language Acquisition.* Amsterdam/ Philadelphia, 1989.
2. HUEBNER, Thom and Charles A. FERGUSON (eds): *Crosscurrents in Second Language Acquisition and Linguistic Theories.* Amsterdam/Philadelphia, 1991.
3. EUBANK, Lynn (ed.): *Point-Counter-Point. Universal Grammar and Second Language Acquisition.* Amsterdam/Philadelphia, 1991.
4. ECKMAN, Fred R. (ed.): *Confluence. Linguistics, L2 acquisition and speech pathology.* Amsterdam/Philadelphia, 1993.
5. GASS, Susan and Larry SELINKER (eds): *Language Transfer in Language Learning.* Amsterdam/Philadelphia, 1992.
6. THOMAS, Margaret: *Knowledge of Reflexives in a Second Language.* Amsterdam/ Philadelphia, 1993.
7. MEISEL, Jürgen M. (ed.): *Bilingual First Language Acquisition.* Amsterdam/Philadelphia, 1994.
8. HOEKSTRA, Teun and Bonnie D. SCHWARTZ (eds): *Language Acquisition Studies in Generative Grammar: Papers in honor of Kenneth Wexler from the 1991 GLOW workshops.* Amsterdam/Philadelphia, 1994.
9. ADONE, Dany: *The Acquisition of Mauritian Creole.* Amsterdam/Philadelphia, 1994.
10. LAKSHMANAN, Usha: *Universal Grammar in Child Second Language Acquisition: Null subjects and morphological uniformity.* Amsterdam/Philadelphia, 1994.